CW01663721

# THE LAST SIAMESE

BY THE SAME AUTHOR

A Print Point of View

The Rise of Asian Advertising

Addresses

The Siamese Trail of Ho Chi Minh

Ode to Manuela of Trento

# THE LAST SIAMESE

## HEROES IN WAR AND PEACE

Teddy Spha Palasthira

TALISMAN

First published in Thailand in 2013 by Post Books
Revised edition 2019 by Talisman Publishing

Copyright © 2013 Teddy Spha Palasthira

All rights reserved. No part of this publication may be reproduced, stored in a retrieval system, or transmitted in any form or by any means, electronic, mechanical, photocopying, recording, or otherwise, without the prior permission of both the copyright owner and the publisher of this book.

**National Library of Thailand Cataloging in Publication Data**
Teddy Spha Palasthira.
THE LAST SIAMESE – Bangkok: Postbooks, 2013. 288 p.
1. History – Biography. I. Title.
808.84

ISBN 978-981-14-3597-3

**Talisman Publishing Pte Ltd**
52 Genting Lane #06-05
Ruby Land Complex 1, Singapore 349560
talisman@adpsing.com
www.talismanpublishing.com

*To my parents who were exemplary Siamese*

# CONTENTS

# FOREWORD

The social and political landscape of Thailand changed forever after three momentous events in the last century. The first happened in 1932 when the world knew our country as Siam: a group of young army officers and officials seized power and forced King Prajadhipok, Rama VII, to give up his absolute powers and accept a constitutional monarchy. It was the nation's first coup d'etat. The second event was the Second World War, in particular the Japanese attack on the American Pacific Fleet at Pearl Harbor in 1941, bringing the war to the shores of Southeast Asia, and the third was when Thailand became a staunch anti-communist ally of the United States, culminating in the Vietnam War in 1965. At the turn of each event, the Thai people were forced to take sides.

This book tells the stories of a select group of people in Siam in the last century who witnessed these events and how their lives were affected, and how some of them unwittingly ended up on opposing sides. The stories in this book cover a span of a century and a broad swath of events – from an era when the young people of Siam were brought up in a world heavily dominated by class, monarchy and religion, to an era when Western imperialism was coming to an end, and finally to the post-Second World War when America became the dominant global power.

This is not a history book nor a collection of biographies, but entertaining essays on diverse individuals. What they have in common is that each person led an uncommon life and each chapter is an exciting adventure that took place in exciting and tumultuous times. Teddy rightly calls this book "Journeys in War and Peace". When I put this book down, I was reminded of the turbulent history of the last century that I lived through and was fortunate enough to survive. I am glad that Teddy has chosen to help us remember some of these events. I hope that this book will help younger readers become aware of our nation's recent past and better understand the way we were.

Anand Panyarachun

Former Prime Minister of Thailand

# INTRODUCTION

*The Last Siamese* comprises twelve stories about prominent people of exceptional talent and vitality born between 1872 and 1930. In those years, foreigners knew the country as Siam, although the Siamese themselves called it *muang Thai* (or "The Land of the Free") and referred to themselves as *khon Thai* ("Thai people"). In 1939, Field Marshal Pibulsonggram, who was also born "Siamese" and is a subject in this book, changed the country's name from Siam to Thailand. This policy was the source of some contention until the matter was decisively concluded in 1949. From that point on the country has been known as Thailand.

I had the good fortune to know some of the characters in *The Last Siamese* and others I met as a child through my parents. They were people of courage and imagination. Some changed the course of Thai history, some were controversial, and still others were unsung heroes who did their best under trying circumstances. All led exciting and adventurous lives, in exciting and adventurous times during the last century, and they were all patriotic people of resolve, leadership and unselfishness, qualities I find sadly lacking in our society today.

I have included one foreigner, Captain Hercules Dennis, who felt more Siamese than British towards the end of his life. Only one figure is still with us: Khamsing Srinawk, a patriotic Isan writer whose work has been translated into nine languages. He sought refuge in Sweden during the witch-hunt for communists in the seventies. Today he is happily retired on his farm in Pak Chong, Thailand.

Some of the characters in the book had conflicting political views. Readers are advised that *The Last Siamese* is not meant to be a scholarly work nor a political treatise, and therefore supports neither side of the political spectrum. Suffice to say, all twelve figures lived during a period of great global and national upheaval. They represented different sides of the same coin. Imperialism, Nazism, Fascism and Communism, as well as the Free Thai, are movements of the past. Let them remain in the annals of history so that writers like me can have some *divertissements.*

I could have called this book *The Last of the Siamese: A Dying Breed,* but I didn't set out to be polemic and needlessly get myself into an argument. I simply wanted to tell some inspiring stories about real people who lived in a very different era from the present one. I myself am proud to be both Siamese and Thai. When I was young I was brought up to respect our Thai name, and the patriotic concept of being "free" was drummed into my psyche. We were told repeatedly by our parents and teachers that we were never colonized. I confess I am not proud to be Thai when our name is used by modern politicians in vain, purely for personal and political profit. I am repulsed by political party names like *Prachakorn Thai* (The Thai People), *Pheu Thai* (For Thais), *Chart Thai Pattana* (The Thai Nation Development), *Thai Pen Thai* (Thais Are Free), *Ruam Jai Thai* (United Thais), *Chart Thai* (Thai Nation), and *Thai Rak Thai* (Thai Love Thai). The last assumes that you do not love your country if you didn't vote for *Thai Rak Thai*. These politicians are far from being the patriots that I depict in my book. We have become our worst enemy. It is times like this that I naively feel Siamese.

In the absence of letters and diaries, except in the cases of Prince Subha Svasti and Captain Dennis, and personal notes from Dr. Samarn, primary research became painstakingly slow and cumbersome (no secretary or assistants). Fortunately, I was able to conduct in-depth interviews with many friends and relatives of my subjects. My research took me to Britain, Sweden, Berlin, Lake Garda in northern Italy, the Plain of Jars in Laos, Vietnam, and in Thailand, to Udorn, Petchabun, Chiang Mai, Prachuab Kirikhan, Tarutao island, Pak Chong, the River Kwae and many other interesting locations. I went in search of new perspectives on some already well-known people, who had each in their own way tried to make our country a better place to live. When I was teaching creative writing at the Missouri School of Journalism in America, I discouraged student reporters from lifting material from the Internet (which they often did). If it's already on Google, there's no point whatsoever in writing about it. I have used Google sparingly, although it was of great help when I needed to check my historic facts, or to look up a word in Swedish or Japanese.

I have endeavoured to liven up some episodes and anecdotes by treating these historic figures as if they were fictional characters, which may well be how they would secretly like to be treated. However, I have always sought to remain faithful to the personality and character of my subject, and to the events as they truly happened. Due to the lack of material on actual conversations during some of these events, I have occasionally given voices to my characters, presenting imagined dialogue in order to bring them to life and to better capture the dramatic mood of the time.

I have used both "Thailand "and "Siam" throughout the book to describe our country, depending on the relevant historic era that is depicted and the circumstances of the story. In deference to Premier Pibul, I have used "Thailand" in his chapter; he would undoubtedly have preferred it that way. Khamsing is, of course "Thai", more Thai than the rest of us, if we recognize that the Lao/Isan people are direct descendants of the T'ai tribes that came from Guanxi province in China a millennium ago.

I could have selected many other great Siamese people for this book, but I was working under a deadline. Writing is a lonely business and I wasn't prepared to take a year off in total isolation to complete such a big project. God willing, I will continue to do research for my next book. *The Khmer Lion* is the current working title.

I have discovered that in the course of writing *The Last Siamese* many kind people have been both sympathetic and encouraging, especially the friends, relations and descendants of my characters. I thank them all. Acknowledgements to these helpful people are at the end of the book, together with a bibliography.

I am grateful to Thailand's former prime minister Anand Panyarachun for kindly writing the foreword. Special thanks go to Nicholas Grossman for his editorial feedback and patient guidance, and to Supakorn Vejjajiva of the *Bangkok Post*, my publisher, for his support and confidence in my work. I am indebted to Prisna Boonsinsukh for her excellent translation for the Thai edition and for keeping me on track with Thai history, and to Teerapong Hoonnirun for the cover design and artwork production. Julian Atkinson again came to my help in typing the manuscript.

One final observation: If you want to find out who your true friends are and you want to enjoy your old age, write a book. It has worked for me.

Teddy Spha Palasthira

Hua Hin, Thailand, 2013.

# PREFACE TO THE REVISED SECOND EDITION

This book began life as *The Last Siamese,* subtitled *Journeys in War and Peace.* It remains *The Last Siamese,* but in the course of making a few additions and corrections for this second edition, it dawned on me that the twelve people depicted in the book not only had exceptional talent and vitality, but each one performed incredibly heroic deeds. The subtitle has therefore been changed to *Heroes in War and Peace.*

Whatever they did, they did not do it for monetary profit or personal gain. They were men of integrity, determined to do the right thing, and dedicated to their cause. Importantly what they did was for their love of Thailand. They were honourable men. They were *heroes*.

In order to appreciate them, it is important to place them in the context of their times rather than judge them by contemporary standards. I also hope that this book can help the reader understand some of the momentuous events in Thai history during the last century.

To make this revised second edition possible, I am indebted to Nicholas Grossman and Yvan Van Outrive for their assistance in securing me a new publisher. Teerapong Hoonirun again came to my help in producing the updated graphic designs.

Teddy Spha Palasthira

2019

# SO SETHAPUTRA
## 1903 – 1970

A mining graduate from England
who found his vocation in prison

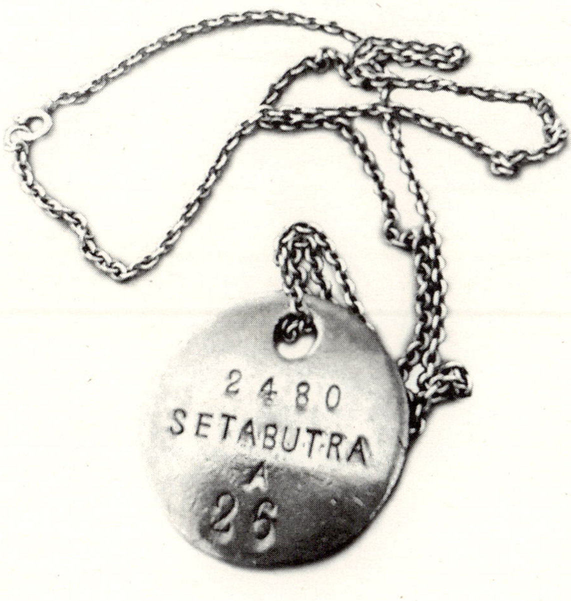

***Previous page***: *Sor's identification tag, prisoner number 26, in Roman letters; there was no Thai language stamping machine in the prison.*

***Above***: *Sor was always well groomed on Tarutao island, where he served part of his sentence from 1939 to 1943.*

# 1

# How to Write a Dictionary in Prison

The prows of two small steamers thrust through the dark rippling waters of the Talo Udang Bay and laid anchor three hundred metres offshore at Tarutao island in southern Thailand. The tide was much too low for the *Adang* and the *Rawi* – converted Japanese fishing boats – to land on the beach. Seventy passengers – all prisoners – waded ashore in complete darkness.

Prisoner number 26, thin, weary, yet in good spirits, was the last to disembark. As he moved slowly through the waist-deep water, a heavy cardboard box precariously balanced on his head, his main concern was the safety of its contents: 22 tins of State Express cigarettes, one tattered 1924 edition of the Concise Oxford Dictionary (minus cover), several English language classics, sixty exercise books, 5 pens and 73 nibs, six bottles of ink, three dozen pencils, and most precious of all, a partially completed manuscript in longhand.

Today, the lonely, untouched island of Tarutao is the headquarters of Southeast Asia's largest marine park. Its forest-clad hills rise seven hundred metres above the intense blue Andaman Sea on the western horizon, its jungles wet with rain stretching down to the beach, while the craggy limestone cliffs on the eastern side of the island plunge dramatically into the ocean. Numerous streams and waterfalls cut through the mountainous interior. A thick canopy of rainforest up to forty metres high provides a secure retreat for wild boar, long-tailed macaques, hornbills and mousedeer. In the azure sea, dolphins, sea turtles, octopus, rays, angelfish, even sponges, thrive undisturbed. The coral reefs of the marine park are some of the world's most spectacular. For holidaymakers, it is paradise.

In 1939, however, for the newly arrived political prisoners who were transferred there from Bangkok, Tarutao was grim and forbidding. They spent the night shivering on the beach, huddled uncomfortably together in an open makeshift lean-to, with just a flimsy palm thatch roof to protect them from the wind and rain. Behind them, the jungle and its dark menacing forest were foreboding. The piercing screams of wild boars and the eerie shrills of the macaws put fear into their hearts. The cold, wet monsoon wind was slapping noisily against the palm thatch, keeping them awake for most of the night. By the time it was dawn, they were too weary to marvel at the first gentle rays of the rising sun streaking the eastern sky with shafts of pink and gold.

The prison camp at Talo Udang Bay, located at the southern end of the island, had been established as a penal colony for political prisoners in 1937. There was already a prison camp for hardened criminals and murderers on the east coast at Talo Wao Bay. These two prison camps were separated by a 12-kilometre track built by the common prisoners. The two classes of prisoners were kept apart, although some of the less dangerous inmates were often called upon to work for the political prisoners.

Tarutao had been chosen for its distance from Bangkok – over 1,000 kilometres – and for its treacherous shark-infested waters. The southwest monsoon that battered the western shore from May to October and the northeast typhoon that hit the eastern side from November to April made travel to and from the mainland difficult and dangerous. Escape was not an option.

So Sveshthaputra (pronounced Sor Sethabud and now written Sethaputra) – Prisoner 26 – had no intention of escaping, although escape had become the main topic of discussion for the political prisoners during their first weeks on the island. Sor[1] had his own agenda. He wanted to finish his life's work.

Sor's life, like those of his fellow political prisoners, had been drastically altered by the events a decade earlier, on 24 June 1932, when a small group of French and German-educated military officers and civil servants positioned a few tanks in front of Dusit Palace and staged a successful coup d'etat against King Rama VII, demanding a constitutional monarchy. They had formed the Khana Ratsadon, the People's Party, and had spent seven years planning the coup. Paradoxically, it took them only half-a-day to change the nation's course of history.

King Prajadhipok accepted their demands without demur and had, in his own words, long "considered making this change" himself, and was already preparing to give up absolute power "for the good of his people." As it transpired, the military faction that seized power did not set up a true democratic constitutional monarchy. Much of the literary and academic intelligentsia of the time, including Sor, had long suspected that many coup leaders were not concerned with the "good of the people."

Back in 1923, Sor, a mining engineering student in England, had learned that the students in France were plotting against the monarchy and even then he had his reservations. He commented in a letter home: "I am afraid that they are not interested in democratic change." He later wrote when he returned to Siam that parliamentary democracy cannot be instituted by military rule; it is a gradual learning process, requiring education, experience and good will.

---

1 To avoid confusion, So's name will be be spelt as it is pronounced - "Sor" - in this chapter.

When Sor returned to Siam in 1926, he did not pursue a career in mining. He was a gifted writer and was more interested in journalism. He worked at the *Daily Mail* as a political correspondent. In 1928 he was recognised by His Majesty the King for his communication and language skills and was appointed Royal Spokesman, today's equivalent of press secretary. He was given the royally-bestowed title of Luang Mahasit Woharn, the "man of great eloquence."

Sor went on to serve the king and queen as an analyst and adviser on current diplomatic affairs, foreign trends and local personalities, and became an integral part of the official secretariat of the Royal Household. Sor shared the same hopes as His Majesty, that a constitutional monarchy supported by a true democratic parliamentary system would one day prevail in Siam. After the 1932 coup that replaced absolute monarchy, Sor resigned his government commission and became a prominent anti-coup activist.

Not all military officers supported the coup. The former Minister of Defence and cousin to the King, Prince Bovoradej, popular among the ranks for his opposition to salary cuts for 91 officers, joined a group of anti-coup loyalists. He was able to raise the victorious royal standard in the provinces of the north and northeast, and expected loyal support from the troops in Bangkok.

On the morning of 11 October 1933, Prince Bovoradej woke up early. In the predawn chill at his Saraburi command post, he prepared for the battle of his life. After reviewing the loyal battalions from seven northern and northeastern provinces, he quickly marched on the capital. By noon, his lightly armed troops had reached the freshly harvested rice fields of Ayudhya, just 50 miles north of Bangkok.

The objective, and the ultimatum, were simple but naïve: to obtain a more democratic government. The much hoped-for support from the Bangkok garrisons never came. On the evening of 13 October, a young and up-and-coming colonel, Plaek Pibulsonggram, opened a heavy artillery attack on the rebels' positions, and two weeks later the rebellion was quashed with a bloody skirmish at Don Muang.

On 4 November 1933, Sor was arrested with 300 other supporters for acting as the rebel's political spokesman. Three months later he was found guilty for ostensibly publishing and distributing "Save the Country" pro-rebellion pamphlets, although the authorities had wanted to put him away long before. The leaflets were simply a legal pretext and Bovoradej's rebellion an official excuse. He was already deemed guilty for his political commentaries and sentenced to life imprisonment for sedition.

Surrounded by a high concrete wall and topped by an electrified razor wire, Bang Kwang prison in Bangkok, where Sor spent the first years of his sentence, was impregnable. Originally a high-security prison built in 1931 for common criminals, after the 1932 coup, Ward Six was rebuilt and redesigned for political prisoners. Each chamber was widened to 20 square metres to house 12 prison cells. An open corridor connected all 50 chambers, to enable the guards easy access.

Many of the political prisoners were members of the educated class, and boasted university degrees from Europe and America. Thirty-three of them decided that the best and only way to use their time in prison productively would be to teach and share their knowledge and learning with other less fortunate inmates. For example, His Highness Prince Sithiporn Kridakorn, brother of Prince Bovoradej, and *eminence grise* of this elite group, was a professional agronomist and a gentleman farmer. His experimental Bang Berd plantation south of Hua Hin had yielded a variety of exciting new produce, including larger eggs, juicy cantaloupes and pumpkins, giant marrow squash and other vegetables. He decided to conduct classes in agriculture and husbandry. Many young hopeful inmates from the countryside became devoted students. Some even opted to learn new skills. Phraya Saraphai Phipat, a naval captain, chose to learn Mandarin from a Chinese prisoner suspected of being a communist. Another senior prisoner gave Japanese language lessons.

Sor volunteered to give English-language reading and writing classes in his small cell. One of his ex-students recalls Cell 42 being transformed into an English language classroom: "Professor Sor Sethaputra, small and frail, with huge eyeglasses that framed his face, sat cross-legged, propped up by a folded mattress against the wall, his students forming a half circle around him." To augment his students' English reading experience, Sor ordered non-political books and picture magazines from outside, and borrowed books from the Neilson Hays Library in Bangkok. Ward Six soon became a small university campus, with daily book readings and classes.

The Thai prisoners had little difficulty reading some English, or for that matter Latin, French, Spanish or Italian, having learned the Roman alphabet from a very early age at school. But there, their skills ended. They understood very little of what they read. Sor was constantly called upon to translate difficult English words and sentences. Sor realized his students clearly needed a good dictionary. The first comprehensive English-Thai dictionary was thus conceived.

At 30, Sor was still in his prime. Realising that he could very well be inside for the rest of his life, he made the momentous decision to embark on what he called his "Life's Work." This immense undertaking kept him focused for the next eleven years and provided him with both intellectual stimulus and a regular income.

For the first time in weeks Sor slept well. He now had a mission to fulfil and he was eager to get started. The question that he kept on asking himself that night was: "How does one even *begin* to write a dictionary in prison?" He thought about all the obstacles that had to be overcome, the materials that would be required, and, most important of all, the help he would need.

All writing by political prisoners intended for outside

readership – other than letters – was strictly forbidden at Bang Kwang. The fundamental problem of writing in secret, often at night, hiding the manuscripts and preparing them for publication was quite easily solved though. Writing under the subterfuge of English classes easily deceived the guards. Every nook and cranny under the poorly constructed ceiling of Ward Six became perfect hiding places. Even the most painstaking calligraphy prepared for the final manuscript was furtively integrated into Sor's English writing class. The delivery of writing paper and instruments into prison was simply a matter of negotiation with the guards.

The single most difficult barrier that had to be overcome was smuggling the completed manuscripts past the guards of Ward Six and the high security checkpoint at the prison gates. The solution came later.

The easy part of writing a dictionary in prison for Sor was its actual execution. Here, Sor was in his element. What better way to occupy his fertile mind than to fully explore his extensive knowledge of the arts and sciences and to use his creative talent to write good English and Thai prose? Sor ingeniously designed and built a functional writing desk and comfortable chair from packing crates. Never short of assistants to do the meticulous physical transcribing, copying and calligraphic work, he instituted a strict daily routine for himself and his team. Up at six, start work at seven-thirty until lunch break at eleven-thirty, back to work at two-thirty until dark. He would often get up in the middle of the night to write a word or phrase that had been bothering him all day.

His organizational skills and self-discipline became legendary in Ward Six. A young member of his team recalls those magical moments: "Sor was the brain and we were the labour. He would sit there, cross-legged, and suddenly burst out with a word or phrase; and we would immediately transcribe it on to paper."

When he reached the letter "G", Sor decided the time was right to market his grand dictionary project. He secretly got in touch with Phraya Nibhon Pojanart, one of his old connections, owner of *Krungdheb Bannakarn*, Bangkok's leading bookstore.

Sor and Phraya Nibhon came up with a brilliant marketing approach and a unique publishing deal. The dictionary would be published in weekly instalments over a period of two years and when the collection was complete, subscribers could bind them together into two volumes, a total of 2,400 pages. Sor was to be paid by instalment, providing him with much needed income.

The political solution was equally brilliant. Phraya Nibon's official line to the authorities was to say that he had commissioned Sor to write the dictionary between 1927 and 1932, *long before* he went to prison.

The first instalments of *The New Model English-Siamese Dictionary* were an immediate success. It was like no other dictionary so far published in Siam. Sor wanted his dictionary to reach out to his readers. Each English word was explained by a simple sentence that vividly rendered its meaning and usage, based on current affairs, Sor's personal life experiences, his education in England and events in Siam past and present. Here are some examples:

| | |
|---|---|
| **abdicate** | His Majesty abdicated |
| **absent** | Freedom of the press is absent |
| **accuse** | They were accused of treason |
| **alma mater** | Suan Khularb was his alma mater |

As a qualified mining engineer, Sor had a sharp mind, inherited from his father, an inquisitive scientist who spent his life inventing new contraptions. His mother was equally free-spirited and independent-minded, one of the few Siamese women at the turn of the last century who could read and write. It was from his mother that he developed a passion for literature, books and writing. Sor was blessed with his mother's support and encouragement; she devoted her entire life to him after his father died.

**mother** Motherly love can never be destroyed

It was his mother Gaysorn who smuggled his manuscripts out of prison, using the outer cylinder of a large Thermos flask to insert and hide the forbidden materials. In order not to arouse suspicion by using the flask once too often, a false bottomed basket was also introduced. Sor must have chuckled to himself when he wrote this entry:

**false** The documents were concealed under the false bottom of the box

Gaysorn was to smuggle almost 2,000 pages out of Ward Six.

After 1937, Sor and his co-inmates were lucky to have Major General Chlor Srisarakorn as their liberal-minded prison warden. He built tennis courts at Bang Kwang so prisoners could have adequate physical exercise. More importantly, he allowed political prisoners out one day a week. Some went to the cinema, others visited friends, but most went home. Sor himself was able to date a young girl working with her sister who owned a grocery store opposite the prison. Sor's first son was born in 1939 from this union. The son, Dr. Chaiya, now a retired surgeon, told this writer it wasn't until 5 years later that he met his father for the first time. Provided the political prisoners were back at Bang Kwang by 6 p.m., they were treated humanely and respectfully, and were free to come and go on their day off.

Although more personal freedom had made life slightly better, conditions inside were now becoming much worse. The guards had been instructed by the paranoid government to make more thorough searches, not just at the prison gates checkpoint, but also inside the cells. Smuggling Sor's material out of prison had become more difficult. Letters they wrote were carefully inspected and censored before being allowed out of Bang Kwang.

These measures were taken, in part, because the political prisoners of Ward Six were increasingly becoming a liability to the state. Their proximity to Bangkok and their political activity inside prison gave them a unique public voice and a new popular prominence. The government discovered that they were *more* of a threat together in prison than they ever were before they went inside. When the prison authority found a radio in Sor's cell, he was falsely accused of communicating with Bovoradej, the rebel prince, who was miles away in exile, in Vietnam. Now that they had more personal freedom to come and go, many were accused of subversive activity and treason. The government finally decided that the only way to exercise full control would be to send them as far away from Bangkok as possible. The Department of Corrections conducted a feasibility study of the most inaccessible islands in Siam. In May 1937 Tarutao was selected. It took a further two years for the Department to get Tarutao ready for the prisoners' transfer. By early September 1939 when they started their journey south to Tarutao, Sor had been incarcerated at Bang Kwang for nearly six years. The dictionary was now up to the letter "T".

Sor was never one for big breakfasts. A cup of tea and the obligatory cigarette would suffice. For the others, their first meals on Tarutao were sickening. The rice gruel was gritty, hardly warm enough to fuel their weak, shivering bodies after a cold night on the beach. The accompanying salted meat was putrid and the preserved vegetables smelt of dead fish.

Right from day one the prisoners split into two distinct groups: those who wanted to escape to Langkawi island five kilometres south across the sea in Malaya, and those who were too old or too frightened, or not prepared to take any further risks.

Sor had been part of an original escape committee formed at Bang Kwang, which also included two of his former colleagues at the *Daily Mail*, Louis Kiriwat, the editor, and Naval Captain Phraya Saraphai, a contributor. They invited many of their close friends at Ward Six to join their cause. Sor's closest friend and confidante,

Prince Sithiporn, a man he respected highly, was also asked to join, but asserted that at 60 he was too old and did not want to be a burden to the group. After much soul-searching, Sor also decided not to join the escape group, even though he was one of the early planners.

On a full moon night, day twenty-nine, five prisoners decided to make their escape to Langkawi by boat, led by Captain Phraya Saraphai. The other four were Louis Kiriwat, Sor's old colleague, Colonel Phraya Suraphan, Chalam Liamphetchrat, a lawyer who was also a keen astrologer and selected the auspicious date for their escape, and Kuhn[2] Asaniratakarn, a railway engineer. It was a sad moment for Sor when they bid their last farewells on the beach. They had worked, laughed and shared sacrifices together for so long.

Why did Sor decide to stay on? He later admitted that he suffered great inner conflict at the time. The main reason he rejected the idea was because his mother, Gaysorn, implored him to stay with two short words, "Don't go". She had communicated to him from Satun on the mainland where she moved to be near Sor. Gaysorn was a practical woman and she was concerned for her son's safety. She also realised that a regular income from the dictionary was the most important priority. After all, Sor was the only breadwinner in the family. He was supporting both his younger brother and sister at university.

Sor also chose to stay in order to complete his unfinished dictionary. He felt a moral obligation to his publisher and subscribers to finish the work. Sor also realised that should his escape come to the attention of the authorities, Phraya Nibhon's printing press would certainly be shut down. After all, how could the government tolerate a book written by a political fugitive and allow it to be published, even if it was just a dictionary? Sor had also received royalties amounting to several thousand baht, thanks to his loyal subscribers.

2 A minor royally granted title, not to be confused with "Khun", Mr.

He could never let them down. Sor's friend and mentor Prince Sithiporn fully supported Sor's decision to stay on. He told Sor that the dictionary would be his gift to future generations.

Those who had made the decision to remain on the island responded with a conscious effort to rebuild their lives. Over the next few weeks they set about improving their living conditions by building new living quarters, decent kitchens and clean latrines. Fortunately, fresh water was freely available from the many streams on the island. Prince Sithiporn put his heart and soul into his work, making the earth more arable, and eventually produced enough vegetables and fruit to keep everyone healthy. The prince became the spiritual leader of the former inmates of Ward Six and continually boosted their morale. He treated Sor like a son and uplifted his spirits, which were now at a low point after the departure of his friends for Langkawi.

It was difficult to work on his dictionary under these trying conditions. Sor was missing his privileged status at Bang Kwang and pining for Sompong, his newly wedded wife. Since he was not a religious person and ceased to believe in God, he did not seek holy guidance in prayer or spiritual meditation like many other prisoners. Instead, Sor took solace in his work, and through sheer determination and strength of character, Sor was soon able to return to his "Life's Work." He hired the common prisoners to build a separate hut for his workplace and designed a new desk. He started to take special care of his personal hygiene and appearance. He never allowed himself to become demoralised. He was always well-groomed and he made sure that even his threadbare clothes – white shirt and Chinese silk trousers – remained impeccable and well-laundered. His hair was always combed and he got one of the common prisoners to give him regular haircuts. He always made sure he felt good about himself.

By June 1940, Sor reached the letter "Z". The giant library edition dictionary was finished at last. It ran to 4,000 pages, 1,600 more than was originally conceived. Now better organised and more mentally alert, he could start work right away on a desk size dictionary, a smaller version, for high school students. He hired some of his fellow inmates to transcribe his notes onto school exercise pads, paying them 25 satangs for each completed book.

In time, Sor came to prefer life on Tarutao to Bang Kwang. The island was beautiful, the air was fresh and clean, and the surrounding nature was peaceful and quiet. Apart from the constant threat of malaria and other tropical diseases, Sor and his fellow prisoners led a relatively healthy life.

Morale also improved. Everyone chipped in to make prison life as pleasant as possible. Prince Sithiporn, with the help of a group of common prisoners, produced enough vegetables and fruit for the island's consumption, and a surplus was marketed at Satun on the mainland. He also baked bread and cakes on an oven that was sent from the mainland by his wife.

Not to be outdone, Sor started to make his own soap, essential for someone as particular about personal hygiene as he was. He soon ran out of State Express cigarettes and started experimenting with different kinds of leaves. This was not a huge success. Although Sor was not a gourmet, he enjoyed cooking and he prepared shark fin soup for his friends. He liked mushrooms and created many new recipes. Other inmates joined in the communal spirit and contributed their individual skills, like weaving and basketry. Soon the prison's production earned an income and a small bank was opened. Talo Udang prison was transformed into a self-sufficient commune.

The biggest problem was the lack of adequate medicine, particularly quinine, as malaria was beginning to take its toll on the prison's population. From the mainland in Satun, Sor's mother managed to send over 1,000 quinine tablets which saved many lives.

Visits from friends and family were strictly forbidden, a major aggravation for the inmates, making life on this beautiful island less pleasant. Throughout the period of Sor's imprisonment at Tarutao, his stoic mother patiently remained at Satun on the mainland, so near, yet so very far. Many relatives on the mainland were in dire economic straits and there were cases where prisoners had allowed their wives to find new husbands who could support them. One even went back to her first husband after the war. Sor was more fortunate than many. He was one of the very few inmates who received a regular income.

In 1942, Siam declared war against the Allies and the war in the Pacific had escalated to Siam, Malaya and Burma. On 8 January 1942, Bangkok was bombed by the British and the Hua Lampong railway station area was badly hit. Martial law was declared and the prisons came under stricter supervision. Sor's publisher, Phraya Nibhon, was killed during an air raid and Sor's completed portable edition did not get published. Sor kept the unpublished manuscript for another 6 years, carrying it with him wherever he went. It was not published until well after the war, in 1949.

Although they were shut off from the outside world, the prisoners at the Talo Udang camp were fully aware that there was a war going on. They learned from the prison guards that Siam had been invaded and occupied by the Japanese and that Siam had put up a heroic stand against the invaders in the southern peninsula where many soldiers' lives were lost on 8 and 9 December, 1941.[3] Being as close as they were to the Malayan border, they frequently heard the sound of heavy artillery and as they cocked their ears to listen, they knew instinctively that it was not the sound of thunder, as the rains never came. Now, there were continuous Japanese sea and air patrols over the thousands of islands that made up the archipelago of the Andaman Sea.

By 1943, the tide of the war was beginning to turn and, aware that the Allies would soon be in control of the Andaman Sea, the

3 See Chapter 5.

government decided to move the political prisoners once again, across the peninsula to Koh Tao, a tiny, uninhabited island, save for a small population of hawksbill turtles, in the Gulf of Siam.

There were only 55 political prisoners left on Tarutao. The anti-Japanese Free Thai resistance was gaining grass-roots acceptance among the populace and the government was afraid that these highly educated and high-ranking prisoners from Ward Six would join the resistance.

Sor spent the next fifteen months, from April 1943 to July 1944 on Koh Tao Island. Like Tarutao, Koh Tao is also a paradise for holidaymakers, with long stretches of white sandy beach fringed by miles and miles of coconut palm trees, surrounded by clear waters and beautiful coral reefs. Unlike Tarutao though, Koh Tao was much smaller and less fertile, with little freshwater resources. The prisoners were confined to an area of 14 acres, surrounded by a fence. A watchtower with a machine gun emplacement was positioned on top of a hill overlooking the compound, allowing the prison guards to keep constant surveillance. Escape was not a possibility.

The newly arrived prisoners would soon discover that Koh Tao was hell on earth. The Department of Corrections had changed their liberal policy and political prisoners under 60 were forced to work like slaves. They were no longer allowed to wander around freely and at night they were locked up.

There was an acute shortage of essential medicines and American submarine patrols in the gulf curtailed regular delivery of basic foods and supplies. Malnutrition became a major problem and there were more malarial cases than on Tarutao. A combination of exhaustive work, sunstroke, severe hunger and malaria killed six prisoners in the first two months alone. They were literally worked to death.

These harsh conditions were not conducive for Sor to continue his work. He was planning to write the life story of King Rama V, but the lack of research materials and writing instruments, the rough conditions in the prison camp, and severe debilitation made Sor give up writing for the first time in his adult life. He was down to 30 kilos and so weak that his friends stood in for him to do the strenuous task of chopping logs for firewood. Instead he was assigned to the lighter job of stacking and counting them.

To make up for the lack of intellectual activity, Sor started new experiments with herbal plants, hoping to find a substitute for much needed quinine. Boiling borapet[4] and shatterstone plants together produced a bitter liquid that increased perspiration and urination and also reduced the fever, but it was no cure for malaria. Sor became chief tester for herbs, leaves, flowers and for just about everything that could be converted to food and medicines. Diced and sun-dried camphor leaves, he discovered, was a poor substitute for tobacco.

Like many thin people, Sor was not one to suffer from acute pangs of hunger. But his hungrier friends ended up eating boiled buffalo hide, pythons, monitor lizards, geckos, and for seafood enthusiasts, the occasional mudskipper. The most sought-after delicacy was turtle meat. Artificial coffee was made by combining red rice grains and borapet leaves.

Accused of participating in a second royal rebellion that failed in 1939, two new prisoners, M.R. Nimit Mongkhon Nawarat and Dr. Chote Kumphan, arrived at Koh Tao from Bang Kwang in late 1943. They were horrified by what they found. They saw prisoners so bony that when they sat down, their kneecaps and elbows protruded from their emaciated bodies. Their bulging eyes popped out from their skeletal sockets. At night they shivered uncontrollably under thread-bare blankets. Koh Tao was not a prison, but a concentration camp.

Dr. Chote was moved to say in his memoirs: "If we were animals we would all have died. Being human made us more resistant and hopeful."

---

4 A type of cactus.

An amnesty for all political prisoners was declared after a change of government in September 1944. By 20 October, the prisoners were put on the Bangkok-bound train at Surat station. The news of their release had been broadcast, and overnight the political prisoners became national heroes. Throughout their journey, people came out to greet them at each stop, bringing them food and clothes, and fêted them with garlands.

Sor discovered two things after his long absence. First, that the Siamese hadn't changed at all. They were the same gentle and kind-hearted people that he loved before he went to prison eleven years earlier.

He also discovered that the Thai spelling of his family name had been simplified from "Sveshthaputra" to "Sethaputra" by the Pibul government, who unsuccessfully tried to modernise the Thai alphabet. Sor decided that he would adopt the new, simpler spelling of his name, in keeping with his modest style.

He wanted people to associate him with simplicity and to remember him as a common man, one who loved his fellow human beings, and he did not want to be confused with the wealthier branch of the family that had reverted back to the original spelling. He often boasted about being the "poor relative."

When Sor arrived at Bangkok Noi station, he was greeted by his old friend Manit Vasuwat, who immediately offered him a board directorship at the Sri Krung newspaper and publishing company.

Also at the station, standing out among the throng of friends and well-wishers, despite her petite stature, was a thinner, older but happier Gaysorn, Sor's mother. He broke down and cried.

After ten years, eleven months and twenty days in prison, Sor was exhausted. He took time off to move into his new house and catch up with Sompong, his wife, and their little boy Chaiya, who he had not seen for five years. He joined Dr. Chote, a former Koh Tao inmate, on a rehabilitation program to get back his health. He rested and then started thinking about his next dictionary project.

Production of the manuscript for the library edition of the "New Model English-Siamese Dictionary" from "A" to "T" took almost five years at Bang Kwang prison. As there were no restrictions on writing at Tarutao, Sor was able to complete the final part to "Z" in less than a year. The portable version took him another year.

The two-volume 4000-page New Model English-Siamese Dictionary was a new kind of dictionary. Previous works were compiled by American missionaries for foreigners wanting to learn Thai. So's "New Model" dictionary was written for Thais wanting to learn English. In the introduction, he wrote that it was to be a "dynamic passport to the English language for native Thai speakers" that "captures the idiomatic, colloquial spoken and written character of English." The New Model Dictionary became the best selling English-Thai dictionary in the last century, including library, desk, school and pocket versions.

In the "L" section of the New Model Dictionary, this is what he wrote to illustrate "labour":

"I did it as a labour of love."

# LUANG PIBUL

Full Name: Plaek Pibulsonggram

1897 - 1964

Siam's longest serving prime minister,
who changed its name to Thailand

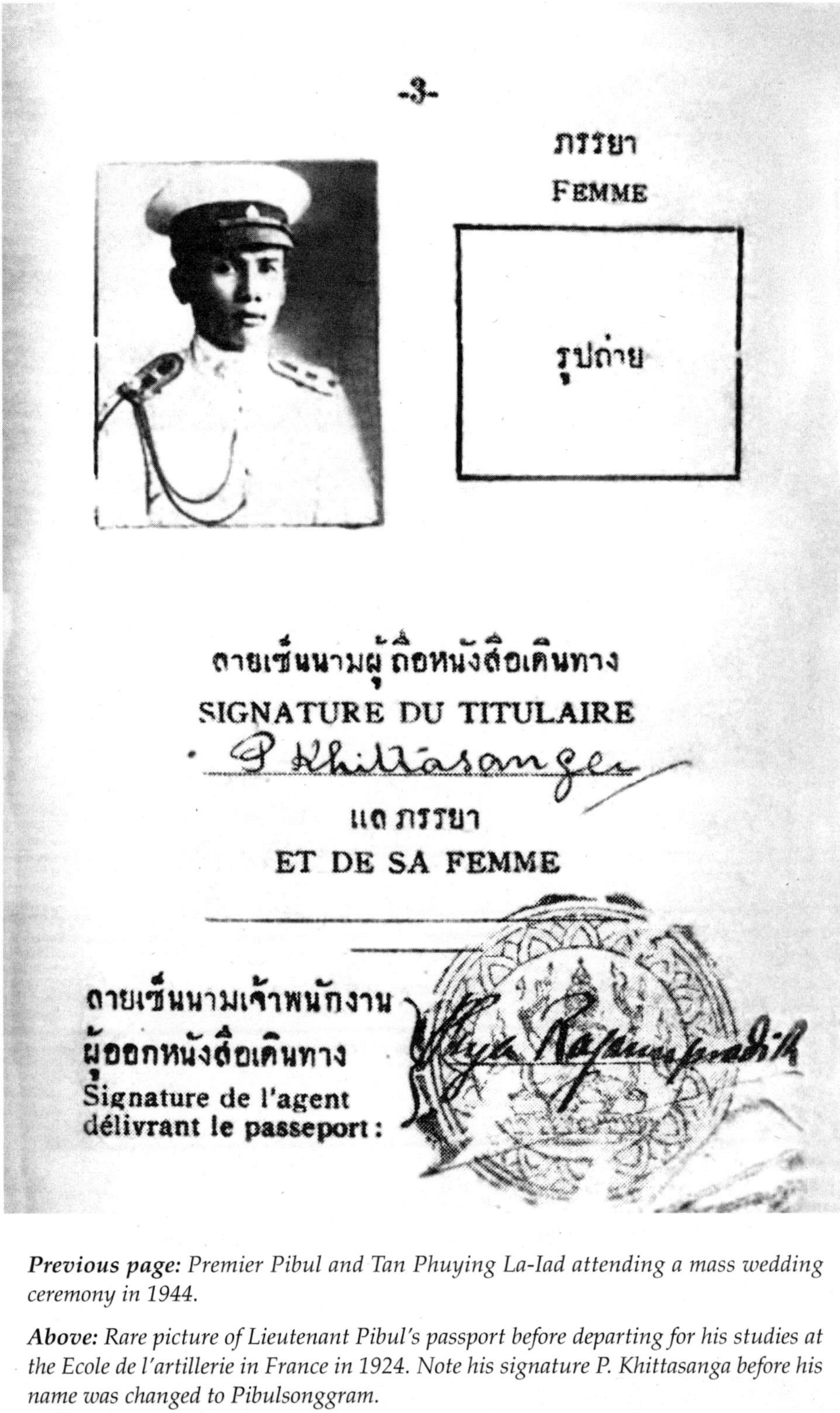

-3-

ภรรยา

FEMME

รูปถ่าย

ลายเซ็นนามผู้ถือหนังสือเดินทาง

SIGNATURE DU TITULAIRE

P Khittasanga

แล ภรรยา

ET DE SA FEMME

ลายเซ็นนามเจ้าพนักงาน
ผู้ออกหนังสือเดินทาง
Signature de l'agent
délivrant le passeport :

***Previous page:*** *Premier Pibul and Tan Phuying La-Iad attending a mass wedding ceremony in 1944.*

***Above:*** *Rare picture of Lieutenant Pibul's passport before departing for his studies at the Ecole de l'artillerie in France in 1924. Note his signature P. Khittasanga before his name was changed to Pibulsonggram.*

# 2

# Pibul's Gold

Midnight, monsoon, 1943. A light drizzle fell on a secluded rice field just outside the village of Taphan Hin, one third of the way to Chiang Mai, where a north-bound freight train had made an unscheduled stop. There, under the cover of darkness, soldiers of the Second Army Division from barracks at Lopburi and Pak Nam Pho, handpicked and sworn to secrecy for this underground mission, were unloading several hundred crates, undetected by Japanese air and land patrols.

The crates were destined to proceed east by the hilly road to Petchabun, on Route 113, along one hundred kilometres of muddy track for three hours, provided they didn't get bogged down by the occasional flash flood, the ever-present sludge and the risk of landslides at Chon Daen, where the road narrows and zigzags before descending into the valley of Petchabun. This clandestine operation had been going on every night for the last three weeks, and there were still 10 more deliveries to be made before the entire consignment reached Petchabun.

It was one of the most secretive and dangerous road and rail logistics exercises ever undertaken in Thailand during the Second World War – and backbreaking work for the soldiers. Many of them did not know the contents of the crates. Only the officers knew each crate contained 100 gold ingots and called it "Pibul's Gold."

Field Marshal Pibulsonggram, or Pibul as he was known, was the Prime Minister of Thailand, the nation's most famous and influential political figure, and a military man. Thailand was occupied by the Japanese at the time, and technically at war with the Allies. Pibul was performing a difficult balancing act, accommodating the Japanese that had invaded his home, while trying to retain the dignity and autonomy of his people during trying war-time circumstances.

On the morning of 7 October 1943, the Field Marshal woke up before sunrise. At 5 a.m., he boarded a special carriage attached to the northern freight train at Hua Lampong station in Bangkok. The secret journey he was about to undertake was part of a crucial campaign of his premiership and its success was fundamental to his anti-Japanese policy. In preparation for a potential showdown with Japan inside Thailand, he was trying to build a secure base in Petchabun, located in the centre of the country and surrounded by protective mountains, where he could also make sure that the country's gold reserves and national treasures were safely hidden from the Japanese. Pibul had heard that Hitler was stealing French and Dutch works of art and shipping them back to Berlin. This kind of wanton plunder, he thought, must not be allowed to happen here. It was his duty to protect the symbols of state and ensure the continuity of the dynasty after the war.

Indeed, over the next eighteen months, Japan was to demand over 490 million baht from the Thai government coffers, several times in excess of the nation's annual budget.[1] They had already shipped forty million dollars' worth of gold to Tokyo.[2] The Japanese war chest was running short of cash, and they needed fuel and armaments for their costly battles with the Americans in the Pacific.

1 Direk Jayanama, *Thailand in Zweiten Weltkrieg*, Erdman Verlag, 1970.

2 In 1949, US President Truman issued special orders to the Japanese government to return the gold to Thailand. Pibul, who was PM at the time, was delighted. (Edwin Stanton, *Brief Authority*, Harper, 1956).

Pibul, however, was particularly determined to protect the sacred symbols of Thailand's history and the revered treasures of the Chakri Dynasty. So in October 1943, the Emerald Buddha, the kingdom's most important Buddhist image since the $16^{th}$ century, several stately thrones and royal regalia, and dozens of ceremonial gold and silver swords, were loaded onto this special train. Pibul would supervise this part of "Operation Gold" personally. Nothing could be allowed to go wrong.

Pibul had been preparing for a Japanese invasion as far back as April 1937 when he called upon the entire nation to arm itself in self-defence, because he believed its security and independence were threatened by a conflict that was about to break out between Britain and Japan in their struggle to impose their domination over Southeast Asia. This was broadcast on radio, five years before the outbreak of war in the Pacific. When the British and Japanese governments heard this speech, they lodged official complaints with the Thai government, denying that they were intending to go to war with each other. Both governments also stressed their commitment to respect Thailand's neutrality. Pibul was not assured.

Pibul made further defensive preparations for a Japanese invasion in September 1940, after the powerless Vichy French authorities capitulated to the Japanese forces in Indochina. Maintaining Thailand's policy of neutrality wasn't going to be easy, with the Japanese army right on the nation's doorstep.

Throughout 1941, Pibul was *obsessed* with Thailand's defences and was often away from Bangkok making inspection tours of the border provinces. Convinced that sooner or later the Japanese would strike from French Indochina, he reinforced the Laotian and Cambodian border areas with additional divisions, and in September 1941 passed stringent laws to control Japanese immigration into the country. Too many of them had recently been entering Thailand posing as tourists, dentists, teachers and merchants, when in fact they were covert military intelligence personnel on spying missions. When the war started, they donned army uniforms overnight.

In addition, the Thai Citizens' Duties in Wartime Act was passed by the National Assembly, instructing the populace to help protect the nation's neutrality in the case of attack through a scorched earth policy, urging them to destroy crops, livestock, provisions and buildings to prevent them from being used by the enemy.

A massive Japanese military and naval build-up in Indochina in July 1941, including the establishment of air bases in Tonkin, warships in Haiphong and troopships in Saigon, confirmed to Pibul that a Japanese attack was both inevitable and imminent. Over the next few months, he futilely attempted to convince the Western powers that the Japanese threat from Indochina was real, and to secure military support from Britain and America. On 4 December he informed the British in Malaya that he had sufficient intelligence to believe an attack would come "within the next four days,"[3] requesting at least the promise of support. In a personal communication to Sir Winston Churchill, the British Prime Minister, Pibul said he was "certain" an invasion of Thailand was coming soon. Churchill replied that help would not be forthcoming and that Thailand was to "defend herself." Pibul later said that he did not understand how Churchill expected "us to fight the Japanese single-handedly."

In the closing months of 1941 the French garrisons in Indochina were neutralised, and the Japanese concentrated their land, air and sea strength in Indochina for their successful onslaughts against British Malaya, Singapore and Hong Kong, American Guam and the Philippines, the Dutch East Indies and independent Thailand.

"The day of infamy"[4] on 7 December 1941, when Japanese planes from six aircraft carriers destroyed six battleships and 188

3 MI6, the British Intelligence Service, also knew of the threat of invasion, but they concluded that due to the monsoon "any attack would be impossible before March."

4 President Roosevelt addressing Congress on 8th December 1941.

aircraft of the US Pacific Fleet at Pearl Harbor, was also the day when Pibul was faced with the toughest predicament of his life. He had been on an inspection tour in the northeast at the time. At 4 a.m. he was awakened and told that since ten-thirty the previous night, General Adun Adundetcharat, the Deputy Prime Minister, had been trying to reach him with the news that the Japanese ambassador, Teiji Tsubokami, requested that Japanese troops be allowed to pass through Thailand. Adun was given three and a half hours to make up his mind; otherwise, the Japanese would invade the country.[5]

By 2 a.m. the time limit had expired and the combined Japanese forces invaded the southern peninsula.[6] Pibul remembered this agonizing moment, the crackling telephone trembling in his hand, as Adun waited for his answer. Like Sweden and Switzerland, Pibul dearly wanted Thailand to remain neutral. His first reaction was to put up a fight, but he knew that it would be futile for the tiny Thai army to resist the Japanese who had years of hardened battle experience in China. He remembered facing the arrogant Japanese ambassador, squat and bespectacled, with his threatening demands after he quickly flew back to Bangkok. Britain and the US had already admitted they could not help after he had requested their assistance. He also learned that the Japanese, as he suspected they would, had also landed at Kota Bharu in Malaya, and was heavily bombarding Singapore. He wondered whether Ambassador Tsubokami realised how much contempt he had for the Japanese on that day.

Pibul had to decide whether to fight the Japanese to the last man, at the risk of laying the country to waste, or surrender and allow the invading Japanese army to seize Thailand, ending 700 years of independence.

*He chose to do neither.*

---

5 A ridiculous request. The Japanese would have attacked anyway, *whatever* Pibul's response, as they did at Pearl Harbor. The Japanese navy *had already set sail* on 26 November with clear instructions to attack Pearl Harbor, Malaya, Singapore, Philippines, Hong Kong and Thailand on the same day.

6 One of the battles in the southern peninsula is the subject of Chapter 5.

Right up to the last week in November 1941, Pibul was hoping for Allied assistance. Had help from Britain and America actually materialized, Pibul could very well have been tempted to join them. Just before the invasion, the British Minister to Thailand, Sir Josiah Crosby, reported to Sir Anthony Eden, the British Foreign Secretary, that "in the absence of a promise from Britain, Siam might be compelled to adopt the role which Denmark is now playing vis-à-vis Germany." In other words, military occupation of neutral Denmark, *without* collaborating with the enemy.[7]

Between December 8 and 9, the Thai forces initially put up a courageous defence of Thailand's southern peninsula, often resorting to hand-to-hand combat, earning respect from their Japanese invaders for bravery and tenacity. Well over 250[8] Japanese and 150 Thai soldiers were killed in action before Pibul ordered a ceasefire. He wanted to prevent the country from becoming a battlefield.

Meanwhile, Churchill had been too proud to the point of arrogance to heed Pibul's warnings about a likely Japanese landing in Thailand and Malaya. The British base in Singapore had strengthened its seaward defensive batteries, expecting an attack by the Japanese navy from the south, not a Japanese army invasion across the Malayan mainland from the north. Britain was caught completely unprepared. Her guns were uselessly pointing in the wrong direction. After two months of fighting the Japanese in Malaya and Singapore, the British unconditionally surrendered 85,000 Commonwealth troops in Singapore on 15 February 1942. This was the most ignominious defeat in British history.

Pibul's next decision was considerably more difficult. The Japanese presented Thailand with a number of unacceptable propositions. The first was for complete political, military and economic cooperation. The second was for Thailand to become a

7 *Siam:The Crossroads,* Sir Josiah Crosby, Hollis and Carter, London, 1945.

8 The Japanese got rid of their dead bodies by burning or burying them before the enemy could make a body count, so their exact losses were never known throughout the war.

full partner with Japan, Germany and Italy as an Axis power. The third was a mutual defence pact without Axis participation, and the fourth to urgently allow Japanese troops the right of transit through Thailand to attack Burma and Malaya.

Pibul realised that a strategic course of action was needed quickly, based on a number of realities:

1. The enemy was already at the gates, yet the Thai army, outnumbered and outgunned, was still under his command.
2. Despite the assurance of the British minister, Sir Josiah Crosby, that "England will help if Siam will fight,"[9] British help did not materialize, and Thailand was therefore under no obligation to assist Britain in defending her Burmese and Malayan colonies.
3. Thailand's geographic location was strategically important for Japan's military conquest of Southeast Asia.
4. Having lost all her alliances in Asia, Japan badly wanted our friendship, a fellow-traveller that had never been colonized.
5. All options considered, it would seem that geopolitically they needed us more than we needed them.

In an address to the nation on 10 December 1939, Pibul had stated that "we must be determined to defend our neutrality" at all costs. Becoming a full partner with Japan would have compromised that position. Partnership was therefore out of the question. Pibul realized that Japanese passage through Thailand was their most pressing and strategically important demand. To temporarily keep them at bay, this request was granted immediately.

In allowing the Japanese to pass through the country, Thailand was perceived as their friend in need and thereby avoided the fate of Korea, the east coast of China, Taiwan and Manchukuo, which had

9 *Thailand and World War II*, Direk Jayanama, Silkworm Books 2008.

become virtual Japanese colonies. While accusations of being a traitor or collaborator were often leveled at Pibul during and immediately after the war, he had always been worried about which side to take for the survival of Thailand's sovereignty. During the confusing years before Pearl Harbor, he had taken into account the shifting political situations around the world: the French supported their leader Petain, and to avoid war, his Vichy government willingly joined the Nazis; Britain seemed about to be invaded; the Italians[10] and the Soviets[11] were allied with Hitler; Japan had brought China to her knees; while the Americans were determined to stay out of the war. Surrounded by powerful rooks on this global chessboard, Thailand was a weak pawn indeed.

Even though Pibul was later forced to declare war on Britain and America to appease the Japanese, Thai sovereignty remained intact and the government under Pibul was allowed complete freedom of action in all her internal affairs, with the executive, legislative and judicial branches of the government remaining autonomous throughout the war, never to be controlled by the Japanese.

Allied prisoners captured by the Thai army, for example, remained in Thai prison camps and were "well treated, well fed, and well housed"[12], unlike the British, Australian and Dutch prisoners-of-war who were worked to death by the Japanese on the Death Railway.[13]

Moreover, Pibul was able to prevent the crushing blow of disarmament by the Japanese. At no time during the war was the Thai army ever placed under Japanese command, unlike the armistice signed between France and Germany on 22 June 1940, when French forces were totally disarmed and three-fifths of the country was surrendered to German control.

---

10 In 1936, Mussolini, the Italian dictator, joined Nazi Germany and formed the Rome-Berlin Axis.

11 In 1939, Joseph Stalin, the Soviet leader, signed a nonaggression pact with Hitler.

12 Sir Geoffrey Thompson, Britain's ambassador in Bangkok, 1947.

13 See Chapter 10.

Of course, Pibul continually had to enter into onerous agreements with the Japanese, but based on the sound principles of *Realpolitik*, he had no intention whatsoever of honouring them. Alliance, if need be, he decided, rather than subjugation.[14]

Indeed, in the years that followed the Japanese invasion of December 1941, the Japanese, militarists at heart, would misinterpret Pibul's leadership as being compatible with their hegemonist aims of conquering Asia. They couldn't have been more mistaken. While Pibul was "outwardly posturing as the pro-Japanese puppet Prime Minister"[15], he was secretly having a dialogue with Free China's 93rd Division Commander at the Lam River on the border of Burma and China. As a token of Thai friendship, General Lu was presented with a beautifully engraved hunting rifle, a personal gift from Pibul. Pibul was making sure that the back door remained open for Allied support should the Japanese decide to conduct an air and ground war against his base in Petchabun. Pibul's peaceful contacts with the Chinese through the Kong Thap Phayap (Northwest Army) whose ostensible mission was to protect the Japanese northern flank was one of the most well-kept secret operations of the war.

Pibul well knew that there was an active Free Thai resistance movement in the country, yet he did nothing to stop it. Instead, he facilitated the resistance's activities by tacitly allowing the movement's build-up in the northeast without reporting it to the Japanese. "Pibul's decision not to betray the resistance movement to the Japanese saved the life of the resistance movement."[16] By feigning obedience to the Japanese, Pibul also allowed Thailand to become the Allies' best listening post in Asia.

---

14 "Being part of the British Empire was no guarantee of safety. Indeed had Burma been an independent state, she would have suffered much less. The Siamese, for instance, had got through with very little damage." *The Last and First in Burma,* Maurice Collis, Faber and Faber, 1956. The Burma campaign was the longest land campaign of the war.

15 *The Thai Resistance Movement During the Second World War,* John Haseman, Chalermnit Press, 1999.

16 Ibid.

Thus Pibul's choices conformed with his goal from the outset of the conflict. Before M.R. Seni Pramoj left Bangkok in 1941 to take up his position as Minister to Washington, D.C., he asked Pibul for clarification on Thailand's foreign policy. "Were we pro-Japanese, pro-English, pro-American or pro-anything? He replied that we were not *pro* any country in particular. We were pro-Thailand."[17]

One of Pibul's powerful dictums to explain his desire for Thailand to remain neutral is well encapsulated in these simple words: "We are not concerned about the war outside the country. We are more concerned about fighting each other. To whom will we sing the National Anthem if we kill each other?"

In another famous dictum, he said that even if we were to be defeated and forced to give up our land, the spirit of the Thai people can never be destroyed.

Today, Pibul's important role during World War II has often been overlooked in the history books. In 1960, HRH Prince Chula Chakrabongse wrote in *Lords of Life,* a story of the Chakri Dynasty, that "apart from avoiding complete ruin to the country, had Pibul not joined the Japanese, British, American, and other allied prisoners-of-war of the Japanese incarcerated in Thailand might not have survived."

In his full Field Marshal's artillery uniform, and his favourite, highly polished cavalry boots, Pibul strutted jauntily up the Hua Lampong station platform followed by his aide-de-camp, a batman and three army officers. The distant sound of chanting monks mingling with the hissing steam of the locomotive could just be discerned in the early morning silence. The train driver was stoking up the engine with coal for the long journey north to Taphan Hin.

As Pibul and his small party approached a special carriage,

17 M.R. Seni Pramoj's memoirs.

the chanting got louder. They boarded the train. Nine chanting monks were seated in a lotus position on both sides of a pedestal in the centre of the carriage, at their head a senior abbot, leading the Buddhist incantations. Pibul prostrated himself at the base of the pedestal in reverence and kowtowed three times, and again prostrated before each monk in turn. Standing vertically on the pedestal on a gold ceremonial tray[18] was a gilded teak box measuring one metre by one-fifty. Inside was the Emerald Buddha, the palladium of the Chakri, the dynasty that has ruled Thailand since 1782.

Realising the implication of this risky mission, Pibul was, for a brief moment, overcome with emotion. Relocating the Emerald Buddha was tantamount to moving five centuries of Thai history. As a military officer who helped lead the 1932 revolution, Pibul himself had played an important role in transitioning the country from absolute to constitutional monarchy that year. In the 1930s, after rising to become prime minister of the country, his government was often at loggerheads with the royalist factions who distrusted his intentions and saw him as an autocratic leader bent on undermining royal institutions and power. Moving the royal regalia might be unacceptable to some in Bangkok. Meanwhile, the current king, His Majesty King Ananda Mahidol, only a minor at the time, was living abroad in Switzerland. Did Pibul even have the moral right to do this? A decisive, determined and a very Buddhist person, Pibul was convinced that protecting the Emerald Buddha was the right thing to do. He would *personally* accompany this most sacred icon to its new resting place in Petchabun.

Twenty other wagons in the railway convoy were stacked with forty crates containing the royal regalia received by each successive Chakri king on his coronation, including swords, jewelled slippers, gilded thrones and other ceremonial items dating back to the first Chakri ruler. And of course, there were also the gold ingots that

18 "Phaan" in Thai.

needed to be kept safe. Each wagon was guarded by a platoon of four trusted soldiers. The station platform at that time of the morning was quiet and eerily empty; public access was forbidden. There was a light mist in the moist air.

Pibul and his party settled down at the front end of the carriage, which was converted into a private suite. At precisely 5.17 a.m. the train slowly chugged out of the station. After Nonthaburi, it picked up speed, and Pibul was at last left alone with his thoughts. He pressed his palms together in thankful reverence as the train passed the town where he was born 46 years before. As always, he was moved by the early glow of the sun, as it started to glimmer on the horizon's rice fields, an emerald green at this time of the morning. Glad to leave behind the hurly-burly of politics in Bangkok, he sat back and relaxed for the first time in months.

Pibul had always been at his happiest when he went on inspection tours of the provinces, and he felt particularly comfortable and secure when travelling by train. This route was a familiar one. Pathumthani, Bang Pa-In, Ayudhya... he passed the towns he knew so well. *This country was to fight for,* he was thinking, *and to save from her enemies.* He reminisced about his days as an army cadet. *The mark of a great soldier is knowing when to apply the iron fist and knowing when to apply the velvet glove.* Pibul recalled his dissertation on one of the Thai army's many powerful strategic principles.

Pibul, or Plaek, as he was then known, was only eighteen when he graduated from the Military Cadet School in Bangkok with honours. He was the top student of his year, the class of 1915, and his superior training officer noticed that this opportunistic but bright and affable young man continually came up with the correct answers, even to the most difficult tactical exercises. He also noticed that during classes Plaek was a master survivor, able to fall on his feet in tight situations every time. Indeed, Plaek always made sure each situation would end in his favour. One day, he was certain, Plaek would come to something.

He also remembered his early career as a junior officer, when life was less complicated. He had taken this very train to Phitsanulok where he was attached to the Artillery Corps. There, he met La-Iad, his future wife, not only the most beautiful girl in the north, but the most intelligent woman he had ever met.

In those days, Pibul was especially diligent, highly ambitious and clever. Clever enough in 1924 to win a government scholarship to further his studies at the prestigious Fontainebleau Ecole de l'artillerie in France. In 1933, back in Thailand as an artillery officer, he used the iron fist to quash the Bovoradej rebellion[19] and made a name for himself outside military circles for the first time. Colonel Pibul became the man of the moment.

The train stopped to take on more troops. He looked out of the window. *Aah… Lopburi.* He immediately felt at home. He could always count on the 2nd Army at Lopburi. The loyal soldiers here loved and admired him. They would trustingly follow him to the ends of the earth…

As the train continued its journey north, its rhythmic motion soothed his nerves, and he began to think about the difficult and eventful year he just had. His decision to relocate the capital to Petchabun was a temporary move to draw the Japanese *away* from Bangkok and to prevent it from being an Allied target should the war escalate the country into a battlefield. This strategy had come to him a few months after Thailand was occupied by the Japanese. He knew that it wouldn't be long before they would find out he was *never* on their side. Throughout 1942, the Field Marshal had shrewdly led the Japanese to believe through his public speeches and ostensibly pro-Japanese policies that he was their ally.

Petchabun was his exit strategy. In early 1943, Pibul had appointed an investigative board of six senior police officers and two army generals assisted by five ministerial-level civil servants to look

19 See Chapter 1.

into the feasibility of building up a new, modern Petchabun, a small town of 3,000, set in a valley surrounded by mountains.

At Petchabun he could establish his military and political base, far from Bangkok and the highly populated central plains, from where he could safely conduct a guerrilla campaign against his true enemy. Petchabun would not only be a secure military command post and a temporary civilian capital, but also a safe hideaway for the Kingdom's treasures. Mountain caves 23 kilometres further north would be difficult for Japanese forces to reach and were not visible from the air by Japanese reconnaissance missions. Meanwhile, Bangkok could safely become an "open city."[20]

On 11 September 1943, the board reported to Pibul and the Petchabun project was set into motion. "Operation Gold" could begin. The logistics were planned and executed by the Army Field Forces Headquarters in Petchabun. Within a month, Pibul was able to combine rail and road transport, an efficient workforce, the necessary cover, as well as a suitable cache for the treasure, into *one single operation, in secret*. Pibul was satisfied that so far his campaign was a skilful military undercover operation conducted right under the noses of the Japanese army. He was pleased that he had successfully outmanoeuvred them.

What was going to be rather more difficult was making the move a *political* success with his own government. Except for his closest aides and La-Iad, however, the Petchabun campaign was totally misunderstood by his government. He was even accused of wanting to abandon Bangkok, when all he really intended was to *save* it.

Now, Pibul's train was approaching the transfer rendezvous at Taphan Hin...

20 Paris and Rome were declared "open cities" whereby all defence efforts were abandoned to save the city from needless destruction.

After a hearty meal of his favourite green chicken curry and rice, Pibul left the train at 2 a.m. and boarded the army Austin 8 staff car that would lead the military convoy carrying the Emerald Buddha, the royal treasures, and the gold to their secret destination across the mountains, arriving before daybreak. It had taken two hours to unload hundreds of crates from the train onto the trucks. Apart from one truck that got stuck in the mud, the journey east from the rice fields at Taphan Hin to the valley on the other side of the mountains was relatively uneventful. Fortunately, they did not encounter any Japanese air or land patrols.

As they approached the valley, about 50 kilometres from Petchabun, the dark profile of the karst mountains towered into view in the early morning light. Pibul was reminded of another strategic principle that he had learned as a cadet:

*If you do not understand the terrain of the mountains, forests and hazardous areas, and the dangers that are present, you will not be able to move your troops and engage in war.*

The mountains that embraced both sides of the valley placed Petchabun in an ideal defensive position. Seeing this forbidding terrain once again convinced him that he had made the right decision.

After a series of hairpin bends, the convoy reached the fertile plantations of Ban Hua Na at the foot of the mountain and continued its journey north to the town of Petchabun, along the valley road and the rapids of Pa Sak River, on Route 21, today called Sammaki Chai[21] road, Pibul's *nom de guerre,* in his honour. Fortunately, it was no longer raining.

He would have liked to stop at the town of Petchabun to inspect the public works in progress, but that could wait. He was anxious to get to the cave. *His cave.* Pibul ordered the precious convoy

21 Victorious in unity.

to proceed without delay a few kilometres north to Ban Boong Nam Tao and the entrance of the cave. The most important journey of his life was nearly over.

With a sudden rush of adrenalin, Pibul leapt out of the car and ran up the 250 steps, two at a time, that led to the cave entrance. His aides followed quickly, barely able to keep up with him. His heart was pounding, partly from the strenuous climb, but mainly from anticipation and excitement. He had long dreamed of this moment. Deep inside the cave he stopped at the niche he was looking for. He fell to his knees in prayer and told his aide-de-camp: "This is where the Emerald Buddha must rest."

One of the elderly villagers, at the time a boy of 10, recalls those eventful forty nights in October 1943. He remembers soldiers – hundreds of soldiers stripped down to a *pakama*[22] loincloth, their bodies gleaming with sweat – unloading the crates in silence and carrying them to the top of the hill, 20 metres and 250 steps above the level of the road. Many local farmers and teenage boys were also pressed into service, helping the soldiers on the ground to complete this brutal work while the officers stood guard and directed operations. The soldiers and workers were stripped to their *pakama* to reduce the temptation to steal the treasures and to obviate the necessity of making body searches. They had to work quickly before being discovered by the Japanese air patrol that routinely flew over Petchabun at around 9 a.m.

By 4 February 1944 mission "Operation Gold" was accomplished. The gold, the royal treasures and the Emerald Buddha were all safely cached away in the caves. The entrance to the cave was sealed off and the steps were heavily guarded. The protective concrete bunkers and fortifications that lined the stairway were so well built that today they are still standing.

Unfortunately for Pibul, however, he did not have the

22 Traditional mulicoloured loincloth for men, folded in such a way as to fit like modern briefs.

opportunity to fulfil his anti-Japanese campaign through the Petchabun project. In July 1944, two of his bills in the National Assembly were defeated and the Field Marshal was forced to resign his premiership.[23]

One of these bills dealt with the establishment of the temporary capital in Petchabun. Because of the campaign's secretive nature, when called upon to explain what the plan was all about, Pibul was not able to publicly defend this bill in Parliament, without giving the game away to the Japanese. The opposition in Parliament did not understand Pibul's intentions and accused him of wanting to abandon Bangkok.

The second bill, to establish a Buddhist sanctuary of peace and safety in the hills of Saraburi, the Buddhaburi Monthon, for Thai civilian refugees fleeing from the Japanese army, should Siam become a war zone, was also defeated.

The author John McNally[24] wrote: "His greatest hope had become his greatest failure – the military base upcountry where he had planned to secretly concentrate enough army personnel to resist the Japanese." Ironically, the very action that Pibul took to protect Thailand's sovereignty and preserve the royal capital was precisely the one that brought him down. He retired to his farm without demur, satisfied that the nation's treasures were safe.

On 23 April 1946, after two years, two months and twenty days, the Emerald Buddha was safely back at the temple of Wat Phra Keo in Bangkok, and "Pibul's Gold" and the royal treasures were restored to the nation, intact.

After the war ended, the national treasures' safe journey home was far less dramatic. There was no longer any threat from a Japanese

23 Curiously for a dictator, Pibul never ruled by decree, and could have easily dissolved Parliament. He never headed a government without a parliament.

24 In his book *Dragon in Paradise*, Doubleday, New York, 1963, page 201.

attack. It was a formal caravan procession to the railway siding at Taphan Hin where the train was waiting, attended by officials from the Royal Household and the Prime Minister's Office, under the protection of the army, with continued pomp and ceremony in Bangkok. When the Emerald Buddha was carefully lifted from its secret hiding place before travelling back to Wat Phra Keo, it was blessed by the Supreme Patriarch's emissary, Phra[25] Chantrsri Chantateepo, who subsequently became Chief Abbot Phra Udomyanmolee at Wat Pho Somporn in Udorn. It was certainly the most devout ceremony he had ever conducted. He often recounted this unforgettable spiritual experience to his acolytes in Udorn. *How many abbots in the country had the unique opportunity to perform prayers for the nation's most sacred Buddha image?* he would proudly ask. It was a humbling moment.

Today, the cave in Petchabun is popularly known as Tam Ruesee Sombad, the "Treasure Cave." The locals are proud it played such an important role in the Second World War. Several Buddha images have been placed there, and prayers and offerings are made by the devout. The local authorities are trying to promote Tam Ruesee Sombad as a tourist attraction, but outside the province of Petchabun, little is known of its historic significance. Until Pibul's heroic journey is given the recognition it deserves, the Treasure Cave will remain a vague footnote in the annals of the Second World War, and at best, a local legend.

25 The formal address for a Buddhist monk.

# NAI LERT

## Full name: Lert Sreshthaputra

## 1872 - 1945

A man who never took no for an answer,
and Siam's first entrepreneur

***Previous page:*** *An early model White Bus, with a Ford engine and passenger entrance at the rear, designed by Nai Lert.*

***Above:*** *Nai Lert was very attached to Tam, his clouded leopard.*

# 3

# A Victorian Siamese

Even before Prime Minister Pibul declared war on Britain and America on 26 January 1942, British Vickers Wellington bombers from Calcutta 225 Group were already making air sorties and attacks on Bangkok. The RAF bombing raids were to continue right to the end of the war. On one particular air raid, two bombs aimed at Bangkok's Makkasan railway junction missed their mark and fell on the property of Nai Lert, narrowly missing the British legation in the adjacent compound, but causing considerable damage to the leading Siamese businessman's villa.

When the frequency of the air raids increased, Nai Lert made sure that his wife, Khunying Sinn, and all the members of his household, were safely evacuated to Soi Prompong in Bangapi[1], several miles away from the military targets in town.[2] Nai Lert himself refused to budge. It takes more than a few bombs to drive *him* out of his own home, he would tell his friends.

During one night raid that totally devastated the villa's terrace and adjacent garden, the explosion was so powerful that loose bricks and tree branches flew in all directions. Nai Lert was hit by falling

---

1 Renamed "Sukhumvit" in the sixties.

2 The Allied bombardment from 1941 to 1945 destroyed many railway stations, power plants and hospitals, yet miraculously none of the city's Buddhist temples were ever hit.

debris and temporarily lost consciousness. When he came to, he tried to see the extent of the damage but he couldn't open his eyes. *I'm blind,* he thought in a panic. Only when help came and ambulance workers removed a large cake of mud that had stuck to his eyes and face did he realise that he had not lost his eyesight. After this fortunate escape, he decided, but not without considerable pressure from Sinn, to move out. A stubborn and proud man, it was not an easy decision. Throughout the war, 14 bombs were dropped on his property.

Later in the war, when the Japanese occupation caused rampant inflation and the economy was at a near standstill, Nai Lert almost went bankrupt. Prime Minister Pibul, an admirer of Nai Lert, offered to help him by requesting Parliament to grant him a soft loan from the Treasury. Nai Lert was invited to present himself before a special Parliamentary Committee set up for this purpose and explain how he intended to invest the money.

"You were once the richest man in Bangkok and now you are bankrupt. How does a man lose so much money in such a short time? What did you spend your money on?"

"I damn well spent it all getting drunk every night on Vat 69[3]." With this acerbic reply, Nai Lert stormed out, never to return. To expect a bailout from the government was demoralizing enough. To be asked how he invested his hard-earned income was just plain insulting. He vowed never again to depend on others to help him out.

One of Pibul's many directives before the war – which were designed to bring Siam into the twentieth century – was his famous dress code legislation. Pibul forbid the public from wearing traditional Siamese costumes, particularly those that exposed parts of the body that were considered immodest by the West. Bare breasts and naked torsos were also no longer allowed. For men, trousers

3 A brand of Scotch imported by Nai Lert's company.

and shirts were *de rigueur* and women were told to wear hats and gloves. The traditional male trousers, the *pha jong-kraben, dhoti*-style calf-length pantaloons, although not forbidden, was also discouraged.

Although he considered himself a modern man and often wore formal black-tie at diplomatic functions, Nai Lert bluntly refused to dress in Western-style shirts and trousers, even when Pibul came to visit. He unsuccessfully tried to persuade female members of his family not to wear hats and gloves. On one occasion towards the end of the war, when his villa and parkland were bombed again, he went with his wife and family to inspect the damage after the raid, and noticed his daughter's [4] curiously designed hat he particularly disliked lying in the rubble.

"Take a look at your lovely hat, dear. It's all topsy-turvy, just like our house!"

They had lost most of their villa, his beloved trees and plants were uprooted and Sinn's precious collection of antique porcelain was in shatters, yet Nai Lert, far from being upset, flippantly asked his wife, "Is there anything left here that we can have for dinner?" Through his mischievous humour, he was always able to keep up the family morale. While life had many ups and downs, it was never the end of the road, he often told them. His humour was legendary and his frequent sarcastic comments and original turns of phrase were often made during the least expected moments. He had a way with the Thai language, and he also had a way with people. Indeed, he had lived a marvellous life.

When Nai Lert was born in 1872, the Suez Canal had just been opened three years before. As a result, the sea voyage from Europe was several weeks shorter than the old voyage via the Cape of Good Hope. The early years of the canal's operation coincided with the

---

4 Tanpuying Lursakdi Sampatisiri.

development of the much faster steamship. The history of Southeast Asia was to change forever.

Nai Lert grew up when King Chulalongkorn (Rama V) fully opened the country's doors to Western ideas and influences and he lived his early years during Siam's transition from a "mediaeval" to a modern state. The first laws were codified, proper control of revenue and finance was introduced, construction of the first railway and road systems began, and by 1890 postal and telegraph services were introduced. In 1893 Asia's first electric tram service was launched in Bangkok.[5]

But even by the start of the new century, the country had still not developed a Siamese commercial middle class. The rice trade, representing two-thirds of Siam's exports, was in the hands of the Chinese, while foreign trade was controlled by the Europeans, who had established exchange banks, shipping offices and merchant houses in Bangkok, a city of 400,000 people.

Nai Lert descended from the establishment Sreshthaputra clan. He did not want to follow family tradition and make a career in government service. He saw new opportunities in the growing commercial sector of the economy. He had a fertile and creative mind full of new ideas, and he wanted to put them into profitable practice. But first he had to gain as much business experience as possible. He had a lot to *learn,* he realised. Being the Victorian minded person he was, he wanted to start from the ground floor. He was determined to learn the hard way.

Not yet eighteen, he volunteered as a trainee with the Windsor trading company and was put to work as the store's errand boy and general factotum. He was introduced to the inner workings of the retail trade and he put his heart into learning about buying and selling. In less than a year he learned about consumer shopping needs and customer habits. Many clients were Europeans so he was able

5 The tramway had 48 km of track and 206 tram cars.

to improve his English. He was expecting a promotion any day and eventually getting a salary, but when he received neither, he left to work at the Tax Department, where he was given a clerical position and learned the skills of accounting, again without a salary. Now twenty, Nai Lert decided it was time to start earning money and he found a teaching position at Sunantalai College. He was paid 20 baht a month.[6] To maintain contact with the expatriate community, and to further practice his English skills, he tutored Thai to foreigners in the evenings at one baht an hour.

One of Nai Lert's expatriate connections, Jane Hay McFarland, wife of an American Presbyterian missionary, took a liking to this bright young man and impressed with his English proficiency, recommended him to Fraser & Neave (F&N), a British soft drinks company from Singapore, where he was given the position of Bill Collector.

By 1893, he had gained three years on-the-job business experience in about the same time it would take today to obtain a business degree with the added benefits of acquiring practical skills and wisdom in the real world. He was now ready, he told his British boss, to become the manager of F&N.

The Englishman didn't quite laugh in his face, but what he said changed Nai Lert's life forever: "You are too young and inexperienced to be a manager of our company. Besides, a Chinaman neither has the *knowledge* nor the *image* to run a European company."

Not one to give up so easily when there was an opportunity to learn something new, he immediately requested transfer to Singapore to work in a similar clerical position in the same company.

In Singapore, he continued his business education. He learned more about F&N's trading operations and he consumed iced drinks for the first time. He decided there and then that he would one day compete with F&N.

---

6 Equivalent to about 10,000 baht today.

He observed that "Chinamen" selected to serve the British – called "compradors" – became the middlemen between the British firms and the locals. They looked and dressed like Europeans and they spoke excellent English. Their *image* was acceptable to the white man. The British merchant, he noticed, could not operate without help from these Western-oriented go-betweens. *Image*, he discovered, was an important business tool. He did not intend to become a comprador in Siam, but he always aspired to become the boss, or *"Nai Harng"* in Thai, the operator of one's own business.

The first step in establishing his new image was to buy a black suit, complete with all the formal black tie accoutrements, from John Little and Co. in Commercial Square. He went across the street to have a haircut and whence to a nearby portrait studio to have his photograph taken. Nai Lert had reinvented himself.

The next step was to spend his free time at the premises of John Little, Singapore's oldest and finest department store.[7] Here he observed that there were products and services that were not available in Bangkok: imported confectionary and biscuits, hams and cheese, musical instruments, as well as a tea room, a beauty salon and a ticket agency on the premises. He also learned about the art of retail display.

His Singaporean "MBA" education now complete, and satisfied with his new image, he returned to Bangkok and within two years launched his own retail business, the Nai Lert Store, at Klong Padung Krung Kasem, at that time Bangkok's commercial district. At this new store, he sold Singer sewing machines, canned meats, and many other imported European food products, as well as carbonated lemonade in bottles with glass stoppers. Every year he introduced new important foods and each year he developed a taste for European delicacies. He enjoyed Western food, and Vat 69 Scotch

7 Established in 1845.

whisky became his favourite drink. Nai Lert became his own best customer.

By 1910, his store had expanded and his new stock now included ice blocks that he manufactured, ice cream, artesian well water, soda water and Shell Motor Oil. He was on his way to becoming Siam's leading businessman.

Such were his entrepreneurial skills that he was to earn the reputation as the person who launched a series of successful commercial "firsts" in Siam.

He was the *first* to build an ice factory in the country and deliver ice blocks to homes and shops all over the city. Ice production and distribution provided employment for hundreds of people in Bangkok. Workers in the ice factory were well looked after and stayed with Nai Lert for the rest of their working lives. When the stock market in the West crashed in 1929, Siam was badly affected and many companies were forced out of business. When his ice factory workers learned that the plant was about to close down, they appeared at Nai Lert's office in tears. They were proud of their work and did not want to leave their jobs. They offered to work at half-pay and forgo their annual bonus.

Confronted by his tearful workers, Nai Lert broke down and started to cry himself. He was now losing money in many of his businesses but he decided that he would not let these loyal people down. He would *borrow* the money to pay them if necessary. With reduced output and lower overheads, the ice plant survived.

All of Nai Lert's employees remained loyal and stayed with him until the very end. A certain Ngee was one of his most trusted and long-serving employees, and Nai Lert allowed him to keep the discarded rice husks that were burned as fuel to power the ice machine. Nai Lert was happy to see that Ngee had the initiative to sell the burnt rice husks and earn a small income. Years later, when Ngee died, his children found thousands of one hundred baht notes stuffed in the mattress.

Nai Lert was also Siam's *first* real estate developer. In 1915 he purchased 65 rai[8] of land in the underdeveloped Ploenchit area from local farmers. The spread extended from the present day Nai Lert Park and the British Embassy on Klong Saen Saeb on one side and Ploenchit Road on the other, reaching east to Soi 5 on Sukhumvit Road. He cut new roads on a grid and subdivided the property into smaller plots that he sold off, keeping a large piece for his new home, soon to be the family's pride and joy, the Nai Lert Park.

His biggest land deal in Ploenchit was in 1921, when he sold a 32 rai[9] plot to the British government for their new legation. The British minister could no longer stand the noisy sawmill near his residence on the river and moved from today's present General Post Office location on New Road to Ploenchit, in those days quiet and rural.

With hundreds of rain trees that he had planted, Nai Lert created an oasis of peace and shady tranquillity, away from the hustle and bustle of the river. A number of colonial-style mansions were built for the expatriate community, the first rental accommodation in Bangkok available on a commercial scale. By 1930 Ploenchit was the most exclusive area in Bangkok. It was also the greenest.

Nai Lert loved his parkland and continually experimented with exotic new plants, and brought over rare trees to his property from all over the tropical and sub-tropical world. He also brought a number of wild animals that he loved to domesticate onto his property. One of his new neighbours was Pibul, the Prime Minister of Siam, who bought a large villa next door. They became friends and often visited each other's homes. On one particular occasion, Nai Lert heard that Tanpuying La-Iad, Pibul's wife, had ordered a tall rain tree that they shared in common on the road to be cut down; she was concerned that the branches were too close to her bedroom and posed a security risk. When a gang of soldiers turned up to cut down the tree, the

---

8 Approximately 16 acres.
9 8 acres.

former clerk at the Fraser & Neave soft drink company grabbed his shotgun and ran out onto the street to confront them.

"Tell old Plaek,"[10] said Nai Lert, pointing his gun at them, "that he need not worry about assassination attempts because I will personally shoot him myself if you cut down this tree!"

The tree was saved and Nai Lert and Plaek remained, as they had always been, good friends. Nai Lert was a passionate nature lover and a committed conservationist until the end of his days. Walk down the lanes of Soi Chidlom and Soi Somkid today, and you will find many rain trees planted in 1915 by Nai Lert still giving shade to grateful pedestrians.

Nai Lert's most successful enterprise was in public transportation. He started in the early 1900s with a fleet of horse-drawn carriages for hire to affluent residents and overseas visitors. Each carriage, chauffeured by a smart driver in a crisp white uniform with shiny brass buttons, was pulled by two handsome white horses. The carriage station and the stables were garaged at the top end of Silom road, near the Oriental Hotel, where many passengers were picked up. Until the arrival of the combustion engine, Nai Lert's hackney carriage service was the most prestigious and comfortable way to travel in Bangkok. The only other transport services available at the time were either noisy trams limited to a small area of the old inner city or bumpy rickshaws pulled by overworked Chinese coolies.

At the same time, he saw an opportunity to improve water transport services on the canals that crisscrossed the city. He had always been fascinated with boats since he was a boy. When he lived in the old inner city he used to go to school in the family's private rowing boat. Those families who did not own a boat might wait for hours at the pier for a passing passenger boat that neither ran on a

10 Prime Minister Pibul's name to his friends.

regular route nor on schedule. Public bus services and ferries as we know today did not exist. Nai Lert launched Siam's first scheduled river and boat transport services in 1918. The White Boat Company's ferry service brought country folk from Chachoengsao to Pratunam in Bangkok for the first time. Over the next 30 years the company's network expanded to all the waterways of Bangkok.

Nai Lert was a keen sailor and an even keener boat designer. He developed and designed a number of seagoing vessels for his own pleasure. He experimented with different models and would spend days at his shipyard inspecting the hulls, prows, keels and rudders, working with his engineers to make the perfect boat. His low draft designs were ideal for plying the shallow waters of the canals during the dry season. His vessels were made of teak wood. He had an aversion to metal construction, which tended to corrode and was prone to dents, holes and irreparable damage. He built a fleet of wooden steamboats that plied the gulf, transporting goods to and from the coastal towns on the Gulf of Siam. The pride of his fleet was the S.S. *Samantao*.[11] Anchored near the company's headquarters at Klong Padung Krung Kasem Canal, it delivered fresh artesian well water to foreign ships berthed at the Port of Bangkok.

In 1925, the Big Flood hit the nation and like the Big One in 2011, many provinces in the central plains, particularly farmland, were as much as three metres under water. The majority of the country's population were rice farmers and Nai Lert pressed his ferryboats into public service and carried thousands of buffaloes and farmers to safety. For this act of courage and charity, Nai Lert was "knighted" by King Rama VI and given the title of Phraya Bhakdinoraseth (Lord Beloved Millionaire).

Nai Lert always boasted that his vessels could easily outrun even the fastest Royal Navy coastguard ship, and jokingly said that his boats would be perfect for piracy and contraband activities. His

11 A name given to him as a child.

rivals would use this to falsely accuse him of evading customs and illegally importing duty free liquor into the country on his boats.

His seamanship skills were legendary and a naval captain that came along on one of his pleasure cruises around the Gulf noticed that he was particularly adept at piloting, the ability to guide a boat through narrow channels and dangerous waters. In his role as captain, he was a master mariner and always gave the right instructions to the engine room below, and precise order to his officers, even though he didn't always use the correct nautical term and official naval language. On the contrary, he preferred to use slang and he would pepper his instructions with naughty sexual connotations. It was, "Bring the little baby in," not "return to port." Or when he gave instructions to anchor, he would say "Drop the goolies."

The SS *Koh Ngor* was his favourite boat, and he frequently took it out on cruises around the islands of the Gulf, loading it up with beer and whisky for long fishing trips, and staffing it with his favourite cook from the restaurant[12] of the Hotel de la Paix, a luxury guesthouse he owned in the Saphan Hlek Bridge area. He would invite his business associates and hard-drinking friends for the ride, and they would party for days. In true naval tradition, he never allowed women on board, not even his wife, her female friends or relatives.

This was the paradox of Nai Lert, who loved Sinn dearly and was never unfaithful to her. He treated her as his partner in life and in business. He never made a business decision without first informing or even consulting her. Yet he would continually swear like a trooper, deliberately using profane language, often in front of his wife, just to tease her. She got used to him, but once in a while she could no longer hold her patience and would openly show her annoyance. He would roar with laughter. The more annoyed she became, the more he swore.

12 It became famous when King Rama VI dined there.

He actually despised men that played around with other women and was, unusually for the era, against bigamy, let alone maintaining a household of minor wives. He was totally against illicit sex. He once allowed one of his friends to use his boat for a pleasure cruise around the Gulf. Without informing Nai Lert, he took a bevy of ladies of ill repute on board. When Nai Lert found this out, he removed every cushion and every mattress, all the carpets and curtains, and had them all burned. He wasn't a prude. He was simply an old-fashioned Victorian male with high moral standards. Women belonged in the home, not out in the streets, he would say.

In 1922, Nai Lert launched the White Bus Company. He ordered Ford truck engines from Bedford in England and built the passenger compartments on the lorry's rear chassis. The buses were made entirely of teak and the bodies were painted white. Nai Lert designed all of them himself and he would often be found on all fours in his workshop drawing his plans in chalk on the cement floor. The early models allowed passengers to climb into the bus on a running board in the rear, and long bench seats were built along each side of the cabin, similar to *song-taew* passenger pick-up trucks today.

The first service started at a new terminal at Pratunam Bridge, one route to Silom, and the other to Yotse Bridge near the Klong Padung Krung Kasem canal. The services were then extended to new destinations all over the city. When this writer came back to Siam in 1949, he always took the White Bus number 101 to school. There were other bus companies but our mothers made sure we only took the "White Bus" because the services were better, the interiors were cleaner, they ran on time and they *never* broke down. The White Bus became the symbol of good, honest and efficient public transport in Bangkok. The safe drivers and courteous ticket collectors wore clean white uniforms and were proud to work for Nai Lert. Female passengers often remarked that the White Bus drivers were the best-looking. Nai Lert's bus company continued serving Bangkokians until 1975, when the industry was nationalized.

One of Nai Lert's many innovative marketing tactics was to allow boat passengers from the countryside to use the same ticket for their onward journey on the connecting bus once they arrived in Bangkok. Another marketing ploy was to name each White Boat after a klong (canal) or a district or the area where the boat plied. For the convenience of passengers, each name was used to describe the route and was easy to remember – "Time to board the Pratunam ferry!" the boatman would shout – giving residents a sense of pride and belonging to the area where they lived.

In the twenties, when cars were first introduced to Siam, Nai Lert imported Fiats from Italy and rented them out complete with uniformed drivers, by the hour. They were Bangkok's first taxi service, following on the heels of his successful hackney carriage business ten years earlier. His taxis were all painted – naturally – in white.

Nai Lert was obsessed with white, his favourite colour. His horses were white, all his boats and buses were white, his taxis were white, and he insisted that all his offices, garages and shops were painted white. White became a unifying element for his company and part of his branding strategy. It symbolised purity, in keeping with his high moral ethics.

The only transportation business where Nai Lert admitted defeat was when he imported Raleigh bicycles from England. He was sure that Bangkokians would take up bikes both as a form of short neighbourhood transport and as a sporty fad for young people. He was wrong. Now, one hundred years on, Thais are finally taking bicycling seriously. He lost a lot of money from this one single shipment. The colour of the imported bikes were black.

Nai Lert was a master in marketing strategy, well ahead of his time. *Image*, one of his early learnings, was to serve his business organization well over the years.

A good image, Nai Lert had learned, came from what consumers remembered, felt and took away from a brand. Every single branded product that Nai Lert imported from Europe carried a memorable "insignia," a trademark, what we call today a "logo." Nai Lert's logo, a red circled cross, was Thailand's *first brand logo*.

Nai Lert instinctively knew about the power of a brand's logo. Once the consumer is sold on the quality of your product and service, then your logo represents that quality, so whatever you sell or provide under that logo automatically assumes an aura of quality. He taught his employees that his logo was his personal guarantee of quality. Nai Lert was arguably the nation's first marketing guru. He didn't invent the design of his logo. He wasn't a graphic artist. He just remembered seeing a similar graphic used by a photographic studio in Singapore that he particularly liked.

Nai Lert was neither academic nor spiritual, although in his later years he liked to philosophize. He was a practical man and he never tried to explain the intellectual or spiritual significance of his logo, as there wasn't one. It was simply a successful commercial trademark that consumers remembered. Later, well-meaning people in his organization intellectualized that each of the four points of the cross represented joy, compassion, neutrality and kindness, probably because Nai Lert demonstrated all these four traits. When he was asked to explain his logo to the general public, he trotted out these four points parrot-fashion, and in time it became the company's mission statement. But in his heart of hearts, Nai Lert believed that no amount of intellectualizing could replace the honest production of creative products and services delivered with quality. Quality and service were Nai Lert's true credo. Once, when he was in one of his mischievous moods, as he often was after several tots of Vat 69 whisky, his friends asked him what the circled cross *really* meant. "Screwing," he said in jest. "Like a man coming together with a woman, screwing."

Nai Lert actually did believe in a number of homespun philosophies and he was quite happy to share them. Here is one of them:

"Human bodies are composed of exactly the same quantity of elements, whether that body be rich or poor, man or woman, young or old. When we are dead, our bodies all have the same value."

It was when we are alive, he believed, that we must do our best to help and understand each other and live together in peace and harmony. Nai Lert was always ready to help people in trouble and was generous to a fault. As an employer, he was fair and he had that unique talent of getting the best from the people who worked for him.

Another philosophy of life he liked to repeat to young people who sought his advice was this one: "Happiness and sadness go hand in hand. Wealth follows poverty. Poverty can lead to wealth."

Nai Lert was influenced by Victorian England and his moral values reflected this. He was an avid reader of English literature, and Charles Dickens was a favourite. In many ways, he was like a business character from Dickens, crusty, hardworking, iron-willed and old-fashioned. But there the similarities ended. Unlike some of the cruel and selfish businessmen depicted by Dickens, like Ebenezer Scrooge or Ralph Nickleby, who lived off the sweat and toil of the working class, Nai Lert was always ready to help and encourage promising young working-class boys (*never* girls) who showed unusual intelligence or athletic potential. A boxer himself when he was young (what did he *not* do?), Nai Lert underwrote boxing lessons for many a young aspiring pugilist.

A touching letter of advice to a young boxer has been published many times. In it, he tells the young man to fight to the end and to win, but once your opponent is down, it is not necessary to go for the kill. A good boxer, he said, is compassionate. You are like a lawyer; you have been given powerful skills that you must *not* abuse. It is a cruel man that uses his power abusively, "worse than a snake." Bravery and strength without honesty is valueless. Furthermore, a good boxer does not play around with women.

Nai Lert's favourite sport was *takraw*, a Thai game played by the masses that involved kicking a rattan ball with the object of keeping it aloft without ever touching it with one's hands. The sport requires speed, accuracy and agility. Nai Lert played *takraw* well into his late sixties. On one occasion, he was playing *takraw* in his garden with a group of young workers from his factory, and oblivious to what was happening around him – he always gave his entire self to the task in front of him – he completely ignored a group of VIP guests who had come to tea. "Simply ignore him," said Sinn, "because he's going to continue to ignore you anyway." That was Nai Lert.

Everyone who worked for him was in a way his replica. He ran an honest company of gentlemen, and he believed that a leader of a country who is a cheat and a liar sends a message to its citizens that it is okay to be the same. Nai Lert had friends from all classes and nationalities, from royalty and prime ministers to farmers and factory workers. He was the same person with them all. There was no guile or pretence. What you saw of Nai Lert was what you got. Here was a man who always kept his word, who never gave up and who never had a hidden agenda.

He also brought passion to everything he did. Even when reading his favourite books, he would underline in red pencil passages that moved him. One of his favourite quotes was from Dickens' *Tale of Two Cities*: "It was the best of times. It was the worst of times," a historical summary of the life and times of Parisians who lived through the French revolution that could well describe the life and times of Siam during his lifetime.

One of his best times, like so many men in the Victorian era, was to spend his free moments with his cronies, drinking, playing poker, telling ribald stories and having a lot of laughs together. Nai Lert was always in a humorous mood. Drinking booze with his friends would be an important part of his evening with the boys. In fact drinking generally, with or without the boys, was a relaxing pastime when he was not working. His doctor once told him that booze would one day kill him. He replied, "that's just as well, because once I'm dead, I won't be able to drink anymore."

His doctor almost gave up on him; he allowed him to drink only one day a week. Every day, he would ask his secretary what day of the week it was, and if it was Monday, he would say, "Ah, *this* is the day when I can have a drink." If it was Tuesday, he would say, "*This* is the day when I can have a drink." If it was Wednesday, he would say the same thing.

In early November 1945, Sinn heard the crashing sound of a falling object on the tiled floor of Nai Lert's bathroom. He had dropped his bathing bowl[13] in the bathroom, which was locked from the inside. Sinn couldn't get a response when she called out "Nai Lert, are you alright?" several times. She always called him – as indeed did the rest of the country – "Nai Lert." The door was locked and nobody could get in to see what was wrong. A little boy[14] that he had adopted crawled through a small window that was left open and unlocked the door from the inside. Nai Lert had passed out and was lying on the floor. He had suffered his first coronary thrombosis attack. He did not survive a second attack on 15 December 1945.

Thus ended the life of a man who was barely five feet five tall yet larger than life.

13 Before the modern shower, bathrooms had large Ali Baba jars from which bathers sluiced cold water over their bodies with their bowls.

14 Dr. Sompong Juisiri.

# CHAMKAD BALANGURA
# 1914 – 1943

Scholar and intellectual,
Siamese patriot to the last

***Previous page:*** *The old quarter of Chungking in 1943, where Chamkad's hotel was located.*

***Above:*** *Chamkad the scholar in his Burberry raincoat, England 1934.*

# 4

# A Hero's Journey

Chamkad Balangura was not a professional soldier. Nor was he a trained undercover agent. He was a scholar – a brilliant one – with a Modern Greats PPE[1] degree from Balliol College, Oxford. In Siam he ran a secondary school with Chalab Chalai, his wife. With his round horn-rimmed spectacles and unassuming appearance, he looked every bit a professor. An idealist, he spent most of his time lost in his reading, his greatest weakness. Yet, it was Chamkad who was chosen to undertake one of the most dangerous missions for Siam in the Second World War.

Chamkad's secret mission was to contact British and American army intelligence in Chungking, and inform them that there was a credible resistance movement against the Japanese in Siam, that neither London nor Washington knew about. Chamkad was instructed by the leader of the Free Thai Movement in Siam, Pridi Panomyong, to inform the British and American Allies, and the Chinese Nationalist government ("Free China"), that the Movement wanted to annul Siam's declaration of war against the Allies as being unconstitutional, and that the treaties of friendship Siam made with Britain and America before the war were still in force. Chamkad was

1 Politics, Philosophy and Economics.

to emphasize that to date no Siamese troops – unlike the French and Italians – had fired a single shot on Allied forces.[2] Most importantly, he wanted them to provide a means of escape by either seaplane or submarine for Pridi and his group of sympathizers in the cabinet, in order to establish a government-in-exile in India. Finally, Chamkad was instructed to request the release of 250 million baht that had been frozen in British and American banks, to finance the movement's activities.

That Chamkad was prepared to travel through enemy territory without proper identification papers or official documents not only reflected upon his courage, but also on his intellectual and political skills. He was able to write several reports on the Free Thai Movement without notes.

Chamkad had no experience in military intelligence – he didn't even know how to handle a gun – so why was he selected for this important assignment?

As secretary general of the Movement and member of the executive committee, he was familiar with all the issues and personalities of the organization. Pridi also recognized that Chamkad was continually exploring different ways to establish contact with the Allies. He was not a civil servant[3] and his absence from Bangkok would therefore not be missed. He had the intellectual and academic qualifications to present the Movement's cause and he knew some people in the British government, important for establishing his *bona fides*. Most importantly, he was a trusted member of Pridi's inner circle.

Chamkad was well aware of the risks when he took on this expedition for the Free Thai Movement. With Japanese intelligence agents operating throughout Siam, and in Indochina in collaboration

---

2 Except on 8 December, 1941 when a British brigade illegally entered Siamese territory from Malaya to forestall the advancing Japanese and met defensive Siamese resistance.

3 He was barred from entering government service because of the anti-military government articles he wrote as a student in England.

with the Vichy French[4], he knew that his journey to Chungking, the new seat of the Nationalist Chinese government in Szechuan where the Allied command had their Far East headquarters, was fraught with danger. He also knew that he would be executed as a spy if he was captured.

What he could never have imagined was that the 2,400-kilometre overland journey from Bangkok through northeast Siam, central Laos and northern Vietnam to Chungking in central China would take 53 days. The direct route by air today with a change of plane at Kunming takes less than 5½ hours.

Fortunately Paisal Trakul-Lee, a trusted Sino-Thai[5], was seconded to Chamkad to accompany him as interpreter, fluent as he was in several Chinese dialects.

## The First 2,400 Kilometres

Chamkad and Paisal started their journey from Bangkok by train on 25 February 1943. Chalab Chalai accompanied them to the Laotian border. Apart from an anxious moment between Don Muang and Ayudhya, when some Japanese soldiers boarded the train and sat in their compartment, the rail-trip to the northeast was uneventful. The Japanese soldiers were polite and only wanted to practice their Thai.

Leaving behind the rich, flat rice plain, now dry from the summer heat, the train slowed down at Saraburi, its wheels grating and screeching on the fifty-year-old track uphill to Korat, where the train split into two. One turned east towards Cambodia, and the other northeast to Laos.

The train now gathered speed across the dry plateau of the

4 The Vichy government in France had allowed the Japanese armed forces to occupy Indochina on 22 September 1940.

5 Chinese name Lee Hui-san, an employee of a rich merchant friend of Pridi's brother.

Northeast, passing small towns with chocolate-coloured corrugated iron-roofed houses, dusty village temples and schools, and the occasional ox-cart carrying rice, salt, pigs, and other local produce to Korat and Udon.

At Khon Kaen, they were met by Tiang Sirikarn, the local Free Thai leader, who arranged their onward journey from Nakorn Phanom across the Mekong River to Ta Kaek in central Laos, and from there to Vinh in Vietnam. When Tiang's wife and sister realised Chamkad was about to travel through enemy territory without sufficient funds, they immediately removed their gold necklaces and wedding rings and gave them to him. Chamkad was deeply moved by this act of selfless generosity. He thanked them and said his farewells. He embraced Chalab Chalai. "I will try and get a message to you when I arrive in Chungking," he told his wife, fighting back the tears, as he wondered if they would ever be reunited.

It was 4 March 1943.

Laos, Chamkad discovered, wasn't much different from Siam. Even the language was similar. Only the hills were higher. The dense forested road from the border to Vinh on a battered old truck organised by Tiang, plunged and curved its way across the Annam Highlands, up to almost 2,000 metres. At Ban Na Pe, the last village that spoke Thai, they stopped at a beautiful pagoda monastery perched on top of the mountain, overlooking the plains down to Vinh. Here, Chamkad and Paisal made an offering to the temple.

From the Ked Nua border pass, the road drops dramatically to the lowlands and the port city of Vinh, today a popular stopover for Vietnamese travellers visiting Ho Chi Minh's birthplace 14 kilometres out of town. Two days later they arrived in Hanoi by train.

At a safe house in Hanoi, they stayed for eight nights, planning their onward journey. They were helped by Professor Georges Cœdès, the Director of *l'École Française d'Extrême-Orient*, and his Siamese wife.

He was the well-known French archaeologist and historian and an old friend of Siam. He was more sympathetic to the Free Thai cause than to his own pro-Japanese Vichy government. They considered the options: travel by land through the hill country to the Chinese border, or by boat along the coast of Halong Bay.

The first option would be to cross the Chinese border by land from Vietnam. Disguised as Hmong smugglers, they could have taken the direct overland route to the Nam Quan pass through the picturesque mountains at Lang Son. This old trading route has been in use for over 2,000 years. It was also the pre-war route used by remittance couriers to deliver money by overseas Chinese to their families. Today it is a favourite southern entry point into Guangxi province by adventurous Lonely Planet backpackers. But in 1943, it was one of the most heavily guarded border posts in Vietnam. This entry point, Chamkad decided, was extremely dangerous. The risks of being stopped, interrogated and possibly tortured, were simply too great.

Instead, they opted for the longer, less convenient sea route from the port of Haiphong to a small fishing village just south of the Chinese border at Mong Cai, today a shantytown Chinese tourists go to for bargain shopping and the sandy beach. With the busy sampan, skiff and steamer traffic in and out of Haiphong day and night, the risk of being detected would be much less.

Professor Cœdès immediately got in touch with the French Chief of Police who instructed his people at the port not to obstruct Chamkad and Paisal, nor disclose their identities to the Japanese authorities.

It was day 19 of their journey. That morning they booked their passage with a private cabin on the SS *Nanning*. Dressed as poor Chinese peasants, they avoided wearing anything that would make them conspicuous. Instead of suitcases, they carried their meagre belongings in cheap canvas bags. Personal effects of real value, such as watches, gold chains and precious stones to pay for their ongoing journey were hidden in different pockets. They wore no socks, and their dirty feet were shod in simple Chinese cloth sandals. Chamkad took the precaution of removing his spectacles when there were Japanese officials about. To blend inconspicuously with the crowd, they waited until late afternoon just before the SS *Nanning* set sail. At that time, the jetty would fill up with local vendors, Chinese merchants, Hmong and Dai hill tribe people, Vietnamese deckhands, porters and fishermen. After boarding, they immediately went into hiding in their cabin. Two Japanese *kempeitai* agents and one French police officer boarded the ship and started their routine check. When Chamkad and Paisal heard the cabin door kicked open, they immediately pretended to sleep.

*"Kippu arimas ka?"*[6]

There was no response. The Japanese soldier shouted his question again, this time more aggressively. They continued to feign sleep. Chamkad was prodded awake by the senior officer's baton. He made signs which he hoped would mean that he did not understand. This time the officer addressed Paisal in simple Chinese and asked him for his ticket. After careful inspection of both tickets, they were told to open their bags. An assortment of threadbare and unwashed farmers' cotton clothes and a few Chinese and Vietnamese coins tumbled onto the floor.

*"Anata doko des' ka?"*[7]

Paisal managed to explain that they were poor chicken farmers from Kwangxi. The Japanese officer was unconvinced and before they could explain further, the French police officer entered the cabin. The tickets and contents of the bag were inspected again. With Gallic flair, the Frenchman shrugged his shoulders and made a rude grimace that clearly told the Japanese officers that they were wasting their time with these two simple Chinese peasants. He then strode angrily out of the cabin.

---

6 "Do you have a ticket?"
7 "Where are you going?"

Although the French Sûreté had also assigned two Vietnamese detectives to keep an eye on them on the voyage to Mong Cai, it was unclear what action they could have taken if Chamkad and Paisal were actually arrested.

"Get some rest. We've had a long day," said Chamkad. They both slept soundly that night.

It was almost midnight. The SS *Nanning* was steaming through one of the world's most spectacular bays. One of many Vietnamese legends has it that an angry dragon threw himself into the sea and the thrashing whiplash of his tail carved the deep craters that today form the limestone islands and caves of Halong ("Dragon Descending") Bay in the Gulf of Tonkin. In 1999 Halong was declared a UNESCO World Heritage site, but in mid-March 1943, Chamkad Balangura and Paisal Trakul-Lee were in no mood to take in the magnificence of Halong Bay, on that night dramatically lit up by the waxing moon. They were too preoccupied with the delicate tasks and potential dangers that lay ahead.

At the Chinese border, thanks to Professor Cœdès, the French police accompanied them across the bridge over River Beilin, this time of the year a dried-up ravine. At last they were in "Free China." It was 19 March. They had been travelling for 21 days.

The Chinese government had been alerted by Pridi of their imminent arrival. At Tung Hing (modern Dongxing) they were met by a smart young lieutenant and four soldiers. This part of Kwangxi province was one of the most bandit-infested regions of south China, not to be explored by anyone on their own. A recent battle between the Chinese and Japanese armies had destroyed many sections of this scenic road. It was a bumpy ride. Soldiers with machine guns stopped their vehicle at each checkpoint. Had it not been for their efficient escort, they would have been delayed for hours. Fortunately, they were always waved on. It was getting towards the end of March and the summer drought was beginning to take its effect. The land was parched and dusty, the earth on the rice fields was beginning to crack and it was now unbearably hot. From Nanning, the onward bus journey, even with their efficient escort, took two more days. Chamkad was beginning to feel the effects of travelling rough. A chronic stomach ulcer sufferer from student days, he now had severe cramps. The pair reached Liuchow by nightfall.

The long delay at Liuchow did not improve Chamkad's frame of mind. He was generally even-tempered, although somewhat impatient; he was missing the comforts of home and good Thai cooking. He'd had enough *congee* rice-soup to last a lifetime. The real difficulty started when he and Paisal were informed that they would not be allowed to continue their onward journey without the requisite stamp on their Alien Registration Forms providing permission to travel on to their next destination. The local Chief of Police only issued the permits after nine days of interrogation and a final cash payment. It was a clever manoeuvre in official blackmail. On 6 April they departed for Kweilin, accompanied by a new escort, one Colonel Lok.

Hundreds of misty karst spires and majestic limestone peaks make a breath-taking backdrop for the old town of Kweilin, a popular subject for Chinese landscape painters and poets, and today one of the most visited spots in China. Exhausted and apprehensive as they were, Chamkad and Paisal were invigorated by its beauty.

Here, in his hotel on the banks of the peaceful Li River, Chamkad set to work. He sent a coded telegram to Washington to inform the Siamese minister and Free Thai leader in America, M.R. Seni Pramoj, of his mission.[8] He also made his first contact with the British Army Aid Group (BAAG). He briefed Colonel Lindsay Ride, head of BAAG in Kweilin, and wrote his first Free Thai Movement

8 His telegram was intercepted and censored by the Chinese government and never reached Washington.

report at BAAG Headquarters. They spent ten days together and became good friends. A fellow Oxonian, Colonel Ride respected Chamkad's intellect and integrity and sent a positive report to his superior, the British military attaché, in Chungking.

The local Chinese authorities were again refusing to issue their onward travel permits. While Chamkad was working with Colonel Ride, Paisal did some intelligence work on his own, and learned that the Chinese were not at all happy that Chamkad was using the good offices of the Chinese government to get British contacts and help. The Chinese had their own agenda; they wanted to increase their own influence in Siam and preferred China to be the key foreign player in assisting the Free Thai.

By this time Chamkad had run out of funds and Colonel Ride generously advanced him enough money to cover 14 nights at his hotel and two plane tickets to Chungking. The British attaché there was also able to obtain the relevant travel permits from the local authorities.

On 21 April 1943, Chamkad and Paisal were finally on the last leg of their journey. They boarded Eurasia's Junker three-propeller aircraft with 10 other passengers at 8 a.m. At 9.40 a.m. the plane touched down on the sandbar in the middle of the Yangtze River, the official airfield in Chungking. They had arrived at last. But Chungking, as they were about to discover, was a difficult city to operate in, and their work was not going to be easy.

## Intrigue in China

After Nanking fell to the Japanese army in 1937, Chungking had become the new seat of the Nationalist Chinese government led by President Chiang Kai-shek. Well protected by a ring of mountains and the formidable Three Gorges of the Yangtze River, it was easier to defend than Chengdu, the cultured capital of Szechuan province. Chiang had used Chungking once before as a successful base against Mao Tse-tung's Communist marchers back in 1935. Here, he now felt more secure against a renewed Japanese land attack. Still vulnerable to air raids, however, Chungking was to become the most heavily bombed Chinese city in the Second World War.

The Nationalists' exodus to west China caused by the Japanese invasion changed both the demographics and the topography of Chungking forever, from a small town of 300,000 to a sprawl that was home to one million in 1943.[9] The main roads now carried more traffic. Those who could afford the fares travelled by rickshaw and sedan chair on the narrow streets of the old part of town, but the steep slopes on the riverbanks were clogged with poorer people scurrying up and down the slippery steps on foot. Overall, it was still a rather backward and dirty provincial town.

When Chamkad arrived in April 1943, Chungking was a hive of intrigue and subterfuge. The British and Americans had conflicting interests and did not cooperate with each other. Britain was concerned with the safety of her Indian colony and Churchill was determined to prevent China from undermining British pre-war influence in Asia. Chiang himself was a vocal supporter of Indian independence and preferred the company of Nehru[10] to Churchill, who referred to China as "four hundred and twenty-five million pigtails."

The Americans, meanwhile, looked to the Pacific and the future, treating China as a key ally against Japan and a bulwark against communism after the war. To the consternation of the Americans, who gave millions in aid to Chiang Kai-shek[11], he was reluctant to commit his best troops to fight the Japanese, keeping them back for the real battle ahead with the Chinese Red Army. Even the American

9 Today, Chongqing is a megacity of 30 million, the result of aggressive development.

10 On a visit to India, Chiang and Nehru horseplayed around in the latter's garden like old friends.

11 The Americans mockingly called him "Cash my cheque".

top brass disagreed with each other over how the war in China was to be conducted. General Joseph Stillwell, the Allied forces chief of staff, a true infantryman, believed in land supremacy. The air force commander, General Claire Chennault, insisted that the war could only be won from the air. Meanwhile the corrupt Nationalist government's only real interest was to stay in power whatever the outcome of the war. There was a prevailing mood of distrust and fear all around.

In this difficult environment, Chamkad had to navigate between the lordly British, the rookie Americans and the cunning Chinese. He soon discovered that the Free Thai cause had a very low priority on the Allied agenda. Siam was only of interest to the Allies as a base of last resort to attack the Japanese in Burma and Malaya should the war go badly for them.

Even the Free Thai themselves lacked direction, failing to fully understand the differing policies of the Allies. Pridi, the Free Thai leader in Siam, wanted British help and offered a long-term *political solution,* while the British were only seeking a short-term *military* one. The British were treating Siam as an enemy whereas the Americans considered Siam as an occupied ally. Chiang distrusted the British and to spite them pledged support for the Free Thais. The Chinese believed that the British were pursuing a separate policy of self-interest from the American and Chinese governments. Indeed, both Pridi and Chamkad had been much encouraged by Chiang Kai-shek's radio broadcast on 26 February 1943, when he openly declared China's friendship and recognition of Siam's sovereignty, calling upon all Siamese to work with China to fight the common enemy.

The only people outside Siam who may have known anything about Pridi's underground operation were a select group of senior members of the Chinese Nationalist government, including Chiang Kai-shek himself. Pridi had made long-lasting friendships in China before the war and was still in touch. The Chinese community in

Siam, themselves admirers of Pridi, were anti-Japanese and more than willing to furnish inside information to the Chinese government. Little is known of the Chinese intelligence network in Siam in 1943. Compared with the western Allies' weak infiltration attempts, it probably was substantial.

## Chinese Support

After the beauty of Kweilin, the mountain town of Chungking, grey from both the mist and smoke that pervaded the streets and the limestone cliffs that the city bestrode, made Chamkad even more homesick. He plunged into a deep depression. *Is this infernal place really Chiang Kai-shek's new capital?*

The Victory House Hotel, the Chinese Foreign Office Guest House on the 2nd Chung Road was just one of many rundown buildings on the slopes of this riverside alley. As non-paying guests of the Chinese government, Chamkad shared a seedy room with Paisal on the top floor until 25 June, when they were moved to dirtier quarters in the basement, situated next to the laundry room and the kitchens at one end and the servants' lavatories at the other. The latrines lacked adequate flushing and were often left to fester for two or three days at a time. The filth, the odours, the rats and the cockroaches made life unbearable. The heat was worse than Bangkok at the height of the dry season. Chamkad described this part of his journey as "living death". His ulcers were getting worse.

The key player in Chamkad's life in Chungking was Chiang's trusted Chief of Intelligence, General Dai Li, who wielded immense power in the government. Suspicious of any clandestine work carried on by the West in his country, he had a particular dislike for the British, who once locked him up for one night in Hong Kong. Captain Milton Miles, the senior American intelligence officer in Chungking, said that "to get anything done in China, you have to work with Dai Li, otherwise he can and will delay you in a thousand ways."

Chamkad discovered the long arm of Dai Li's power on his first day in Chungking. He was immediately placed in "protective custody" – tantamount to house arrest – in his hotel and agents were assigned to spy on his movements. Dai Li knew perfectly well that Chamkad was Pridi's special emissary, but for the next three months Chamkad was given the run-around and was refused permission to contact representatives of the British or American embassies and intelligence agencies. Dai Li held absolute control of Allied operations directed into Siam from China and over the dissemination of much of the intelligence. He deliberately prevented the delivery of Chamkad's letters and reports to M.R. Seni in Washington, to the U.S. State Department and to the British Foreign Office. Dai Li had his own agenda.

Meanwhile, Chamkad was losing valuable time. He was particularly concerned that the chances of getting Pridi out of the country before the monsoon were getting slimmer. Three months of isolation in a hotel room, particularly in a filthy basement, is a long time to wait for events to happen. Chamkad wrote copious letters and lengthy telegrams, but to no avail. None of them reached their intended destinations. His ulcer pains were becoming unbearable and he was starting to haemorrhage blood every time he used the toilet. He had never been under such severe stress.

On 25 May, he was summoned to the Chinese Foreign Ministry, to receive the devastating news that would change his attitude towards the British forever. Despite Colonel Ride's positive report on Chamkad's intentions, the British Foreign Office in London was less receptive to Chamkad's proposals. The following message from the British government was relayed to Chamkad through Dai Li's office:

*His Majesty's Government thinks that Balankura has gone off at half cock and has come out with no carefully laid-out plan. His Majesty's*

*Government proposes to continue with what it has been doing.*[12] *The Foreign Office thinks that time is not ripe to support an active Free Siamese Movement at present.*

Chamkad read this message with despair. It must have been a great blow to him. He had always been pro-British and naïvely expected a positive response from them. Despite the respect he had for him, Colonel Ride had commented in the same report that Chamkad was "inexperienced", particularly in dealing with the Chinese, who were too wily and clever for him. "He made the elementary mistake of giving far too much away in his efforts to overcome Chinese official brick walls," wrote Ride. From the British point of view, Chamkad's proposals were of a political rather than of a military or "resistance" nature. His talk with Colonel Ride about "getting armies out and marching down through the north of Siam" was seen as naïve. There was nothing in his proposal about the practical task of organizing resistance to the Japanese on the ground. So much for the cynical, unhelpful British.

After Dai Li learned that the British had turned down Chamkad's proposals, he immediately reported this to his superior, Chiang Kai-shek, who was delighted. Dai Li then began to put the Chinese plan into motion.

On 28 June 1943, Chamkad and Paisal had a private audience with Chiang Kai-shek. This historic meeting was engineered by Dai Li and kept secret from the British and Americans. Dai Li's stalling and delaying tactics were designed to prevent Chamkad from getting in touch with British and American intelligence representatives *before* his meeting with Chiang, thus enabling the Chinese and the Free Thais to come to a separate agreement without Western interference.

---

12 i.e. to continue *not* to recognize the Free Thai and to veto any plan to set up a government-in-exile.

At 10 a.m. a Dodge military saloon car arrived at the Victory House Hotel to take Chamkad and Paisal to Chiang's official residence, a redbrick villa in the same compound as his headquarters in the north-western heights of Yuzhong District.

At the villa, Chamkad was kept waiting for almost half-an-hour in Chiang's ante-room downstairs. He observed that Chiang's military aides were unhelpful and inhospitable. Chamkad was beginning to have serious doubts about the meeting and was becoming nervous, but he needn't have worried. Chiang was cordial and friendly. The meeting was in his well-appointed office upstairs. He stood up from behind his desk, erect and smartly tailored in a slim-fitting, high-buttoned khaki military jacket, extended his hand in greeting and then sat in a high-backed Ming chair at the head of a long conference table. Apart from the occasional question through his interpreter, Chiang let Chamkad do most of the talking. Shao Yu-lin from the Foreign Ministry and an interpreter were the only other people present. Chamkad was hoping to meet Meiling Soong, Chiang's wife and the most powerful woman in China, but she was away on her famous American tour, drumming up US support.

After briefly relaying Pridi's respects and confirming Siam's continued friendship with China in response to Chiang's radio broadcast earlier in the year, Chamkad got to the point. Siam's treaty with the Japanese was made under duress, he said, and therefore null and void. Furthermore, the Free Thais were ready to fight the Japanese enemy shoulder to shoulder with the Chinese army at all times. Chiang smiled in appreciation. Chamkad went on to state that the British were not supportive and were imperialists at heart. Pridi was a true democrat, a follower of Sun Yat Sen's "Three Principles of the People"[13] doctrine, and more suitable, Chamkad said, for Asian countries. At this, Chiang chuckled and whispered to Shao Yu-lin. We may never know what he whispered, but we do know for sure

13 *Nationalism, democracy and people's livelihood:* Sun Yat Sen, the "father of modern China" and Chiang's mentor.

that Chiang decided that it would be in China's best interest to help Siam by limiting British influence in Asia after the war. There is now evidence that the British Colonial Office had formulated a plan to annex southern Siam at the Kra Isthmus and append it to Malaya at war's end.[14]

Chiang officially accepted the Free Thai's proposal to set up a provisional government outside Siam and even offered Free China as an alternative location. Chiang also gave permission for Chamkad to travel to Washington and discuss these proposals with M.R. Seni, the Free Thai leader in America. Other than Chiang's benevolent support of the Free Thais, China never had a specific Siam policy. Now, the Siamese door was open, and China decided "to enter the field."[15] The meeting lasted 30 minutes. As they were exchanging their goodbyes, Chiang urged Paisal to make sure that all the Chinese in Siam join the Free Thai movement.

This meeting with Chiang was to have portentous significance on Siam's fortunes after the war. On the night of 3 November, 1943, before the Allied summit in Cairo convened to agree on the defeat of Japan, Chiang had a private dinner with Roosevelt, the American president, and together they discussed the future of Korea, Indochina and Siam. Without the presence of Churchill (who was not at the dinner), they reached an agreement that both the US and China would guarantee Siam's sovereignty after the war, as well as support Korea and Indochina in their fight for independence from their colonial masters. This accord became part of the greater "Cairo Declaration" of 1 December 1943.

This was followed by another broadcast by Chiang on New Year's Day, 1944, confirming his government's commitment to help the Allies defeat the Japanese, and again pledging his support for Siam's sovereignty.

---

14 Professor Nicholas Tarling, *Atonement before Absolution: British Policy Towards Thailand in the Second World War* (1977).

15 Prince Subha Svasti, memoirs.

China did "enter the field" and decided she *would* play an active role in Siam after the war. In September 1945, after the Japanese surrender, China's 93rd Division stationed on the border of Burma and China were preparing to march into Siam to disarm the Japanese army. Two events stopped them.

The first was the appointment of M.R. Seni Pramoj, the leader of the Free Thais in America, as the new prime minister. Seni was able to persuade the Americans to prevent the Chinese from entering Siam.

The other was Mao Tse-tung's powerful Red Army that was quickly moving down from the north. The 93rd Division was forced to defend Chiang Kai-shek's southern flank. The final phase of the bloody civil war between the Communists and the Kuomintang Nationalists had begun.

By 1949 Chiang had lost the country and fled to Taiwan. Remnants of the 93rd Division fleeing the victorious Red Army took refuge in Northern Siam and settled in the villages of Mae Aw in Mae Hong Son province and Mae Salong in Chiang Rai province. They are still there today and their descendants have become Thai citizens.

## The Final Journey

After Chamkad's meeting with Chiang in June, Dai Li relaxed his policy of isolation and finally allowed Chamkad to make contact with the Allies in Chungking. In early July, Captain Milton Miles, head of OSS operations in China, was the first Allied officer to meet Chamkad. At last Chamkad was able to hand over a lengthy report with an emotional covering letter requesting American assistance. It would reach OSS[16] headquarters in Washington intact, *the first accurate report of the Free Thai movement's activities inside the country ever to arrive in a Western capital.*

16 Office of Strategic Services, precursor to the CIA.

In August, Prince Subha Svasti, also known as Major Arun, was the first Free Thai outside Siam to meet Chamkad. Chamkad was encouraged to learn of the existence of the Free Thai movement in Britain from Arun, and that a group of Siamese volunteers, some of them old friends from his student days, were now trained and given commissions in the British Army as part of a military detachment called Force 136. It was being trained to operate against the Japanese from bases in India and Ceylon. Thanks to the helpful information Chamkad provided to Major Arun on the Free Thai's activities in Siam, Force 136's morale and efficiency were boosted. It was the first time that the Free Thais in Britain knew that there was an active resistance movement in their own country.

The past four months in Chungking had not been easy for Chamkad. By September, he could hardly eat, he was quickly losing weight and had difficulty sleeping. He was suffering from severe stomach pains and rectal haemorrhaging rendered him weak and almost immobile. Without informing the Allies, Dai Li spirited him away from the guest house and placed him in a Chinese military hospital. In Chamkad's weak condition, Dai Li tried to "bribe him to form a nucleus of a Thai government in exile based in China."[17] When the British discovered where he was, Major R.J.H. McMullen, posing as a doctor, ordered the "watchers out of the room whilst he made a thorough examination of the patient" and arranged for Chamkad to be moved clandestinely to the Canadian Mission Hospital. It was 20 September.[18]

On a dark, foggy day on 7 October 1943, Chamkad died at the Canadian Mission Hospital in Chungking. He was only 29 years old. The death certificate stated that Chamkad died from cancer that had spread from his liver into the stomach. Major Edmund Grut, a senior British officer attached to the SOE, suspected foul play, and wrote in

17 *Siam Becomes Thailand,* Judith A. Stowe, University of Hawaii Press, 1991.
18 *Thailand's Secret War,* E. Bruce Reynolds, Cambridge University Press, 2005.

a report that "Balangkura's death was brought about by the Chinese to delay any coordination of British and Free Siamese plans." In this tense atmosphere of American-Chinese collaboration and Chinese-British hostility, even Milton Miles suspected that Chamkad might have been disposed of by a Chinese type of assassination "where finely chopped pigs bristles are fed to a person for a period of weeks and eventually he succumbs to perforated intestines and dies."[19]

An autopsy was never conducted and the true circumstances around Chamkad's death remain a mystery, although it was certainly caused by cancer. He died before the British could help him get away to a hospital in India.

Chamkad did not live to witness the events that soon unfolded in Siam, much of them as a result of his persistence and courageous work. Chamkad's continuous flow of reports, telegrams and letters were the *first accounts* of the Free Thai resistance movement in Siam to reach the outside world. Without his determination to contact the Allies in Chungking, they would not have known until much later about the extent and viability of the movement, and incredibly, that Pridi, the Regent of Siam, was their leader.

Chamkad's uncharted overland journey also showed the Allies that infiltration into Siam from the north was possible. Guarantee of Siam's independence at the "Cairo Declaration" was partly due to Chamkad's successful half-hour presentation to Chiang Kai-shek.

Tos Patumasen, a Siamese volunteer officer in Force 136 and fellow student in England in the thirties, later said that he never for one moment imagined that this nerdy, unkempt, long-haired, bespectacled scholar, forever lecturing him about a better Siam, would one day become a heroic undercover agent.

19 E. Bruce Reynolds, Ibid.

# MOM LUANG PRAVAS CHOOMSAI 1909 - 1966

The remarkable life and times of an aviator

***Previous page:*** *The Curtiss-Hawk, one of the fighters assigned to defend the south.*

***Above:*** *M.L. Pravas in his full dress Wing Commander uniform, 1942.*

# 5

# The Courageous Aviator

*"Tora! Tora! Tora!"*

Major Kisoyoshi Utsunomiya, commander of the 2nd Battalion, 143rd Infantry Regiment, 55th Division of the Imperial Japanese Army, gave the battle cry to attack the town and airfield of Prachuab Khirikhan in southern Siam. It was 3 a.m. on Monday, 8 December 1941[1].

The attack had been planned months ahead. The invasion fleet of 29 troopships, escorted by the battleship *Haruna*, supported by 5 cruisers and 7 destroyers, sailed across the Gulf of Siam from the Indochinese ports of Saigon, Phucoq and Camranh, which were made available by the collaborating Vichy French government, in late November. Ten days later 70,000 hardened Japanese troops landed on the peninsular east coast towns of Pattani, Singora[2], Ligor[3] and Prachuab Khirikhan in Siam, and Khota Bharu in Malaya.

Only three troopships carrying 4,000 men, the smallest regiment in the entire fleet, were assigned to land at Prachuab Khirikhan,

---

1 At that very moment, across the international dateline in Hawaii, when it was still 7 December, a Japanese force of six carriers was launching two strikes on the US Pacific Fleet at Pearl Harbor. Over 183 Japanese planes destroyed six battleships and 188 aircraft, damaged and sank 10 other ships, and killed 2000 servicemen.

2 English for Songkhla.

3 English for Nakorn Srithammaraj.

capture the town, and destroy its airfield and eight Siamese fighter planes. Very light resistance was expected. The main thrust of this huge armada was preparing for much greater opposition further south, particularly in Malaya, from several divisions of British and Australian troops.[4]

On the previous evening of 7 December, the Japanese naval commander assigned to the landings at Prachuab Khirikhan scanned the horizon of the Gulf of Siam with his binoculars and slowly shook his head. He sucked through his teeth with a long rasping sound as he always did when things weren't looking good. *"Akutenkou"*[5], he muttered to himself. He reported to Major Utsunomiya that the weather was foul. The monsoon rain was coming down in sheets and the sea was choppy. Clouds hung low and there was no hope of the sun coming out. It was not a good omen for the Japanese soldiers who believed that seeing the sunrise would bring them luck. But the 143rd Regiment was highly trained in landing operations and the Prachuab airfield was considered an easy target. They were confident that the whole operation would be over by noon that day, despite the weather. In the early hours of 8 December, three transport troopships dropped anchor five kilometres offshore and the invaders silently prepared to board their landing crafts. It was 3 a.m.

---

4 Some British officers' memoirs recounting their defeat in Malaya stated that Siam "capitulated" to the Japanese without putting up a fight. *It was the British who capitulated* in Singapore on 15 February 1942, handing over some 85,000 British, Australian and Indian military and civilian prisoners to the Japanese, after abandoning Penang and many Malayan towns, whose local populations had to defend themselves without weapons. Many Chinese and Malays who survived remembered that all the "white people disappeared" when the Japanese landed. It was the most ignominious defeat in British history. The small Siamese army put up a courageous and honourable fight against the Japanese invaders, not only at Prachuab Khirikhan, but also at the southern coastal towns of Nakorn Srithammaraj, Chumpon, Surat, Songkhla and Pattani, with a total loss of 150 lives, inflicting far greater casualties on the Japanese invaders (approximately 250). The fiercest battle raged over the defence of Pattani River bridge where an entire Siamese platoon was wiped out. At Tha Phae in Nakorn Srithammaraj province, the two hour battle was so fierce, the Siamese resorting to hand-to-hand combat after running out of ammunition, and suffering 38 losses, that the Japanese invaders praised their Siamese adversaries for their bravery and tenacity.

5 "Bad weather".

Pilot Officer Srisak Sucharittham was trawling for fish and squid in a small fishing boat with ten of his men a few kilometres out to sea at the time[6], and thought he saw the faint , shadowy outline of a ship in the distance, but he wasn't sure. The rain squalls and the dense fog made visibility impossible. After he'd returned from fishing, he thought to himself, he would report this to the superior commanding officer of the 5th Siamese Air Corps of Prachuab airfield, Squadron Leader Mom Luang[7] Pravas Choomsai.

Commander Pravas was a strict disciplinarian, a feared but highly respected leader. He once cashiered a guard for abandoning his post. When Pravas was put in charge of this base, he was told that Prachuab Khirikhan was the country's first line of air defence for the south and was therefore instructed to be in a permanent state of preparedness. Eight open cockpit and lightly armed but highly manoeuvrable fighter biplanes, four Curtiss Hawk IIIs and four Vought V-93 Corsairs, were primed and prepared for action at the western end of the runway near the pilots' quarters, ready for take-off whenever necessary. Pravas made sure that the 40-strong air corps of pilots, gunners, mechanics and ground crew under his command, as well as the infantry guard detachment of 100 men, were at their posts at all times. Two heavy 77 millimetre machine gun nests were positioned at each end of the runway and three 66 millimetre light machine guns were positioned to protect the Ao Manao bay, one on the southern beach, the other on the small hill of Khao Ta Hluek overlooking the airfield, and the third on the road connecting the airdrome with the command building.

The Ao Manao promontory would not be easy to defend. It is a 500 metre long spit jutting out to sea and both the north and south beaches on either side were dangerously vulnerable to attack. Only the eastern tip of the promontory that directly faced the open

---

6 Trawling is often done at night.

7 Title given to the last person of royal line before becoming a commoner in the following generation, addressed simply as "Khun", or Mister.

sea of the Gulf afforded adequate protection, a steep rocky hill, the 270 metre Khao Lom Muak.

Major Utsunomiya ordered the 143rd Regiment to split into three attacking battalions.

Four armoured Daihatsu flat-bottomed landing craft unloaded the first battalion on the wide beach of Prachuab Khirikhan and headed straight for the town. Military intelligence had informed them that this sleepy little seaport town of less than 3000 people would be defended by a small police force and were not equipped to offer any serious resistance. The invaders arrived in the small hours of the morning while the town was fast asleep, and silently dug several trenches at key strategic locations to launch a surprise attack at first light. It started to rain again so it was too wet to raise the Japanese flag in front of the local town hall.

As the sun was trying to pierce through the heavy grey clouds on the horizon at 4.30 a.m., a Japanese officer went up the stairs of the police station intending to inform the officer on duty that they had captured the town and that all its citizens were now prisoners of the Imperial Japanese Army. At the top of the stairs, he was stopped by a police guard, bayoneted rifle at the ready. The Japanese officer started to shout arrogantly, waving a document, and commanded him to give way. The provincial Siamese policeman had never seen a Japanese person before and thought he was Malayan. A tussle ensued and he stabbed the Japanese to death with his bayonet. When the Japanese platoon saw what had happened to their officer they shot the guard, waking up 20 policemen who were sleeping inside.

Still wearing their *pakama*,[8] some policemen made a hasty escape through the back door, while others tried to grab their guns,

8 Traditional loincloth folded in such a way as to resemble modern male briefs; also a common swimming and sleeping garment.

but before they could fight the attackers, two grenades were lobbed into the station, killing all those who were still inside. By this time, the whole town was awake, and other policemen not on duty that night quickly tried to overcome the Japanese who were well concealed and protected in their newly dug trenches.

The local Yawachon Taharn, a quasi-military teenage auxiliary, joined the few remaining policemen to fight off the invaders.

At around 5 a.m. Pravas instructed Sergeant Puen to drive into town to see what the commotion that woke him up was all about. He returned with the bad news of the invasion at the same time when Pilot Officer Srisak was making his own report after his fishing expedition.

One police officer, Lieutenant Sngob, had managed to escape the Japanese cordon and make his way to the airfield. When he reached Pravas' office a few minutes after Sergeant Puen's report, he confirmed to Pravas what he now knew, that the Japanese had attacked the town. Badly wounded with deep sword cuts and bullet injuries, he passed out immediately after leaving Pravas' command post and died.

By 6 a.m. the town had been captured. Thirteen policemen lay dead and many more were wounded. The town hall, the police headquarters, the post and telegraph office, and the railway station were in enemy hands. It took a Japanese brigade of 1000 men three hours to capture a small town protected by 30 policemen.

While it was still dark at the airfield, the Japanese invaders launched their *second* landing, quickly wading ashore from two landing crafts at the northern end of the runway. They silently overcame the light machine gun emplacement guarding the planes, stabbing the entire platoon to death with their samurai swords without a single shot being fired. The northern flank of the airfield where the planes were parked was now left completely undefended. A Japanese machine gun nest was now positioned on the tarmac. At 6 a.m., Pravas ordered a bugle call to arms, piercing the quiet, early morning darkness.

Pandemonium broke out. The pilots, who had no experience in combat whatsoever, scrambled to their parked aircraft, but they were sitting ducks. The first pilot to reach his plane, Pilot Officer Prom Chuwong, together with two flight officers, managed to take off in his Hawk III. But as the biplane was lifting off from the ground, Japanese ground fire brought it down, killing all three instantly. Two more Hawks were destroyed by gunfire as they were taxiing along the runway, fatally wounding the pilots and flight crew. As the ground crew were removing a bomb from a Vought V-93 Corsair and fitting it with a machine gun, they were attacked by more Japanese soldiers; and Sergeant Porn's hand was severed from his arm and the gunner, Sergeant Sathit, was shot in the leg. Another two V-93s were surrounded by the enemy platoon and prevented from leaving the ground, wounding the entire squadron with their swords. Only Pilot Officer Man Prasongdee managed to get airborne. He took off in a Hawk III armed with four 50kg bombs and pointed his plane east towards the sea. He wanted to bomb the invading troopships anchored in the bay. The thick fog and the blinding rain reduced visibility down to less than 10 metres and he circled several times but couldn't find his targets. Rather than surrendering his plane to the enemy, he flew on to Hua Hin and landed at Bo Fai airdrome.

Meanwhile, Pravas realized that he could no longer defend the airfield without reinforcements. He sent airman Pan to the radio control room to alert the other air bases and request for some planes to help fight the aggressors. Radio communication from the Prachuab field was rudimentary, only equipped to contact Don Muang airfield headquarters but not with the outside world. Pravas could not communicate with Bangkok or indeed with any government department. Pan staggered back with several deep samurai sword cuts on his back and shoulders. He only managed to report that the radio control room was now in Japanese hands before he fainted.

Pravas was now preparing to fight to the end. But he could not allow the families belonging to the flight crew and military guards living in bungalows on the airfield to be captured or killed.

As the southern flank was still well defended, he ordered all the women and children to quickly evacuate the airfield and hide in a cave 150 metres up the Khao Lom Muak hill at the eastern end of the Ao Manao promontory.

Pravas looked at his watch… 7 a.m. It was raining hard and the sky was still overcast. He ordered the bugle to sound the evacuation order and under cover of the hazy darkness he gambled that the Japanese would not notice the moving mass of people nor realize what was happening. He ordered the machine gun emplacement on Khao Ta Hluek hill to give them fire cover.

The sound of the bugle had the effect of alerting the Japanese to be on the defensive, and to expect a Siamese attack, temporarily putting a halt to their offensive. They were clearly sensitive to alien sounds and strange noises, especially when having to operate in such poor light and on unfamiliar terrain.

The gamble paid off and the evacuation, which took most of the day, was successful but not without some incidents.

One mother of two temporarily lost her baby as she climbed the steep hill. After depositing her three-year-old child safely in the cave, she went back down the muddy dirt track and miraculously found her baby happily nestled in the bushes. The elderly, weak and soaking wet, often slipped and fell, and many lost the few belongings they managed to save at the last minute.

Young teenagers became the heroes of the day, helping the children and older people make the dangerous climb. They were familiar with the territory and voluntarily undertook to run errands for the families who needed food and water.

At 9 a.m., just as the sun was finally beginning to break through the clouds, three more Daihatsu landing craft were lowered from the troopship and headed towards the southern end of Ao Manao bay.

The Japanese were now launching their *third* attack.

Pilot Officer Srisak saw this and immediately ordered 10 of his best marksmen to spread evenly across the beachhead and lie under cover, aiming their rifle sights at the first landing craft. Each rifle had 4 rounds, and as they were getting short of ammunition, they had to make sure each shot made its mark. They were able to pick out 40 Japanese soldiers, and shoot them off one by one as they waded ashore. The marksmen wiped out the entire Japanese platoon without reloading. It was the only Siamese victory of the day.

When the Japanese sailors on the second landing craft saw what was happening, they immediately turned their vessel sideways so that its armoured body faced the marksmen on the beach, shielding their soldiers within. Because the Siamese were no longer able to get a good shot at this new position, airman Maen immediately threw down his weapon, stripped off his uniform and before any of his comrades could stop him, ran down the beach; he waded quickly into the water and pushed the Daihatsu craft into a vulnerable frontal direction. All 40 Japanese on board were then shot and killed. When the soldiers in the third craft saw what had happened to the two boats ahead of them, they immediately turned back to sea towards the safety of their troopship. It was starting to rain again.

It took a bit of time before the Japanese were able to regroup, giving Pravas enough breathing space to plan his next move. He took command of the area south of the hangars and administrative buildings and ordered his men to fire on anything that moved from the beach. Another group was stationed by the officers' houses at the northern end of the bay and trained their guns on the road leading from town. Now, in heavy rain, the Japanese were landing more troops on the undefended northern beach, including a number of tanks to give them armoured cover.

The Siamese machine gun emplacements continued to defend their weakening positions for the rest of the day. The ammunition dump was at least 200 metres away from their protected positions and they were getting short of food and water. More boys came down from the mountain caves and volunteered to help the defenders. They knew each nook and cranny of their home terrain and were able to sneak and run undetected to get food and water, and carry ammunition to them. They also acted as messengers to maintain contact with Pravas' command post. A young boy of 13, Boonying Sirisathien, a Prachuab high school student, lost his life while helping to arm a machine gun platoon with ammunition. He was posthumously awarded the title of Flight Sergeant for bravery, the youngest Siamese to ever receive such a decoration.

Four machine guns had run out of ammunition. Pravas ordered his men to continue firing blanks, making as much noise as possible, as if they were firing real live bullets. It worked in the pouring rain. But he couldn't fool the Japanese for very long.

As darkness fell, the airplane hangars and Pravas' command post were in Japanese hands. To make sure that the Siamese planes would never fly again, they were totally destroyed by the Japanese. Meanwhile Pravas ordered[9] all the remaining buildings to be set on fire. The control tower's instruments were smashed, and all the important documents were either destroyed or burned. The fuel tanks and store rooms, and even the hospital, were set alight. The patients were moved up to the caves.

There was a rumour about, that Siamese naval reinforcements would soon arrive. This gave Pravas another idea. He encouraged this rumour to spread through the ranks and was able to temporarily uplift their spirits. In this mood of bravado he ordered every man, woman and child to shout *"Chaiyo! Chaiyo! Chaiyo!"*[10] at the top of

---

9 Pravas had been acting upon a standing government decree stating that all Siamese citizens should fight "to the last man" against all invaders that threatened the nation's neutrality, followed by a scorched earth policy to destroy all food supplies, fuel and property, should the tide turn against them. This was the Siamese Citizens' Duties in Wartime Act passed by the National Assembly in September 1941, when Siam was determined to maintain her neutrality.

10 Victory! Victory! Victory! In peacetime Chaiyo means "Cheers" normally after making a toast to honour or congratulate someone, similar to "Hip- hip- hoorah!" in England.

their voices at regular intervals throughout the night. It was the brave youngsters who ran with these instructions to galvanize the defenders to shout in unison from all the different directions.

Their victorious shouts echoed across the bay. The Japanese were terrified and believed they were ancient Siamese warriors' battle cries. Intoxicated by the frenzied sound of their own rallying shouts, the Siamese defenders were fired up with courage and they were prepared to fight to the end. Pravas' ruse had the desired effect.

Pravas and his men fell back to the base of the Khao Lom Muak hill and dug in for the night.

By 9 a.m. the following morning, Tuesday 9 December, Pravas realized, that while he could not know the enemy's strength with certainty, he knew he was outnumbered. The Japanese were, in fact, landing fresh troops in the thousands. Both beaches in front of the airfield were now littered with Japanese equipment and stores.

At 10 a.m., two vehicles arrived on the road from town, one with a white flag carrying two Siamese soldiers, and the other flying a Japanese flag with two Japanese soldiers. Prime Minister Pibulsonggram had ordered a ceasefire. Seeing the two flags flying together, both sides thought this was a trick and fired several rounds onto the two vehicles. One driver was killed and several soldiers were wounded. They made a hasty retreat.

The fighting resumed and the invaders mounted new assaults with even greater energy and determination. The Siamese defenders fought back from their base at Khao Lom Muak hill. The last machine gun emplacement had been taken out. His men had completely run out of ammunition and many of them had been killed. Pravas realized that he had lost the battle.

Wing Commander Pravas checked his .38 Webley service revolver, making sure all six chambers were fully loaded. He never thought it would come to this: one bullet for each of his five children and the last one for himself. Thank the Lord Buddha his wife Sutha, and Suwanna, their little one, were safe in Bangkok. He ordered all his officers to do the same. Fight to the very end but keep one last bullet. Just don't get captured. Pravas had heard that the Japanese treated their prisoners in China very cruelly, and that it was even worse for civilians. In Nanking they had gang-raped thousands of women and children, and even bayoneted little babies just for the sport of it. Pravas had told the women and children to escape during the night but they refused to abandon the men.

At noon, a wet and exhausted postman from Prachuab, his drenched uniform clinging to his body, waded onto the northern shore of Ao Manao beach and crawled all the way to Pravas' position. He opened a waterproof satchel, produced an official telegram from the Prime Minister himself, announcing the official ceasefire and presented it to Pravas. The brave postman, one Kachat Chalipnakul, had swum three kilometres across Prachuab Bay to deliver this historic message. He was anxious to put an end to the bloodshed and realized that only he had the power to do so. After he saw the two bullet-riddled vehicles that failed to announce the ceasefire order three hours earlier, he decided not to deliver the message by road. He didn't relish being shot at. Nobody, he noticed, was firing in the direction of the sea towards the north. So he jumped in the water fully clothed and safely took the telegram across the bay. Kachat must surely be the bravest postman in Thai history.

The battle of Prachuab airfield officially ended at 12.35 p.m. on 9 December 1941.

At Prachuab airfield, the Japanese had planned a simple mop-up operation, not a battle that would last almost 30 hours. The death toll was considerable, more so for the invaders than the invaded. The Siamese lost 38 airmen and soldiers, one policeman, two female civilians, one of whom was pregnant, and one boy volunteer, a total of 42 deaths. A further 27 were wounded. The Japanese claimed to have lost 115 soldiers but Siamese estimates put the Japanese losses closer to 217 dead and 300 wounded. The true numbers will never be known.[11]

Pravas was quietly removed from the scene. He was a hero but he could not officially be recognised as one. For the Thai government to award a medal to someone who had recently killed so many Japanese soldiers would not have been politically acceptable. To maintain some semblance of sovereignty during the Japanese occupation, Thailand would have to appease the Japanese. Pravas was transferred to a less strategically important air base in Korat for the rest of the war.

It is one of history's small ironies that Pravas did not become a hero for doing what he could have done best during the Japanese invasion, and that was to fight the enemy from the air. Indeed, before World War II, Pravas had been one of Siam's pioneering aviators. In the mid-1920s he was charged with training new pilots for the fledgling Royal Siamese Flying Corps. Established in 1913, it was one of the earliest air forces in the world. In 1917, King Rama VI declared war on Germany during the First World War and sent a small expeditionary force of 1,284 volunteers to France, including a contingent of Siamese Air Corps who trained at French army flying schools. In 1918, over 95 Siamese officers qualified as pilots, and returned home to teach their flying skills to new recruits. Pravas was one of them.

In 1928 Pravas piloted the first plane to the new Chiang Mai airfield. He was received like a hero by hundreds of local citizens who had never seen an airplane before. One of them was Srisak Sucharittham, a young high school student at the time. So impressed

11 There is a grisly story of one particular way the Japanese dealt with their dead. The writer heard about this from a veteran soldier who worked with the Japanese. Apparently, after each battle, they put their dead in boiling water and removed the cooked meat from their bodies, leaving the bones to be sent back to Japan or buried in a common grave. The Japanese *never* allowed the Siamese to make a body count of their dead.

was he with Pravas' flying performance and his dashing uniform, helmet and goggles, that he was determined to become an aviator himself after he graduated from school.

He did not meet Pravas personally on that day. It was not until 1939 when he was assigned to the 5th Air Squadron in Prachuab and put under the command of Pravas, his role model from boyhood, that they finally met and became not only fellow aviators but also lifelong friends, despite their age difference. Srisak, like Pravas, had fought the Japanese on the ground, even though they were first-rate pilots.

Pravas' command posts at Prachuab Khirikhan and Korat were not what he had really wanted from his career. He would have preferred to serve his country as a pilot. He was trained to be a line officer and was not happy in administrative positions. Yet, after the war ended in 1945, he was promoted to Director General of the Royal Thai Air Force's Pilot Training Command, a desk job in Bangkok, where he shuffled more paper and people than planes and pilots.

He was then transferred to the newly established Thai Airways as Chief Pilot where he was at least able to test-fly new aircraft. Unfortunately, one of the planes under his command crashed and he was held responsible. This was followed by a public enquiry and an unpleasant court case, and he was called upon to pay the costs. Not a man to shirk responsibility, he looked for more gainful employment to help settle his debts. In 1957 he was offered a better paying job by General Thao Ma, Chief of the Royal Lao Air Force, as a consultant and chief trainer. The Laotian government had recently purchased a fleet of T-28 fighters to provide air support to the Royal Lao Army. The General sent Pravas to the small airfield at Luang Prabang and put him in charge of setting up a squadron of Laotian pilots, gunners, engineers and ground crew.

In 1959, former Pilot Officer Chalermkiart Wattanakun, the airman who lost his pregnant wife during the battle of Prachuab airfield in 1941, was now Air Chief Marshal and head of the Royal

Thai Air Force. He was on an official visit to Luang Prabang airfield, at the invitation of the Royal Lao Air Force. It was a happy reunion of former comrades-in-arms, but Chalermkiart was sad to see his former commanding officer in circumstances not befitting a war hero. He persuaded Pravas to return home and he was able to place his old friend as a senior pilot with the domestic arm of Thai Airways.

Back in Thailand he found that all his wartime colleagues who had served under him during the war had been promoted, and some were now his superior officers at Thai Airways. He was not a happy man. In 1963, Air Chief Marshal Chalermkiart died in an air crash. Pravas had lost his patron and good friend. Times had changed and he decided to leave the airline, much to the relief of many of his former colleagues who now served above him. Pravas was still heavily in debt, but better days lay ahead.

On 3 June 1964, Pravas joined Air America, a private airline run by the CIA as part of their covert anti-communist operation in Laos during the Vietnam War. Pravas landed on a scheduled flight at Udorn airfield and reported for duty to American Major Drexel B. Cochran, chief of Detachment 6 of the 1st Air Command Wing of Air America, code named *Water Pump*. The word had got around that Pravas had left Thai Airways and General Ma recommended him to join Air America. It was a challenging and dangerous assignment that entailed flying missions over Southeast Asia's roughest terrain. Whatever the season, there were always low cloud ceilings and fog, and in the monsoon between June and October one could expect torrential rains and freak thunderstorms. Add the continuous threat of enemy gunfire from the Communist Pathet Lao and Vietnamese forces to the equation and Pravas' new job with Air America could certainly be considered one of the most dangerous in the world. Only candidates with rare flying skills and steely determination should apply, he was told. But the pay was good.[12]

"Siddown Captain and welcome to *Water Pump*. We've put you up at the Sri Udorn hotel until we can find you a bigger place near the airfield."

A veteran of the Korean War, the Major was in his mid-fifties, big and burly, and a serious man who didn't mince his words, though he was friendly enough. In short, he was Pravas' kind of man. The only thing he needed was to get used to the *accent*. All the Americans he met at Air America's office at the USOM[13] North Sathorn Road headquarters in Bangkok where he was interviewed spoke a different kind of English from what he was used to. But language difficulties aside, he knew he was going to get on well with the Major.

"You're gonna be flying mostly C123Bs and C46s with full fuel loads and cargo weighing several thousand pounds on the way out and as soon as you empty those babies you gotta turn around *quick* and head back home," the Major explained. "Those commies on the ground have heavy Russian 12.7 millimetre guns but their aim ain't so hot. Our outfit has a good track record and we run a tight ship. Most of our boys get back."

With that piece of reassuring news Pravas saluted his new commander and said "Thank you, sir".

"Good luck. And call me Drex!"

The Fairchild C123 "Provider", a heavy duty cargo plane, was being prepared for take-off from the runway of the Udorn military airfield under the vigilant eye of Captain Pravas. He watched the fuel truck drive away into the stormy darkness of the monsoon season. The cargo doors of the plane's open aft fuselage were closing and the

12 Some pilots could earn up to five thousand dollars a month, a considerable sum in 1964. Joshua Kurlantzick, *The Ideal Man*, John Wiley, 2011.

13 United States Operation Mission. To the amusement of American officers who knew the Thai language well, U-som meant "You fix it".

loading ramp was wheeled away. Hundreds of tons of rice sacks on pallets had been loaded into the huge whale-like bowels of the C123, known as the "heavy lifter", its two reciprocating propeller engines enabling it to land on short runways and unprepared fields hacked out of the jungle.

Pravas picked up his flight plan and boarded the airplane. Inside, Lieutenant Thavee Phuttanand, his copilot, was busy studying the flight checklist, while behind him, Captain Chuck Dempsey, the crew's navigator, was plotting their route on a map of northern Laos.

"How is the course?" Pravas asked the American navigator.

"It's gonna be wet and bumpy all the way and as usual we'll be flying over the planet's most unfriendly country. Otherwise everything's A-Okay!"

Pravas checked with Joe Agnelli, the flight engineer who appeared at the cabin door.

"Everything's fine and dandy in the back, Captain. The pallets are all secure and the boys are ready to rock n' roll when we arrive at the DZ."

"The boys", three young Royal Lao Air Force trainees, were hired as "kickers"[14], whose job was to push cargo – on this flight, the pallets of rice – out of the plane onto the drop zone, often a mountain side or a marked location in the jungle.

Pravas checked the instruments and looked out at the driving rain belting down on the cockpit windscreen. He had his trusted crew on board who flew with him on all his missions so he was confident.

"All right, let's get this plane into the air!"

The first engine sputtered to life in a cloud of smoke followed by the second one. The chocks were pulled away from under the wheels and Pravas taxied the plane onto the wet runway.

---

14 The kickers have a dangerous job. On this flight they had to push pallets of rice out of the aircraft hold through the open aft fuselage for an 800 feet free fall by parachute to the drop zone. To prevent falling out of the plane, they were held back by straps, and in cases where the straps did not hold, they would parachute down, often into enemy country.

"*See Saw* to control tower. Ready to take off. Over."

The control tower acknowledged Pravas' request and the Mickey Mouse nose of the C123 pushed through the rain. The brakes were released and the plane started to gather speed. Pravas saw the red lights of the runway and at one hundred and twenty knots he felt the plane lifting off the ground. The landing gear was pushing up into the wheel wells with a shudder and at two hundred knots the altimeter was showing three thousand feet. *See Saw* was airborne.

Pravas was back in the air. He was on his 29th mission for Air America.

Udorn airfield in northeastern Thailand, not far from the Laotian border, was originally an old laterite runway with a small wooden hangar used by the Japanese in World War II. With the arrival of three C46s in September 1955 to deliver food, medical supplies and emergency aid to anti-communist forces in Laos, Air America started its operations here. A new hard-surface concrete runway was built for heavy traffic and the airfield was upgraded to an air force base. Udorn became the Asian headquarters for Air America. The CIA also had an office in Udorn, called the 480 2nd Joint Liason Detachment under the chief spook, James Lair, who ran the entire covert operation from here.

Air America was a vital component of the agency's covert operations in Laos. Its primary task was to airdrop refugee supplies, mainly foodstuffs such as rice, salt and cornmeal, as well as medical supplies, to the Hmong hill tribes fighting the communist North Vietnamese and the Pathet Lao forces.

In 1963 the Pathet Lao North Vietnamese-backed rebel army – "*rebel*" for the CIA, "*freedom fighter*" for those who were anti-French-colonial communists – gained control of half the country. A strategically important area in the far northeast was Sam Neua province bordering North Vietnam. The population of this area, the intensely independent Hmong[15] hill tribe people, were historically anti-Vietnamese and had fiercely opposed the communists' efforts to take over their homelands. For the Hmong, Sam Neua is their sacred territory and their ancestral ground for centuries, and they "don't take lightly to interference with their tribal customs."[16] Due to its proximity to North Vietnam, Sam Neua was one of the first areas to be attacked by the communists and throughout the sixties the struggle for the control of this rugged, yet fertile country, was both bloody and continuous.

Apart from the food drops, known as "rice drops", Air America was frequently called upon to perform paramilitary tasks, transporting and air-dropping ammunition and weapons – euphemistically called "hard rice" – to friendly forces. Pravas delivered construction materials on one mission, and a jeep on another. The mercenary pilots never questioned their superiors about the CIA's political agenda and were proud of their motto, "*Anything, anytime, anywhere – professionally.*"

If the pilots carried opium, as has been widely reported, they didn't know about it. It did not appear on the cargo manifest, and the illegal drugs would have been secretly planted on the plane, to the total ignorance of the pilots. The pilots at Udorn were well-paid mercenaries, apolitical perhaps, and certainly daredevils who enjoyed the ride. They were occasionally gun runners for the American cause, but *never* drug carriers, at least not on the humanitarian cargo transport runs *out of Udorn.* Pravas thoroughly inspected the cargo hold before each mission. If he found any *yud sai*[17] opium, he would, as did all the pilots, immediately report it to Drex. If a pilot was found guilty of trafficking drugs, he was fired. The rank and file of Air

---

15 *Meo* meaning "barbarians"is the Chinese name for the *Hmong,* which for them means "free men".

16 Frank Viviano, *Dispatches from the Pacific Century,* Addison-Wesley, 1993.

17 Secretly stuffed in the cargo.

America pilots and commanding officers in Udorn refused to allow opium to be transported on their planes.[18]

In July 1966, Pravas became involved in one of Air America's riskiest operations of the CIA's secret war in Laos. During the previous year's monsoon, the Royal Lao troops under the command of gutsy General Vang Pao, the Hmong warlord who was elevated from the rank of Lieutenant by the CIA to win respect and support from his people, temporarily gained the upper hand and was now in control of his homeland in Sam Neua province. Although he spoke "a sometimes bewildering mix of French, English, Lao, and Hmong", Vang Pao was considered by the CIA as a "military genius" who understood Lao and Vietnamese tactics better than the Americans.[19] In response to an appeal from Vang Pao for reinforcements, Air America was requested by the CIA to transport several platoons of Thai Special Forces to help Vang Pao's much depleted army to help defend his position against advancing Pathet Lao and North Vietnamese convoys heading towards Sam Nuea and the Plain of Jars.

The Thais had been in Laos since the fifties, but in limited numbers, under the guise of "volunteers". The standing instruction in the event of capture was that they were to identify themselves as "mercenaries"[20]. In July 1966, four Curtiss C46s were selected and several air missions were planned for landing and unloading the Thai reinforcements on the Hong Non dirt strip airfield on the Plain

18 True, it was known that heroin produced by the Hmong hilltribes were transported from the Plain of Jars to Long Tiang for processing on Air America aircraft between 1965 to 1971, but not from Udorn. It was a separate CIA operation solely to help move the Hmong's cash crop of heroin to market, without which they would face economic ruin. It was also politically expedient for the CIA to turn a "blind eye" (Christopher Robbins, *Air America,* Macmillan, 1979) to their clients, senior Royal Lao Army and Air Force generals, who ran the opium business in Vientiane.

19 *The Ideal Man,* Op.Cit.

20 By 1970, seventeen thousand Thai troops were to serve in Laos. The US government was spending about a hundred million dollars a year to support the Thai Special Forces helping Vang Pao. *The Ideal Man,* Op.Cit.

of Jars 12 miles south of the town of Sam Nuea during that month. Air America was not normally used for landing armed troops on the front.

Captain Pravas was supervising the loading of his plane personally, as he always did before a mission. He was glad that he had his trusted team on board: copilot Thavee, navigator Chuck, and Joe his engineer. Six crew-cut members of the Thai Special Forces and their equipment boarded his aircraft. They were fresh from Thailand, carrying full battle gear, and wore smart new uniforms without identifying insignia. Pravas welcomed them aboard and made sure they were comfortable in his C46, Pravas' favourite airplane. He'd flown thousands of miles on this rugged wartime cargo transport. It was especially effective in mountainous areas where a good climb rate and high service ceiling was required. He inspected the landing gear to make sure there were no mishaps when the plane touched down on the Hong Non landing strip.

*Sandra Dee,* as the plane was nicknamed, took off at precisely "zero light thirty,"[21] on 19 July 1966. The mountains were misty, as they always are in Laos, but at least it wasn't raining. One hour later, Pravas lowered the landing gear and prepared to make a smooth run towards Hong Non's postage stamp of an airfield. At one thousand feet he heard the sound of gunfire. The aircraft lurched and he grimaced at the acrid smell of an electrical short circuit. The plane was hit by ground fire, probably by the 12.7 millimetre guns that he had been warned about. Pravas had never been shot at in a plane before. This was not turning out to be the routine flight he was expecting. Headquarters did not realize that the town of Sam Nuea had just been retaken by the Pathet Lao forces and was now their new base.[22] More bullets ripped through the fuselage and the C46 started to vibrate as Pravas put the heavy plane back on full-throttle.

---

21 Slang for 12.30 p.m.

22 The town of Sam Nua was to become Pathet Lao's national headquarters, with a munitions factory and a cadre training camp.

The *pingk-pingk* sound of bullets punching through the metal of the plane's fuselage reminded Chuck of his boyhood in Tennessee when he used to take his .22 rifle to the woods near his home for target practice at a line of tin cans. Joe was wounded in the shoulder and two Thai soldiers were hit and their harnessed bodies slumped forward in their seats.

"Abort landing!" yelled Pravas, as he raised the wing flaps and got the plane to immediately ascend. *You gotta turn around quick.* The aircraft shuddered and cleared the runway, and started to climb to three thousand feet. But even with full-power, there was no way the heavy plane could maintain that altitude for long. But at least it was out of the line of fire. The plane began a long and impossible climb towards the four thousand feet peak of the Pha Thi Mountain five miles north of Sam Nuea. But then, it suddenly lost power. Both Pravas and Thavee felt helpless as the trembling aircraft started to pitch uncontrollably. The only thing Pravas could do, by adjusting the engine-cowl flaps and throttle settings, was to prepare for a wheels-up landing on a paddy field. Thavee strained his eyes through the windshield searching for a level piece of ground.

To this day, the fate of the *Sandra Dee* remains a mystery. No trace of the plane and its passengers was ever found. Did the plane crash-land onto a muddy rice field? Were there any survivors and if so, were they captured? Did they smack into the Pha Thi Mountain, explode into a fireball and burn to a cinder, or even manage to clear the mountain and break into pieces over the uncharted and remote jungles of northern Vietnam? One of Pravas' student air cadets back in the thirties, Air Marshal Dhawee Chulasap, said at a Royal Thai Air Force remembrance ceremony, that he is now in heaven, happy in the arms of a beautiful Vietnamese girl.

The passing away of Pravas marked the end of the pioneering era of aviation and the romance of flying. The early biplanes that Pravas flew, some parts of which were sometimes made of wood, were small, fragile and equipped with only a few instruments. The French Breguet 14B2 that he flew to Chiang Mai in 1928 had an altimeter and tachometer, simple gauges for air speed, fuel, and temperature, a compass and a clock. He flew without radio or sextant, no oxygen supply or parachute, and from his open cockpit, he was so close to the ground that he could see farmers harvesting their rice below. They waved to him and he would wave back. It must be remembered that only the year before, in 1927, Charles Lindbergh, the famous US aviator, was the first to make a non-stop solo flight across the Atlantic. The Hawk III at Prachuab had a few more gauges, twelve to be precise. A modern jetliner has dozens of instruments, gauges and monitoring screens, and pilots today are trained to trust their instruments implicitly. But in situations where a technical failure occurs, as it did in 2009 when an Air France Airbus 330 went down in the Atlantic, these instruments can give false readings. It is often claimed that today's pilots, unlike Pravas, are not really pilots, but system operators. Apparently, the Airbus pilots couldn't tell from the instruments whether their plane was climbing or descending. Aviator goggles, leather kits and the wind and rain in the pilot's face are a far cry from modern aviation, and nostalgically remind us of Pravas' pioneering spirit.

It took 68 years for the government to finally pay tribute to the bravery of the pilots, soldiers and civilians who died at the battle of Prachuab airfield on those two fateful days in December 1941. On 15 March 2010, their names were engraved on a commemorative monument on the airfield. Mom Luang Pravas Choomsai was recognized for his courage in the face of the enemy and a museum next to the monument where his brave actions during the battle of Prachuab are recorded will hopefully help us remember one of Thailand's most courageous aviators.

# STRATFORD HERCULES DENNIS
# 1899 - 1979

Forgotten war hero in Britain,
well remembered in Siam

***Previous page:*** *Happy days at the Sports Club where he was Secretary; on New Year's Eve, 1950. Chada is far right.*

***Above:*** *Hercules and wife Chada.*

# 6
# Hercules to the Rescue

On the eve of the biggest seaborne invasion in history, Lieutenant Commander Stratford Hercules Dennis of the British Royal Navy made a thorough inspection of his ship, the HMS *Prince Charles*, to make sure that everything on board was shipshape. He inspected the engine room, the conditions on all the decks, the guns, even the cabins and galleys, in preparation for transporting several battalions of the 1st US Infantry Division across the Channel from Weymouth on the English southern coast to Omaha Beach in Normandy.

The *Prince Charles* was originally a 2,950-ton merchant ship from Belgium, converted by the Royal Navy into an infantry-landing ship, capable of carrying 8 LCPs (Landing-Craft Personnel) and 300 troops. Commander Dennis knew that sooner or later he would be called upon to take part in Operation Neptune, the naval portion of the Normandy campaign – called Operation Overlord – to land 160,000 allied troops in one single day on the beaches of north western France and start liberating the European continent from the clutches of Nazi Germany.

Dennis had been preparing and training his crew for this operation for several months. He was solicitous about the welfare of his men and built up a relationship based on loyalty and genuine affection with them since the Allied landings on the Salerno beachhead for the Italian campaign the year before, on 9 September

1943. Some of his men had served with him as far back as the historic evacuation of 338,226 British, French and Belgian troops trapped by the German army in Dunkirk in May and June 1940. Indeed, Commander Dennis and his crew had become experts in rescue and landing operations.

His best friend on board the ship that day, though, was Nelson. Born from a family of animal lovers, Dennis could not bear to be separated from his beloved Alsatian during long periods at sea. It was against navy regulations to bring pets on board, and during the Salerno campaign he suffered immensely without the company of his dog. How he managed to smuggle Nelson on board the *Prince Charles* remains a secret between Dennis and his crew, who came to love the dog as much as their commander.

Five invasion assault forces – British, American, French, Polish and Canadian – had boarded 6,000 landing ships to attack Hitler's "Fortress Europe" in Normandy. General Eisenhower, Supreme Commander of Operation Overlord, originally scheduled the invasion for 5 June 1944. The only thing that held them back was the English weather. The sea was choppy and the wind was blowing strong, far too hazardous for the 125-mile journey across the English Channel. Cold, cramped and seasick, the soldiers were packed like sardines into 49 invasion convoys, waiting for Ike[1] to issue his command to sail. A slight break in the weather was forecast and Ike made his historic decision, with these three words, "Okay, we'll go." The next day, 6 June 1944, would go down in history as "D-Day."

On 4 June, Commander Dennis watched from the rails as hundreds of American troops boarded HMS *Prince Charles*. He was immediately reminded of Operation Avalanche at Salerno the year before, when he was in command of HMS *Prince Astrid*, landing several battalions of the US Fifth Army onto the Italian beaches. He remembered the hundreds of fresh-faced Mickey Rooney and

1 Dwight Eisenhower's popular nickname.

Van Johnson look-alikes, innocent country lads from small towns in Illinois and Iowa, and from the farms of Kansas and Missouri, barely half his age, ignorant of the dangers ahead. But some of the men who were now boarding *Prince Charles* were a different lot. They were not young, regular conscripts, but the US Army's Special Forces, the 2nd Ranger Battalion, specially trained to scale the cliffs at Omaha Beach with grappling irons.

Because of Commander Dennis' experience at Dunkirk, Dieppe and Salerno, he had earned the reputation for successfully evacuating and landing troops on difficult terrain and under dangerous conditions. For Operation Neptune, he was entrusted with landing 300 elite corps of the 2nd Ranger Battalion who would assist the raw recruits of the 1st US Infantry Division to secure Omaha Beach.

The crossing was rougher than expected. Even crack troops like the Rangers can vomit, and they did. So sickening was the stench on board that many of them could hardly wait to get off the rolling ship and land. Commander Dennis' crew, not normally squeamish, were beginning to feel sick themselves and kept on yelling to the "Yanks" to puke *away* from the wind, "to leeward, mate – leeward!"[2] But the real danger was not seasickness, but the groundless fear of attack from enemy aircraft, which never came, and the occasional floating mine that could sometimes brush against the ship's hull. It needed just a slight knock to set off one of these mines and the *Prince Charles* would be obliterated.

Commander Dennis was familiar with these floating minefields and, with his able pilot, the *Prince Charles* safely reached the disembarkation point twelve miles from the coast in poor sea conditions. Now came the tricky bit: transferring three hundred men safely on board the LCPs. This was one of the most difficult parts of Operation Neptune, as the landing craft and the troopship

2 Alex Kershaw, *The Bedford Boys*, Simon & Schuster, 2003.

were lashed by 8-foot waves and connected by a narrow gangplank. Many men often slipped and drowned. The principal task of the troopship's commander was to ensure that the soldiers boarded their LCPs safely and without losses. Commander Dennis successfully transferred all 300 Rangers onto their landing craft without a single mishap. The bloodiest fighting of the day was about to begin at Omaha, where the US 1st Infantry Division was pinned down by the Germans from a high cliff. The *Prince Charles* was to lie offshore to take back the wounded. A gale was blowing and, on the way back to England, the *Prince Charles* lost three landing craft but fortunately no lives.

There were thousands of heroes on that day. War historians normally attribute the success of Operation Overlord to the bravery of the fighting men on the beaches, to the airmen who gave them cover and to the naval gunners that shelled the German artillery's coastal defences. The heroic role of the seamen manning the transport ships is often overlooked; without these men Operation Neptune could not have been successfully executed. Stratford Hercules Dennis was such a hero, a skilled and courageous commander. By then, he had been awarded two DSCs (Distinguished Service Crosses) by the Royal Navy for bravery in Dunkirk and Salerno, as well as the Polish Cross of Valour for exceptional service on board Polish ships in 1941. He was awarded another DSC in Normandy for bravery under fire. But Stratford Hercules Dennis had not always been a hero.

Son of a well-to-do horse breeder and British army officer, Colonel Meade Crosbie Dennis, and the Honourable Alice Handcock, a member of the Irish peerage, Stratford Hercules Dennis was born in a large manor house overlooking the Solent Channel on 11 November 1899, in Portsea Island, Hampshire, England.

The Dennis family was part of the Anglo-Irish landowning class of absentee-landlords from Kiltegan, County Wicklow. Stratford's grandparents moved to southern England where they established their second home at the turn of the 19th century when life in Ireland after the potato famine became unbearable, even for the well-off.

As a boy, Stratford longed to go beyond the sea that he enthusiastically gazed at everyday from his bedroom window. It was only natural that this sea-loving lad received his early schooling on the Isle of Wight, and at 16 was admitted as a naval cadet to the prestigious Royal Naval College at Dartmouth, in Devon.

Dennis was a born sailor and his happy-go-lucky personality endeared him to his commanding officers. *I think he will do well and is suitable for a destroyer* – went one commendation from Captain Hyde-Parker, after Dennis displayed his skills and courage as a midshipman on a battle-cruiser at the Battle of Jutland in the North Sea on 31 May 1916, aged only seventeen. Other commendations were equally complimentary. *Energetic officer of a most cheerful temperament and should do well* – Captain French. *A very keen officer, should do well if he took more trouble. Absolutely to be relied upon* – Commander Robinson. This report in 1919 seemed to indicate that the easy-going Dennis did not take things seriously enough when he should have. By the next semester, according to Commander Norris, he managed to pull his socks up: *I think he does take the trouble*. By 1920 Dennis was promoted to Acting Lieutenant. Captain Mackenzie, his immediate superior, was well pleased with his progress, and described him as *zealous and intelligent*.

Dennis was popular; he had the support of his senior officers and a bright naval career ahead of him. Why then, was such a promising young officer placed on the retirement list *at his own request* on 16 July 1922? The problem with Dennis is that he had a surfeit of talents, enough at 23 to make him undecided as to his future and what he wanted to do for the rest of his life. He tended to spend more than he earned from his meagre naval salary and thought he could make more money on civvy-street. He was also a keen equestrian and was five times a jockey in the Grand National horse race. He thought he could do better on his own.

The next seventeen years were to become a period of serious financial difficulty and professional uncertainty, the *first* unsuccessful phase of Dennis' adventurous life.

After leaving the Navy, Dennis returned to his family home in Ireland and, according to a family history, "spent the ensuing years living without any visible means of support and had a reputation of being something of a cad – he lived on his wits rather than through any military connections and set himself up as a racecourse trainer."[3]

To his credit, he never called upon his father, nor his brother Meade Edward Dennis, for financial help or moral support, nor did he use their senior military positions to further his interests. Stratford had always been a proud and independent man. Despite being continually short of money he was able to pursue his passion for dogs and invested in a pack of hounds, which he maintained at Grogan's Kennels at Slaney Park near his family home in County Wicklow. His mother did not know about this expensive hobby even though she was always wondering, "What is this filthy smell?", whenever she caught whiff of the hounds' dinner, stored on their estate near the Slaney River. Although Stratford made a name for himself in equestrian circles, in February 1929, *The Times* declared that "S.H. Dennis, Esq., trainer of racehorses" was bankrupt.

In 1930, he rented out his home in East Sussex and moved to Hollywood, California, to try his luck there. He had heard that the American film industry needed well-trained horses, and many a Western movie must have featured some of Stratford's "hosses." On the film set, we can well imagine "Commander Dennis" charming the boots off film cowboy legends like Gene Autry and Roy Rogers.

A horse-training stable requires frequent injections of capital and although Dennis tried his hand at breeding racehorses for various American derbies, he found himself stretched too thinly. His Irish luck had finally run out and he admitted that "the coin fell

3 From a family biography posted on the internet.

heads when it should have been tails."

By 1938, married to an American named Sheila Watt, with whom he had two children, he was in financial difficulties. Bankrupt again, he was obliged to leave behind his wife and work his passage home on board a German trans-Atlantic steamer, on which he was able to gain valuable insights into the naval tactics of his future enemy by working close to German naval officers in the ship's control room.

His brother Meade, a successful career soldier, soon to become general and the hero of the Battle of El Alamein in North Africa under Field Marshal Montgomery, was ashamed of Stratford and was continually making excuses for his frequent absences. When he came back from Hollywood, Meade told friends that Stratford was back on leave from government service in India. But his father was furious. "Whether anyone accepted his stories of 'endless rotten luck' or not, Stratford was in disgrace."[4]

On Sunday morning, 18 March 1939, Stratford was staying with his brother at Fort Granite, their family seat, in Baltinglass, Ireland. As the two were talking in the garden, a servant girl came rushing out of the house shouting, telling them that she had just heard on the radio that the German army had invaded Czechoslovakia. At this, Meade later recounted to his son Piers, how "all the awfulness of the First World War passed before my eyes and I turned to my brother and said, 'How very terrible, what are we to do!' But Stratford looked at me and said, 'Thank God! At least I can now go out and enjoy the navy and salvage my reputation.'"[5] Within that same month, Stratford was appointed Lieutenant Commander on board the HMS *Caledonia*. Stratford, older and wiser, was back in action.

Stratford's war record was spectacular. He received his first DSC for his heroic efforts in relieving the British Expeditionary

4 Memoirs, Piers Dennis, son of General Meade Dennis.
5 Piers Dennis, Ibid.

Force from Dunkirk in 1940 and the Polish Cross of Valour in 1941. In between large-scale evacuation and landing operations, Stratford ferried agents into occupied France on small boats and trawlers across the Channel. The operations were done in secret, so there are no official records of these dangerous missions. We can only imagine Stratford wishing them "good luck" as he deposited Allied spies on the beaches of northwestern France in the middle of the night. By May 1944, Commander H.S. Dennis had two bars[6] added to his DSC for his role in the landing of the American GIs at Salerno and the US Rangers on Omaha. His final campaign was in the Aegean Sea in 1945, for the relief of Greece and the liberation of that country from Axis occupation. On 14 August 1945, Commander Dennis received his last MID (Mention in Dispatches).

A war hero, he decided to make a permanent career in the service of the British Royal Navy. But superior naval skills in the field of battle become superfluous in times of peace. Dennis was undoubtedly a leader of firm conviction and unwavering moral fibre, but his new naval career, as we shall see, would require professional skills in diplomacy, keen political experience and the ability to practice the art of Realpolitic. Dennis was neither trained nor experienced in any of these competences.

Whilst on leave in England between Operation Avalanche (Salerno) and Operation Neptune (Normandy), he met and married his second wife, Betty Helyar, and fathered a son, Shane Patrick, and a daughter, Ann Caroline. He was looking forward to his new life in peacetime, which he hoped would finally be on an even keel.

Dennis was now promoted to Captain. In early 1945, he was transferred to the Royal Navy Base in Bombay and served directly

6 Further awards of the same decoration were shown by a bar on the ribbon of the cross, meaning that Dennis had been awarded again.

under Admiral Lord Louis Mountbatten, the Allied Supreme Commander. Dennis was appointed SEAC's[7] deputy head of Combined Operations, a well-earned advancement. In this capacity, he accompanied Mountbatten on several official missions to Siam and met Pridi Panomyong, leader of the Free Thai Movement.[8] It was September 1945. Dennis and Pridi were to become firm friends and Dennis immediately fell in love with Siam. His life was not to be the same again.

One of Dennis' first assignments in Siam in late September 1945 was to help the Allied army supervise the surrender of the Japanese troops and the decommissioning of Japanese arms and materiel with a platoon of Gurkhas. It was a delicate job for Dennis, as there was also a prevailing and not totally unfounded suspicion abroad, particularly within the American State Department, that Britain wanted to colonise Siam[9] and establish a Protectorate,[10] reminiscent of Britain's pre-war hegemonic days of empire. The presence of British colonial troops in Siam made Dennis' job even more difficult. It took all of Dennis' leadership and social skills to fulfil his first duties in Siam with professional aplomb.

In the following year, Dennis received orders from the Admiralty to remain in Siam. *Would he like to be Britain's naval attaché at the embassy in Bangkok?* he was asked. Dennis never had a desk job in his life, neither was he a career diplomat. But he said he would give it a go.

His first task as attaché was easy. He was invited by the Siamese government to advise the Royal Thai Navy. Part of this assignment entailed getting to know the Thai Navy's top brass. He socialised with them and built strong relationships with many Thai admirals and captains, some of whom were to remain close friends for the rest

---

7 South East Asia Command.

8 See Chapter 4.

9 Professor Nicholas Tarling, History Department, University of Auckland, *Rice and Reconciliation: the Anglo-Thai Peace Negotiations of 1945.*

10 Churchill indeed considered taking over the Kra Isthmus.

of his life. Discovering that it was difficult to remain aloof from their problems and at the same time be the dispassionate career diplomat that this assignment called for, however, he was soon to become the victim of local politics.

To a newly arrived expatriate, Siam's position in the world was confusing. Here was a nation that played an unusual role in the Second World War. She was neither a defeated country like Germany nor a liberated one like France. Despite the uneasy alliance[11] between Siam and Japan, the majority of Siamese were anti-Japanese, but they weren't exactly in love with the European powers either, in particular France and Britain, who had annexed some of her territories earlier on in the century.

The local politics were even more confusing. Following the war's end, there were many different camps vying for power and there was no shortage of intrigue. The year before Dennis arrived in Siam the Pibulsonggram government was defeated by the National Assembly[12] and when the Second World War came to an end, Pridi Panomyong, the Regent and leader of the Free Thai Movement within the country, issued a proclamation repudiating the declaration of war on Britain and America,[13] paving the way for M.R. Seni Pramoj, ex-Minister of Siam to Washington, DC, and leader of the Free Thais in America, to become Siam's first post-war Prime Minister.

Seni was followed by a series of premiers, none of whom remained in power for very long. On 8 November 1947, Luang Damrong, the last Prime Minister who was supported by Pridi and the Pridi-alligned Navy, was deposed in a bloodless coup d'état by the army.

When two opposing forces face each other in Parliament, acrimonious words are hurled back and forth. When the opposing forces are the army and the navy of the same country, one can well

---

11 See Chapter 2.
12 See Chapter 2.
13 See Chapter 4.

expect flying bullets to take their place. The Siamese army and navy were to be pitted against each other over the next five years.

There was chaos and confusion throughout the country, and indeed throughout the post-war world. In Austria, the cities had been laid waste in rubble, there was an outbreak of typhus and the country was about to be carved up into British, American, French and Russian military zones. In Belgium, King Leopold was accused of being too friendly with the Germans and had to abdicate. In Italy, the timid King Victor Emmanuel III, who had enabled Mussolini to rise to power, also abdicated before a referendum turned the nation into a republic, and there was a real fear that the Communists led by the Soviets would take over. France had slid into anarchy, as towns and villages set up local tribunals and summarily executed thousands of wartime collaborators in a frenzy of revenge. In China, a civil war was raging between the Communists in the north under Mao Tse-tung and Chiang Kai-shek's Kuomingtang Nationalists in the south, tearing the country apart.

If the reader is confused by these events, one can well understand Dennis' predicament. He sympathised with his new friends in the navy and he had great respect for Pridi. It must also be said, judging from his wartime experiences, that Captain Dennis had an appetite for intrigue and looked for adventure. He was beginning to enjoy his new assignment.

Dennis had become a regular on the diplomatic cocktail circuit and made many friends with other foreign diplomats, in particular with his counterpart at the American embassy, Commander Skeats Gardas, the US naval attaché, who was to play an important role as a fellow conspirator in an undiplomatic incident that almost cost him his job.

At one Siamese Ministry of Foreign Affairs function on "Constitution Day", 10 December 1946, Dennis met a Thai lady who was to become the most important person in his life in Siam. The daughter of Phraya Prakit Kolasat, and a member of the distinguished Kanchanavanit family, who had served His Majesty the King's government for many generations, Chada was vivacious, beautiful and outspoken. Dennis was immediately drawn to her and certainly met his match. Her forthright responses to his light-hearted flirtation intrigued him.

Chada's initial reaction to Dennis' advances, meanwhile, was *Who does this presumptuous yet charming British officer think he is?* Captain Dennis was, at 47, fit, handsome and, in his white naval uniform, must have presented a dashing figure. After a whirlwind romance, Chada was bowled over. Dennis was the most exciting person she had ever met. Yet when he proposed to her, she refused to marry him until he divorced Betty. Chada was herself a divorcee. They got married in 1947 after Dennis went on home leave to divorce his second wife.

On the morning of 8 November 1947, Captain Dennis unsuccessfully tried to get in touch with Pridi by telephone to discuss progress on the dredging project at the mouth of the Chao Phraya River that he was working on. The army's bloodless coup d'état, ousting then Prime Minister Damrong, had just begun. Pridi, with advanced warning the night before, had already left the city. This coup, led by a military clique that would hold on to power for many years to come, would leave Pridi on the outside looking in for the rest of his life and forever change the course of the country's history.

At times like this, foreign missions need to wait and see, before deciding which "government" to recognise. "To the question as to whether the British would support Pridi and Damrong with material aid in overthrowing the rebels, there was an emphatic *no*."[14] By 9 November, it was all over. The army was in power and formed the new *de jure* government.

---

14 Dennis' memoirs, page 59.

Ten days later, at 6 a.m., Dennis was woken up by a man in naval uniform at his front gate. "Ruth[15] is here! May he come in?" he blurted out. Five naval officers stepped out of a large naval staff Austin that was now parked in his driveway. One of the officers was a marine commander wearing a large-size cap, thick glasses, and a moustache that ringed a hollow-cheeked face. As soon as this person stepped into the house and removed his cap and glasses, and put in his false teeth, there stood before Dennis his old friend and former comrade-in-arms, Pridi Panomyong.

"I need to leave the country immediately! Could you please help me?" While Pridi was asking Dennis to help him escape, the four naval officers were bringing in a considerable amount of armaments, including Thompson sub-machine guns, pistols and grenades. Not wanting his house to turn into a battle zone, Dennis immediately locked this arsenal up in a closet.

"I would like to help you very much but I must first consult my ambassador," Dennis said, and then provided Pridi and his party with a spare bedroom next to his study as well as a large English breakfast of bacon, eggs, and coffee, followed by much needed refreshments of whiskey and soda. The party looked tired and bedraggled, having travelled 300 kilometres overnight from their upcountry hiding-place.[16]

By 8.30 a.m., Dennis roused the ambassador and appraised him of the situation. Because of Pridi's special relationship with Mountbatten during the war, Dennis and ambassador Sir Geoffrey Thompson felt that the British government owed Pridi the assistance he requested. Dennis also suspected that Pridi had come to him, rather than seeking refuge in the embassy compound, because of his prior relationship with Mountbatten. Both men had an equally amicable rapport with the British admiral. Wartime friendships are hard to sever.

---

15 Wartime codename for Pridi Panomyong.

16 Sattahib naval base beyond Pattaya on the east coast.

Due to army and navy rivalry, Dennis' plan was to spirit Pridi away by sea, rather than escape by land. Dennis knew from his friend, William Adam, an ex-prisoner of war on the Siam-Burma railway and the head of Shell Oil, that the M.S. *Fusus*, a tanker, was about to sail for Singapore and they arranged that Pridi board this ship *outside territorial waters* in the Gulf of Siam.

Dennis and the ambassador proceeded to the US embassy to get the Americans on board for this operation. Commander Skeats Gardas, the American naval attaché, immediately offered his official motorboat to take Pridi to the ship, under the deceptive guise of a "fishing trip" with his wife, provided Dennis accompanied Pridi to the motorboat's landing at the Port of Klong Toey. Dennis returned home and after failing to persuade Pridi *not* to go ahead with this "grave step of leaving the country,"[17] he told him of the escape route and the plan to board the American motorboat at 1.30 a.m. the next day. It was now only 10 a.m.

It was like waiting for Ike's command to sail for Normandy on the HMS *Prince Charles* on D-Day, 1944; the next fifteen hours wait was just as stressful. To keep his mind occupied, Dennis decided to catch up with his paperwork in his study. It was prearranged that if uninvited visitors came to the house, Dennis would knock at the bedroom door three times, instructing his guests to lie low, keep quiet and not go near the window.

As it turned out, a visitor *did* make an appearance, none other than a military officer of his acquaintance. He had come to see Dennis to get the latest on Pridi. "Do you have any information as to the whereabouts of Pridi?" he asked. Reports had reached him that Pridi had returned to Bangkok and was attempting to get away by river. "Have you heard anything to this effect, Captain Dennis?"

He later wrote in his memoirs: "I had to think quicker than I had ever had to think before or since and I took a quick and desperate

17 Dennis' memoirs, page 74.

decision. Yes, I replied, I have heard the same and my informant is usually reliable. I hear he arrived this morning very early and embarked or was about to embark on some fast motorboat and go *upriver* towards Ayudhya – at a small jetty at the exact opposite to our planned place of departure!"[18]

Now that Pridi's pursuers were hopefully put on the wrong trail, Dennis, dressed in civilian clothes, and Pridi, back in disguise, together with three loyal followers, boarded an embassy car and drove down to the landing where the American boat was waiting. It was 1 a.m. The night-time journey through town did not have as many roadblocks as expected and they reached their downriver embarkation point within half-an-hour.

By the early morning of 20 November, Pridi was safely on board the Shell tanker bound for Singapore. When the authorities found out that Pridi had slipped through the army's cordon, they blamed the British and American embassies for facilitating Pridi's escape. This was immediately denied and they allowed Captain Dennis to take the blame. Dennis, in his own words, was "sacrificed on the altar of diplomacy."[19]

It was time for Dennis to go on home leave. It was just as well as he needed to lie low for a while. When he returned, he took up his new position as His Majesty's Consul in Songkhla in southern Siam. In addition to performing normal consular duties, he was to carry out liaison work between the Malayan and Siamese authorities in the suppression of banditry on the frontier, the controlling of cross-border contraband and illegal entry, and assisting the British government with the communist insurgency raging in Malaya.

In the spirit of bonhomie and through the force of his personality, and with the help of his charming wife Chada, Dennis

18 *Op. cit.*, pages 76-77.
19 *Op. cit.*, page 82.

created an atmosphere of friendship and understanding between Siamese and Malay officials, often through relaxed informal meetings and friendly dinner parties. As the most senior British official in the south covering 14 provinces, Dennis felt like being on active duty again. He was the commanding officer and responsible for all final decisions.

He acted independently on two occasions that "very seriously affected my career."[20] The first occasion, Dennis admitted in hindsight, was foolhardy. Here is a short account of the incident. A secretary of Damrong, the deposed Prime Minister, and a friend of Dennis, with strong connections with the navy, was on the run. Asked by his friend for help in getting to Malaya to seek political asylum, Dennis found it difficult to refuse.

At great risk, Dennis squeezed him into the boot of his car and drove him nearly 100 kilometres to the border. At one roadblock, when his car was stopped and given a perfunctory search, he was asked to give two policemen a lift into Haad Yai. "Although their presence assured a clear passage, there was a distinct danger of my other passenger disclosing his presence by banging on the door of the boot, a prearranged signal in case he was suffocating."[21] After dropping off the two policemen, the rest of the journey via Sadao proceeded without incident, and once in Malaya, Dennis was asked to identify him and confirm his claim to political asylum.

The second incident, Dennis later justifiably claimed, was in the line of duty. A dangerous Malayan bandit, who was at large, had crossed the border, and sought refuge in Siam. Captain Dennis approved a request by the Malayan police to cross the border in hot pursuit of this much-wanted criminal. When the ambassador was informed of this, he sent a telegram to Dennis ordering him to *Withdraw Malayan patrol forthwith* and summoned him to Bangkok to explain himself. The ambassador told Dennis that he was most

20 *Op. cit.*, page 114.
21 *Op. cit.*, pages 116-117.

"presumptuous as a consul to authorise foreign troops to belligerently enter a sovereign and independent state."[22]

Born and bred a gentleman, with an old-fashioned outlook on rules of conduct, yet paradoxically with a devil-may-care attitude, Dennis tendered his resignation. He was guilty of getting involved in local politics once too often, and he knew it. He had been a line officer throughout his naval career and was used to making snap decisions in the heat of battle. As it turned out, the Siamese government gave permission to the Malay police to cross the border the very next day. But it was too late. The notorious bandit was never caught, and Dennis' resignation had already been officially accepted.

Dennis spent the remaining years of his time in Siam assuming a variety of roles: Secretary to the Royal Bangkok Sports Club, bee farmer at his DDD Farm in Soi Sethabutr lane, opposite this writer's home, and a British naval retiree in Sussex where he wrote his memoirs.

These were not easy years. It was during Dennis' tenure as Sports Club Secretary that his home on the club's premises, now a restaurant, was shelled, a few months before he left for England. The incident occurred in June 1951, after the navy made its last bid for power with an attempted *coup*. Premier Pibul was attending an official ceremony to accept the *Manhattan*, a dredger from the US government that was docked at the Royal Landing on the river. Naval officers kidnapped Pibul and escorted him at gunpoint to the navy flagship, *Sri Ayudhya*. But Pibul escaped from the battleship where he was kept hostage, swimming safely ashore after the ship was attacked by the air force.

The ensuing battle between the army and the rebellious navy raged for several days and this writer remembers that the sound of gunfire could be heard throughout Bangkok. It was rumoured that Dennis' home was targeted by the army for being a "navy meeting

22 *Op. cit.*, pages 120-121.

place". Dennis survived the stray shells and did his best to quell the rumours that he was involved, which of course he wasn't.

Back in England, Dennis began to miss the country he had come to love, and he returned to Siam as a none-too-successful farmer in Sriracha on the Gulf of Siam, where he could be near his old naval friends. He brought up his three Thai daughters, Radklaow[23], Alice[24] and Doodee[25] there. He had come to love Radklaow, his stepdaughter, as much as his own. In his later years Dennis went totally native and always donned a Siamese sarong. He was often told off by Chada for spoiling their daughters and raised his hand to protect them when Chada wanted to spank them. Whenever she was in one of her finger-pointing moods, he would immediately stand to attention, give his naval salute, and sing the *Thai* national anthem. He also became a heavy drinker.

In 1977 he was diagnosed with liver cancer, yet true to character, he never told a soul. When he was dying at the Bangkok Nursing Home, he made his one and only request to the British government with whom he had long lost touch, and that was for them to help pay his medical bills.

On 2 September 1979, aged 80, Dennis died. He was cremated at the temple of Wat That Tong with honours. A photograph of him in his crisp British naval uniform and the returned war medals that the British government had confiscated after he had left the service were put on full display.

Born the scion of the Anglo-Irish landowning aristocracy and devoted during his lifetime to the rescue of men in danger, Captain Stratford Dennis was a courageous man in war, a reckless maverick in peace, and by the time of his passing, an honoured member of the Siamese elite.

---

23 Radklaow Suebsang.
24 Alice Viratsilp.
25 Doodee Dennis.

# H.S.H. PRINCE SUBHA SVASTI

## a.k.a. Prince Chin
## a.k.a. Major Arun

## 1900 – 1967

A Siamese soldier in exile and the true leader of the Free Thais

**Previous page:** *After more than ten years absence, Tan Chin stealthily returned to Siam on a Shorts S-25 Sutherland flying boat and landed off the coast of Cha-am on 28 April 1945.*

**Above:** *Tan Chin in his British officer's uniform in 1943, when he operated with his wartime name of Major Arun.*

# 7

# The First Free Thai

For the first time in his 43 years, Major Arun was trembling with fear. He was dizzily following instructions from the British Sergeant Major in charge of parachute training on top of the 120-foot jump tower at the Special Operations Executive[1] (S.O.E.) training camp in Chaklala, near Poona, India. It was April 1943.

"For God's sake, roll when you hit the ground! We don't want to lose our legs now, do we sir?"

Major Andrew Gilchrist, a British officer attached to Force 136, Siam Country Section, looked at this scene with amusement. Before the war he was a diplomat in Bangkok and knew the country well, and he reluctantly accepted to look after Major Arun, a newly commissioned officer in the British army. Gilchrist took Arun for parachute training and remembered he was "weeping with apprehension"[2] just before the jump.

"And one more thing, sir. *Always* look down, especially when approaching the drop zone! The last thing we want to do is land on a tree!"

The Sergeant Major didn't know that his frightened Asiatic trainee, Major Arun, was the *nom de guerre* of His Serene Highness Prince Subha Svasti, also known as Tan Chin, brother-in-law of Rama VII, the late King of Siam.

---

1 British wartime organization for clandestine warfare.
2 Sir Andrew Gilchrist, *Bangkok Top Secret*, Hutchinson 1970.

On 24 June 1932, King Prajadhipok, Rama VII, was forced by a small group of military officers and civil servants to abandon his absolute powers and give way to a constitutional monarchy. It was Siam's first *coup d'etat.* His Majesty initially accepted the new constitutional order expecting a more democratic Siam. He was prepared to cooperate with the coup leaders and help look after the interests of his people. Although he retained the throne, the king lost all his prerogatives except the right of pardon, and he was unwilling to accept the restrictions placed on his sovereignty. He was not even allowed to have an active role in the democratization process. The new era of freedom and democracy that was promised by the coup leaders did not materialise. The repository of power that was supposed to be with the people ended up with whoever had the backing of the army.

In 1934, much disillusioned, King Rama VII went to England for an eye operation, and in 1935 he abdicated the throne and went into voluntary exile[3]. Among His Majesty's entourage was his consort, Queen Rambhai Bharni and her brother, Prince Subha Svasti, known popularly as Tan Chin.[4] Tan Chin was a former Siamese army officer and chief of palace security. He was accused of being involved in the failed Bovoradej rebellion[5] against the coup leaders in 1933 and was considered a royalist diehard. He certainly would have been arrested if he returned to Siam. Rama VII died in May 1941 and the dowager queen and her brother remained in exile at Compton House in Virginia Water.

At the very moment when Prime Minister Pibul was anguishly deciding what to do with the invading Japanese army on 8 December 1941,[6] halfway across the world, in Virginia Water, England, Tan Chin had already made up his mind.

---

3 See Chapter 1, Page 5.
4 Tan means His Highness.
5 See Chapter 1, Page 6.
6 See Chapter 2, Page 29.

Chin was the archetypal Siamese prince. British-educated, haughty, self-righteous and patriotic to a fault, he was, like his brother-in-law, King Rama VII, a graduate of the Royal Military Academy in Woolwich, on the River Thames. Like many royals at the time, he was inclined to be pro-British.

The reality on the ground in Siam was very different from that of England. With the Japanese enemy at the gates, Pibul was faced with many difficult decisions. An exile from Siam for many years, the solution for Prince Chin was clear. Fight the Japanese from England.

The total destruction of the US Pacific Fleet at Pearl Harbor, Hawaii, by the Japanese First Air Fleet on 7 December 1941 and Britain's subsequent ignominious defeat in Singapore by the Japanese land forces had a different effect on each of them.

Pibul decided that it would be far wiser to accommodate the superior forces of the Japanese as much as possible without compromising Siam's independence and prevent the country from becoming a battlefield. He allowed Japanese troops the right of transit through Siam to attack Burma and Malaya. Sweden had made a similar decision in 1940, allowing the German army free passage across their country to Norway of armaments, and of soldiers on leave travelling between Norway and Germany, and for a division to cross Sweden to attack Finland.

Not quite under the same pressures, on 8 December, Tan Chin addressed a personal letter to the Prime Minister of Britain, Sir Winston Churchill, and offered his services to the British government "in any capacity." A reply from 10 Downing Street dated 1 January 1942, requested Prince Chin to "transliterate" the War Office's maps of Siam. A later request from the British Ministry of Information was for an update on the current political situation in the country. Up to that point, Siam and Britain were not yet at war.

Prince Chin's paper, *The Development of Siamese Politics*,[7] would

7 *Subhsvasti Century (Neung satawat Suphasawat), 2000*, pages 69-123.

put an ambassador whose job was to write such a report, to shame. The fifty-nine pages were so detailed in its content, so insightful in its descriptions of the key personalities, and so complete in its historic background, that anyone picking it up for the first time would get a comprehensive picture, although somewhat innocuous and biased, of contemporary Siam. The Far East Section of the Ministry wrote in its letter of thanks, "It is an admirable and clear exposition of your country, and is one which is highly appreciated by those concerned in this Ministry."

On the 25 January 1942, Siam declared war on Britain and America.

On that same day, across the Atlantic, the Thai Minister[8] in Washington DC, Mom Rajawong[9] Seni Pramoj, refused to obey orders from his government to declare war on the United States, and formed the Free Thai Movement in America. Minister Seni made an official announcement in Thai and English, that as far as he and the Free Thais in America were concerned, Siam was not at war with the United States. To make his point, he told Cordell Hull, the Secretary of State, that he was not going to hand over his government's declaration of war. It was made, he said, under duress.[10] His announcement was broadcast by the BBC Overseas Service to Britain and around the world.

When the Siamese students in Britain heard Minister Seni's announcement, they too wanted to form an equivalent movement.

---

8 In those days, the head of the diplomatic mission was the "Minister" heading the "Legation". Today all legations have been upgraded to Embassies, headed by the Ambassador.

9 Mom Rajawong, M.R. for short, is a royal rank for a son or daughter of a prince.

10 There are many versions of this story. One was that he tore up the declaration in front of Hull and threw it into the waste paper basket. Another that he kept the declaration in his pocket without handing it over. After the war, Pridi accused Seni of fabricating this myth to minimize Pridi's importance in the wartime resistance. Another myth was that Seni kept the declaration document hidden in a drawer. Whatever the story, Seni *was* certainly responsible for preventing the US from recognising a state of war with Siam.

But they did not have a leader. Tan Chin felt that he would have been the most efficacious. A military graduate of Woolwich, his credentials and his image with the British government were impeccable. His relationship with the late king, however, prevented him from becoming their leader. Many students were reluctant to accept him, fearing a return to absolute monarchy.

M.R. Seni Pramoj sent his representative Manee Sanasen to London to recruit Siamese volunteers to join the Free Thai Movement (F.T.M.). Tan Chin did not know that Manee had his own political agenda. Even after Tan Chin realised that he would not be accepted by the students as their leader, he still volunteered to become a Free Thai. But Manee spread the misinformation that Chin was not to be trusted and was only interested in restoring absolute monarchy.[11] Manee had deliberately ignored Chin's request to join the F.T.M. and made no mention of Chin when he reported back to Seni in America. The putative power struggle to become the leader of the F.T.M. in Britain was, in the final round, unilateral. Chin removed himself from the ring and Manee became the F.T.M.'s self-styled leader.

Son of the Siamese Minister to the Court of St. James in the 1920s and called to the English Bar, Manee could only claim to have all the right British connections. As the king's brother-in-law, the doors of British society were actually opened to Chin, and as a result, he was the only Siamese to have a direct line of communication with no. 10 Downing Street.

Chin was *already* working with the British Ministry of Defence when Manee arrived on the scene, assisting them to formulate a war plan against the Japanese in Siam, but for security reasons he was pledged to secrecy. Neither Manee nor the student volunteers knew this. Not able to actively promote himself, Chin was sidelined from the F.T.M. until mid-1943.

---

11 *Subhasvasti Century*, page 226.

By June 1942, 58 Siamese nationals[12] had decided to remain in England and formed the local Free Thai Movement. They had survived the *blitz,* the terrible havoc caused by the German bombing raids over England in 1940 and they realised even then that the Axis powers, Germany and Japan, were intent on dominating the world militarily. They had seen from newsreels that the Japanese were committing even greater atrocities in China. They were eager to fight the Japanese enemy. Thirty-six Siamese students who passed the medical examination[13] were sent for training in Poona, India, to join Force 136.

Force 136 was part of the SOE (Special Operations Executive), a British secret service operation set up to promote subversive warfare in enemy-occupied Burma, French Indochina and Siam. The Siam Country Section of Force 136 was headed by Major Peter Pointon, an older man who had been awarded a Military Cross in the First World War, and an ex-teak *wallah* in Siam in the 1920s. He was assisted by Captain Nicholson, also an old Siamese hand, and Major Andrew Gilchrist, a former first secretary at the British legation[14]. They all spoke Thai. But Force 136 needed a senior Siamese who understood the British military mind and was at the same time capable of leading the Siamese in the field. They were looking for an experienced officer with gravitas. Tan Chin, they thought, was just the man.

Chin, prevented from joining the Free Thais by Manee, was paradoxically the only senior Siamese who was truly acceptable to the British. His credentials appeared to be proof enough, and as a professional soldier in Siam he was eminently qualified to lead the volunteers into battle. But according to Captain Chapman Walker and Captain Guise, British officers assigned to the F.T.M., it was Manee who told them that Chin was only interested in restoring absolute monarchy after the war ended.

---

12 Including this writer's father working at the Legation.

13 The writer's father was one of the original volunteers but failed the medical. Instead, he was assigned to the BBC to broadcast on the short wave into Siam.

14 *Thailand's Secret War,* E. Bruce Reynolds, Cambridge University Press, 2005.

Under a separate agreement with the British government in July 1943, Chin was appointed Chief Adviser to Major Pointon, with additional duties as Conducting Officer for the student volunteers. He was given his new code name: Major Arun. His task was to go through all the training programmes on the day previous to their execution, to enable him to advise the instructor as to any alterations required to suit local conditions. The training programmes were originally developed for subversive activities in German-occupied France and needed to be re-adapted to suit conditions in the tropical jungle.

Prince Chin arrived in Poona in April 1943 under his new alias of "C. Arun". Arun was soon to discover that his task in India was not without difficulties.

Most British officers who were unaware of his role assumed he was Burmese and they found difficulty in accepting his rank as a major in the British Army. In a letter to his wife he complained that, "We are not a subject race, but we get the same treatment"[15] as if we were their colonial subjects. The British high command did not fully respect the Free Thai student volunteers either. Chin was able to correct this irregularity and arranged to have their status changed from mere privates in the Pioneer Corps[16] to commissioned officers in the British Army upon successful completion of their training course.

But he was still politically unacceptable to the student volunteers when they discovered that he was now serving Force 136 as their superior officer. Throughout the rest of the war, he was continually called upon to deny accusations by his compatriots of wanting to restore absolute monarchy in Siam.

Arun himself was found not to be adequately trained for guerrilla warfare and was sent for a short combat training course, including

15 *Subhasvasti Century.*

16 A wartime unit for men who had been turned down by the regular army, for conscientious objectors, and for non- British subjects. They ended up doing menial jobs. Also referred to as "Alien Companies" because it was composed of up to 25 nationalities.

parachute jumping, under the watchful eye of Major Gilchrist.

Even Gilchrist himself was not certain that Arun was the right person to lead the Siamese volunteers. Gilchrist spoke Thai and knew the country well. He thought Arun was out of touch, having left his country ten years before. Gilchrist felt he was far better qualified to lead the student volunteers himself.

The biggest tactical challenge for Force 136 now was making optimum use of the Free Thai volunteers. The effectiveness of Force 136 very much depended on the answer to one crucial question:

*Did the Free Thai Movement really exist as an active anti-Japanese organization within Siam itself?*

Unless and until the existence of the F.T.M. on the ground was *proved*, there was not much point in training thirty-six Siamese volunteers for dangerous infiltration and underground activities.

It was up to Major Arun to find out.

The key moment occurred on 13 April 1943. Major Arun learned from the office of Force 136 in Chungking, China, that an emissary of Pridi Panomyong, the regent of Siam at that time, had arrived there to make the F.T.M's existence and purposes known to the outside world. This emissary, named Chamkad Balangura, was confirming that Pridi was not only the regent but also the leader of the anti-Japanese resistance.[17]

In May, Arun sought permission from the Chinese government to interview Chamkad in Chungking, to find out the true situation on the ground in Siam. The Chinese were uncooperative and took their time before issuing him a visa. They wanted to isolate Chamkad from British influence.

Chamkad himself had tried and was unsuccessful in getting an official appointment with British and American military and

17 For Chamkad's full story, see Chapter 4, Page 78.

diplomatic authorities in Chungking. He was prevented by his Chinese custodians from doing so before an audience with Generalissimo Chiang Kai-shek could be arranged on 28 June. It was only after this historic meeting that the Chinese government allowed him to make contact with the outside world. But even then, the British ambassador doubted Chamkad's authority to represent his country and refused to meet him.

When Chamkad knew that Tan Chin was due to arrive in Chungking, he was relieved. Finally, here was someone who could vouchsafe his identity and help him get Pridi's message across to the Allies. They had known each other in England before the war, although he was unaware of Tan Chin's new code name of Major Arun. When he discovered C. Arun's true identity, he immediately sent off a letter, informing Tan Chin that "if Your Highness desires to see me, I shall only be too glad" and "only when we meet, shall I be able to inform Your Highness what has really happened."[18]

Major Arun arrived in Chungking from India by plane in late July 1943 and was given accommodation at SOE headquarters. It was a city of conspiracy and subterfuge. The Chinese secret service was unwilling to supply Arun with any information as to Chamkad's activities and whereabouts, and only after a bribe of a packet of gold and rubies was Chinese access and coordination made possible. The Chinese government's official obstruction to Arun meeting Chamkad stemmed from its putative belief that Britain was pursuing a separate policy to that of the USA and China in their support of the F.T.M., and were planning to restore an absolute monarchist government under British auspices after the war.

This perception became even more entrenched when the British remained completely silent after the Generalissimo's broadcast to the Siamese nation in January 1943, stating that China had no territorial designs on Siam and would respect Siam's independence. President

18 *Subhsvasti Century*, page 279.

Roosevelt of America, in contrast, immediately endorsed the declaration.

When Arun was finally allowed to meet up with Chamkad on 6 August, he found that the quixotic scholar from Oxford University was still the firebrand he had known in England. But now he looked thin and unwell – and much, much older.

On the following day, Arun presented his SOE credentials to the British ambassador and introduced Chamkad, vouching for his official F.T.M. identity. They sat down to discuss the following matters: First, that Britain had no post-war colonial designs on Siam[19]. Secondly, a Free Thai government-in-exile should be set up in India as soon as Pridi and a number of his cabinet ministers could be spirited out of Siam by either submarine or seaplane and thus get recognition as the only lawful Siamese government, and lastly, for the British and American governments to release frozen Siamese funds, so that the monies could be used to underwrite F.T.M. resistance activities against the Japanese.

Chamkad and Arun also discussed ways to improve wireless communications between Force 136 personnel in the field and SOE headquarters in India, and to prepare to receive the first group of "White Elephants," as the Siamese volunteers were now called, who would be coming in by submarine and were expected to land on the west coast of the Siamese peninsula south of Ranong in December 1943. They would clandestinely bring in equipment so that a radio transmitter could be installed to ensure continuous contact with SOE headquarters in India.

Until radio contacts could be made, microfilmed messages dispatched from Chungking by the overland route were the only way the two parties could communicate with each other. F.T.M agents were to arrive from Siam to undertake this operation. In a letter to Chamkad on 23 August, Arun gave instructions on how to retrieve

19 Which proved to be untrue, see Chapter 4, page 78.

the secret microfilm concealed in the agent's body: "Ask them to wear a belt and tell them that in order to get at the message, all they have to do (is) use a safety razor blade, and slit open the thin edge of the belt. The message (for Pridi) is hidden in the belt's body about three inches from the buckle."[20]

Chamkad was extremely pleased to learn from Arun that Force 136 was the subversive arm of the Free Thais in Britain, and that many of his former friends from student days in England, including his brother Kamhaeng, were members of this outfit.

Arun returned to India and reported to Major Pointon with the encouraging news that indeed there was an active resistance movement in Siam, and with a local network of F.T.M. resistance fighters on the ground to receive SOE agents, infiltration and underground activities were now possible. Furthermore, Pridi, the Regent of Siam, was *secretly the leader of the F.T.M.*

Arun advised the SOE that the resistance was ready to receive wireless communication and that radio transmitters should be set up all over the country by parachute units of the Whites[21] immediately. This was to be followed by other agents who would land by submarine in less exposed areas on the beaches of the southern peninsula.

By early 1944, several radio transmitters were put into place in parts of the country not yet under Japanese control. From there, the Whites' Force 136 infiltrators were now able to report on enemy troop movements and activities to SOE headquarters. In March they observed elephants dragging 30-inch wide trees from the jungle that were used to build a bridge to cross the river Pai to connect a strategic road to Burma from Chiang Mai. They were able to report increased

20 *Subhasvasti Century*.
21 As the White Elephants were now called.

Japanese activity in the north, from where the enemy were planning to transport several new divisions to Burma in order to strengthen their weakening position there.

By June 1944, thanks to the Whites, the Free Thai's clandestine radio network was well entrenched and right through to the end of the war they were able to transmit encoded messages both to Chungking and Poona, reporting on Japanese troop emplacements, locations of supply dumps and other enemy installations. The Free Thai underground were also able to help downed Allied pilots and prisoners-of-war to escape for the first time. Most important of all, they reported on the progress of the Siam-Burma railway line under construction by the POWs from Kanchanaburi to the Three Pagodas Pass on the Burmese border.

Several strategic plans of attack to hinder the Japanese advance into Burma were discussed and formulated at SOE headquarters. An operation to parachute into Mae Hong Son during the February moon of 1945 to recruit friendly Karenni tribesmen was aborted, or rather vetoed by Major Arun, on the grounds that this north-western border area was too remote from the rest of the country to successfully extend a guerrilla campaign to attack actual Japanese lines of communication and traffic. Pitsanulok, further south, he felt, would be a better location from which to extend the organization and recruit local farmers. Besides, none of the Whites, least of all Arun, spoke Karenni. This put Arun into direct conflict with Major Gilchrist, who came up with the plan. Describing Gilchrist in a letter to his wife (without mentioning his name), Arun wrote "We all had to fight against the caprice and unreasonable obstinacy of this man, so much so that the work was almost in direct harm's way."[22] Arun was to have many disagreements with Gilchrist on matters of planning and execution.

---

22 *Subhsvasti Century.*

Gilchrist himself was later to describe Arun as "that awkward Prince" who "worked like a beaver" but "caused considerable confusion".[23] The enmity between the two men lasted three decades after the war, right to the end of both of their lives.

On 15 April 1945, Major Arun, now Lieutenant Colonel, was promoted to be Force 136's Military Liaison Officer with the Siamese Army General Headquarters.[24] This new position, ironically enough, was coveted by Major Gilchrist, who considered himself a Siam country expert and right for the job. He was, for a while, quite bitter at being passed over.

It was time for Force 136 to officially join forces with the F.T.M. on the ground to prepare for "Operation Zipper," Mountbatten's plan to liberate Southeast Asia from the Japanese by a massive land invasion of Siam. Admiral Lord Louis Mountbatten based in Kandy in Ceylon[25] was Supreme Allied Commander responsible for all Allied operations in Southeast Asia during World War II.

Arun's new mission, arguably Force 136's most critically strategic of the war, was to now land in Siam and immediately get in touch with Pridi and inform him of Mountbatten's plan. The seaplane, such as the Short S-25 Sunderland, a reconnaissance and maritime four-engine amphibian with long-range fuel tanks and high cruising speed, was recommended by Arun as the perfect landing craft. Ideally, this mission should be undertaken between October and April before the northeast monsoon.

Arun also decided that landing at Cha-am on the east coast of the peninsula was safer than Gilchrist's plan to land on the west coast north of Phuket. Cha-am was his home territory where he had a holiday home, and where he could count on help from friendly locals, should the mission run into any difficulties.

Major Arun was ready to go.

---

23 *Bangkok Top Secret*, Op.Cit.

24 Pibul was no longer Prime Minister nor head of the armed forces.

25 Present day Sri Lanka.

On the morning of 28 April 1945, Arun boarded the RAF Sunderland seaplane at Colombo harbour, Ceylon, accompanied by Brigadier Victor Jaques, a lawyer[26] in Bangkok before the war, a highly decorated veteran of World War I and one of Force 136's most senior officers. The mission also included several other senior British SOE officers.[27] As the boat-shaped hull and floats of the aircraft planed across the water and lifted off, Arun started to think about his journey home. He hadn't been back for over ten years and he was apprehensive. He had qualms about returning to Bangkok where he could very well get arrested. He had to rely on Pridi's protection.

Returning to Siam was also an emotional experience. After flying more than one thousand miles over endless blue sea, his heart skipped a beat when the plane approached the Burmese coast at Mergui just as the sun was sinking behind him, turning the rugged mountains of the Tenasserim range that separated Siam from Burma into an undulating sweep of jagged, jungle-clad, saw-toothed ridges the colour of burnished copper. It is one of the unfriendliest landscapes he had ever seen. The plane crossed the peninsula into Siam as the last rays of the sun shone on the white sands for a brief moment, long enough to make Arun realise how much he had missed his country and his beloved villa on the beach of Cha-am.

The fifteen-hundred mile flight across the Indian Ocean and the Andaman Sea was without incident and the seaplane landed safely off the coast of Cha-am on the night of 28 April where they were picked up by a navy launch[28]. After all the risks that Arun had taken with parachute training, he thought it was absurd that now he was to land by seaplane, considering he had no training in this skill whatsoever. At least it was safer than jumping by parachute and less risky than landing from a submarine.

The launch carried them along the coast from Cha-am to the

26 With Tilleke & Gibbins, Thailand's oldest law firm.
27 *Thailand's Secret War*, E. Bruce Reynolds, Cambridge University Press, 2005.
28 Arranged by Pridi who had the support of the Siamese navy.

mouth of the Chao Phraya River under the cover of darkness. But from there the journey up river became dangerous and they had to carefully dodge several Japanese patrols. They arrived safely on the morning of 29 April 1945, and that evening Arun and Jaques enjoyed a very satisfactory dinner with Pridi[29] at his riverside villa in Bangkok. They agreed on a common strategy to fight the Japanese, with Allied officers serving alongside the Siamese troops on an equal basis, gaining Allied trust and thus paving the way for an Allied invasion.

Arun wisely recommended that the F.T.M. and the Siamese army strike first before the Allied invasion and thus give credibility to Pridi's role as the true liberator of Siam; otherwise it would seem as if the British were setting the country free.

In July 1945, Colonel Arun went on to Tak near the Burmese border to consolidate the Siamese army there. He then proceeded to the southern peninsula to start a new support force in preparation for an Allied landing on the coast of the Bay of Bengal. Three more Whites assigned to assist Arun landed by submarine at Phang-Nga on the Andaman coast, but sadly there was no one to meet them. The welcoming party sent by foot across the jungle by Arun failed to arrive in time. They were captured, like so many Whites before them.

Southeast Asia Command in Kandy, Ceylon, was convinced that "the Far Eastern War would last well into 1946 if not into 1947."[30] In Siam, the Japanese Imperial Army was digging in and preparing to make its last stand against the Allies. Arun was fully prepared to fight the Japanese to the very end.

A new plan to evacuate the Pridi government and the royal family of princes to India was introduced, while F.T.M. leaders and some cabinet members would disperse to guerrilla camps in Tak and Suphanburi. A British Airborne Division would capture the military

29 It is interesting to note that Pridi, the revolutionary, and Tan Chin, the royal exile, got on well with each other despite their past differences.

30 Bickham Sweet-Escott, *Baker Street Irregular*, page 261.

airdrome at Don Muang, which would become a supply base by air and for further military reinforcements, as well as serving as a flank guard for the Bangkok garrison.

Colonel Arun was at his jungle headquarters in the southern Srithammaraj mountains organising a fresh defensive unit when news came of the Japanese surrender. The dropping of the atom bombs on Hiroshima and Nagasaki in Japan in August 1945 brought the planned joint operations of the F.T.M. and the Allied forces to a close.

The war was over.

When Arun was first assigned to the Whites in mid-1943, he was not initially well received by the young Siamese volunteers. He was twice their age, he was a royal and as a commissioned officer in the British army, he did not have the potential for being a popular leader. They perceived him to be on the British rather than on the Siamese side.

By 1945, Arun had completely turned around that relationship. He had gained, through leadership by example, not only their trust, but also their loyalty and respect.

He prepared three easy-to-understand strategic papers for "The Boys," as he fondly called the Whites: *Guerilla War and the Art of War*, *Personality of the Commander* and *Guerilla Intelligence*, which became their standard textbooks.

By war's end, when the Whites disbanded, their endearment to what they now willingly recognise as their senior officer was sealed. Back in Siam after the war, they were to have frequent reunions with their wartime senior officer at Suan Sema, Tan Chin's seaside retreat in Cha-am.

Prince Chin was a true professional soldier. But as a politician, he was, as he often admitted, a miserable failure and hugely misunderstood. He was not able to deal with the human intrigues and political machinations that came with the job. The Siamese students in

London were never quite sure why he offered to help Churchill. Was it because he was intending, with British support, to restore absolute monarchy in Siam after the war? Was it because he wanted to get his own back on Pibul, whom he disliked so much because he felt that Pibul should have put up more of a fight? Or maybe it was because of his hatred for the Germans and the Japanese?

Little did he know on 8 December 1941, the day of the invasion and the day he wrote to Churchill, that Siam was *already* defending herself against the Japanese, and even repelled a British garrison that had illegally entered Siamese territory from Malaya to forestall the advancing Japanese.[31] None of this was known in Britain at the time, and certainly not to Prince Chin, that the Siamese defence forces initially resisted the Japanese, following Pibul's long-standing policy for Siam to protect her neutrality. Brave Siamese troops had fought along the Southern peninsula for two days and incurred heavy casualties.[32]

Manee was never quite able to form a united front of Free Thais from London and Washington, so a rift developed between the two groups. They worked independently from each other and never cooperated in the field.

Chin later learned that Seni distrusted Pridi, suspecting him of being communist. By 1944, two Free Thai factions had developed. Seni's group in America were reluctant to work with Pridi, whilst the students serving the SOE with Chin in India were keen to establish contact with him.

Similarly, there was very little cooperation between the British and Americans. "The present relations between British and US organizations in Asia are characterized by intrigue, suspicion, and by absurd duplication of activities in all fields."[33] The rival firms of the

31 The Siamese army was instructed to defend the nation's neutrality from *all* invaders, British and Japanese alike.
32 See Chapter 5.
33 Sir Andrew Gilchrist, *op. cit.*, page 191.

British SOE and the American OSS, precursor to the CIA, continued to keep well apart right throughout the war.

Another conflict that frequently arose was the divergent points of view that the Free Thais had with the British officers, particularly with regard to field operations in Siam. It was a great source of annoyance to be told what to do and how to do it *in their own country* by those British who had spent only a few years in Siam before the war. The young Whites often felt like "beggars," having to depend on the magnanimity of their British hosts.

Chin was over-sensitive to these conflicting issues and naively tried to get all the parties together to work under one single command. Called the Free Thai Co-ordinating Committee, consisting of Siamese from both sides of the Atlantic, including Seni and Manee, they were to act as "a medium to induce the SOE, the OSS and the Chinese to meet and discuss a method to co-ordinate the work in Siam. The existence of such a committee is purely for the war effort. It has nothing to do with politics."[34] His proposed mechanism, however, was potentially *fraught* with politics and was doomed to failure from the start. Both the SOE and the OSS were to appoint a liaison officer to the committee, and the British Ministry of Defence and the Chinese government would each send a delegate to attend committee meetings; their joint recommendations were to be sent on to Lord Louis Mountbatten's SEAC[35] headquarters in Kandy, Ceylon, for approval.

Not surprisingly, this unwieldy committee never got off the ground. Chin was far too ingenuous to even consider that such a project would not become highly politicised.

Now that over seventy years have gone by, it is time to re-evaluate Prince Chin's role during the Second World War. By immediately offering to fight the Japanese from day one, he can

34 *Subhasvasti Century*.
35 South East Asia Command.

justifiably be considered in history as Siam's *first* Free Thai.

Prince Chin's motives were very different from what was popularly believed by the student volunteers at the time, no doubt fuelled by certain quarters that believed he was a threat to their leadership.

Lieutenant-Colonel Prince Subha Svasti was *the first and only* Thai to have been awarded the military Order of the British Empire in "recognition of gallant and distinguished service in the field." The British government, through the *London Gazette* of 29 August 1946, officially announced that Prince Chin was the Senior Siamese Officer of Force 136.

# DR. SMARN MUNTARBHORN

## 1914 – 2001

### Siam's first heart surgeon

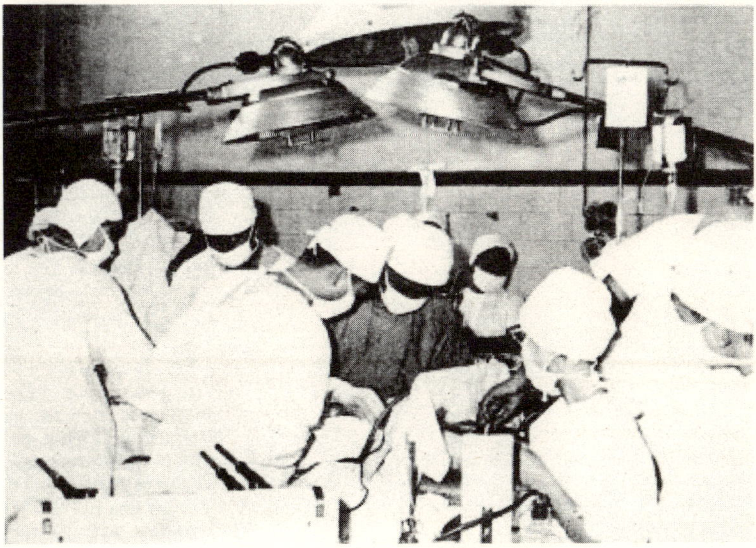

***Previous page:*** *Dr Smarn, in dark surgical gown, performing an operation at the Chulalongkorn Hospital operating theatre in 1963.*

***Above:*** *The prize winning athlete Smarn at the Manchester Grammar School in 1934.*

# 8

# Anatomy of a Fighting Surgeon

The night of Sunday, 29 December 1940 was to be remembered by Londoners as the Second Great Fire of London. The first one was in 1666, vividly described in Samuel Pepys' diary:

> ... in corners and upon steeples, and between churches and house, and as far as we could see up the hill of the city ... a most torrid, malicious, bloody flame, not like an ordinary fire.

In 1940, contemporary observers witnessed a similar scene from Westminster Bridge. The City of London – the English capital's famous square mile – was silhouetted in red and the Thames was transformed from a river of water to a sea of fire.

It was the night when one hundred German Heinkel III bombers dropped more than 300 incendiary bombs a minute over London's square mile.

In August 1940, German bombers had started an aggressive push designed to destroy Britain's air strength by blasting airfields and vital industries, in preparation for *Operation Sealion*, Hitler's planned invasion of Britain in September. By November, the Royal Air Force had prevented the Germans from gaining superiority in the air and the Battle of Britain was won. Hitler's invasion never came. Germany's response was to bomb London into submission. The Blitz over London lasted 114 days and nights. The worst attack came on the terrible night of 29 December when the Luftwaffe[1] set the City of London ablaze with 10,000 incendiary bombs, the most ferocious raid of the Blitz. It was the night when the River Thames was at its lowest and earlier in the evening German aircraft had destroyed the city's water mains.

It was also the night when St. Paul's Cathedral miraculously remained standing, relatively unscathed, becoming a beacon of hope for Londoners and an icon of Britain's finest hour, strengthening the public's resolve not to give in. Every building, every street and every shop in the vicinity of St. Paul's was totally put to the torch, including Guy's, one of England's oldest teaching hospitals, next to London Bridge station, across the river.

On that Sunday morning, in the bitterly cold, grey light of an English winter, Smarn Muntarbhorn was warm and comfortable, as he sat quietly, deep in concentration, at his usual place in the library of Guy's Hospital. He was swotting for his final medical exams, which were set for eight days later, on Monday, 5 January. The obligatory tin helmet and gas mask were by his side, next to his medical textbooks and lecture notes. He decided to skip lunch and study right through the evening until the blackout was enforced, pitching the entire hospital into darkness. As the failing crepuscular light through the library window was starting to get dimmer and dimmer, Smarn spent an indeterminate time, as he often did at this hour, being alone in the library, enjoying the pleasure of his thoughts, which were mainly focused on the final exams ahead. He also thought about home. He'd been away from Siam for seven years, yet it seemed as if he'd just arrived the year before. So much had happened, and so quickly…

1 German air force.

Without warning, at 6.13 p.m., as he was preparing to go downstairs for a light supper in the hospital canteen, the air raid siren went off. A minute later, he heard the eerie, screaming sounds of diving firebombs as they plunged towards their targets. Quickly grabbing his helmet, Smarn rushed to the window. He saw a forest of barrage balloons – large blimps to protect the city from air attacks – on fire, and wave upon wave of Heinkel bombers silhouetted against the flames lighting up the night sky. Within seconds, eight bombs had exploded in the Hospital grounds and a shower of incendiary bombs then rained down, non-stop, for fifteen minutes. An "uncontrolled fire[2]" had gripped Guy's Hospital.

Around the entire area of London Bridge station, there were raging fires blazing out of control. While unsuccessful efforts were made on the telephone to get the Fire Brigade to help, the Hospital's air raid wardens tried to extinguish the fires as best they could on their own with rapidly dwindling hospital water supplies.

The main entrance to the hospital was now blocked by a turbulent fire at Down's Brothers, London's largest surgical instrument shop where Smarn had often bought many of his supplies. There was chaos everywhere. The area was full of smoke and falling debris, with blinding sparks and black, hot ash flying in all directions. People were screaming in panic, running across the courtyard on St. Thomas Street, diving for cover. Many people on their way home were burned alive. A petrol station on the edge of the Hospital's property on Newcomen Street had just blown up. The water supply had completely run dry and the Hospital was now surrounded by an expanse of rampant flames.

Within an hour, the four-storey surgical block, the nurses' home, Jesus College and the students' dormitory where Smarn slept were totally gutted.

2 Commander Aylmer Firebrace, ex-head of the London Fire Brigade and ex-fire chief of London Region.

The Hospital's immediate concern was for the safety of the patients. Smarn joined the warden, the medical staff and fellow students to help in their evacuation. The fire trucks finally arrived and the firefighters' main task now was to immediately clear a path *away from the fire* to provide a safe corridor for the staff and patients to evacuate. Ambulances had already arrived to quickly take patients to other hospitals. The orderlies, nurses and doctors were next to leave through this gap in the fire, leaving behind the Matron and Superintendent, the air raid wardens and the younger ward sisters and medical students, who insisted on staying on to assist the firefighters. Smarn was one of them.

It was a miracle of the Blitz that not a single life was lost at Guy's on that dangerous night, although many were wounded. The next morning, with the few possessions they could save, the last evacuees tramped through the streets, their exhausted bodies covered with perspiration and their faces blackened with soot. Weary though they were, they were jubilant and in high spirits. Smarn joined the English students in a chorus of uplifting songs, clutching a small satchel of personal belongings. All that he owned, including his valuable textbooks and lecture notes that he had diligently saved over the years, had been totally lost in the fire. The final exams were just one week away. The students were temporarily evacuated to Lambeth Junior School nearby, but the makeshift bedrooms were uncomfortable. Smarn was unable to focus properly on his studies.

In his diary, he jotted down in English "homeless for 7 days." It was the worst week of his life. For the first time since he arrived in England in 1932, Smarn was homesick. He missed his simple life in Siam.

Smarn Muntarbhorn was proud of his small-town roots. He was brought up in Ban Don, present-day Surat, in southern Siam by a forthright, religious father, and a hardworking mother. As a boy, his father was a bright, diligent student at the monastery school of Wat Dhammabucha temple in the 1880s. He excelled in his studies, and was one of only a few to reach level 8, the highest that could be attained in the land at the time.

In the $18^{th}$ and $19^{th}$ centuries, the tradition for young men in Siam who wanted to learn, particularly those living in upcountry provinces, was to obtain their education at Buddhist monastery schools. These schools were the rough equivalent to Catholic seminaries in Europe. The enlightened King Mongkut (Rama IV) was himself educated in a monastery school, "a democratic place, for the monks were drawn from all classes."[3] It wasn't until later in the century that lay schools were introduced, either by the government, or privately. Christian missionaries also opened new schools in Bangkok and Chiang Mai.

It wasn't easy to get admitted to a monastery school. One needed recommendations and connections with the right people. Those without the necessary recommendations could enter as a young acolyte, and through diligence and academic performance, move on to higher learning. Maha Wan, Smarn's father, followed this path. He had the brains and he was hard-working. When Maha Wan left the monastery school, he initially set up shop selling Buddhist ceremonial accoutrements, religious artefacts, and scripture books. As he made more money, he and his wife invested in the only comfortable hotel in Ban Don. Important royal travellers, senior government officers and religious leaders on their way to the south would stay at this famous hotel. Maha Wan became a well-known personage in the province and through his guests made many important connections in Bangkok.

Smarn inherited his father's intelligence and character, and obtained his primary education at the Sri Sawatmongkol school

3 H.R.H. Prince Chula Chakrabongse, *Lords of Life*, 1960.

at Wat Dhammabucha temple in Ban Don, where he performed with such distinction that his father was able to obtain the support of one of his important senior government connections, one Chao Phraya[4] Charnchart Khadaisaman, to recommend him to complete his high school education at the prestigious Suan Khularb College[5] in Bangkok. At Suan Khularb, in 1932, Smarn won the prestigious King's Scholarship to study in England. He was just 19 years old.

Smarn boarded the Danish motor vessel *Erria* at Penang and arrived at Tilbury Docks on a bright autumn day in September 1932. Seeing London for the first time, he was moved by the realisation that from this day onwards he would need to become complete master of his destiny. He also instinctively felt that his life would never be the same again. That he would not return to Siam for another 13 years would have surprised him. He was looking forward to the challenges of his new life and within two years at the Manchester Grammar School, he was already able to make his mark. A good two years older than his English classmates, he was not daunted by the amount of extra English language tutorials he had to attend and the new Anglo-Saxon culture he had to absorb in such a short time.

It normally takes an English student at least two years of high school to get through the Matriculation Exams ('O' Level today). Smarn earned a top Division I pass after just one year, even in English Literature, passing a written exam on Shakespeare's *Henry IV* and John Milton's *Paradise Lost*. The following year, his last, he was able to cram two years study into one (Lower Sixth and Upper Sixth[6]). For the winter term school exams, he came first in his class in Physics and Biology; in the spring term, he came first again in Physics.

---

4 Equivalent to "Lord".
5 Siam's Eton.
6 Twelfth Grade in America; Premiere Classe in France.

In the summer term, on 9 July 1935, less than three years after his arrival from Siam, he was able to obtain three First Class Distinctions, in Maths, Physics and Biology, and a credit in the German language, at the national London Matriculation Exams, today's equivalent of "A" levels in England and the Higher Level International Baccalaureate. Such was Smarn's strong-willed determination and fighting spirit, that were to stay with him for the rest of his life.

On the 31 July 1936, Smarn won Guy's "Confined Scholarship in Science prize of 100 pounds", at that time enough to cover his educational expenses for another year, yet he was still receiving his King's Scholarship stipend from Siam.

But Smarn was *not* a bookish nerd. Good looking and athletic, he was on the school's second eleven football team, winning matches against other schools in Yorkshire. He also won several prizes at his school's athletic events for high jumping and steeplechase racing.

Like all resolute men, Smarn was not a dreamer either. In Siam, he had long decided that he would one day become a doctor. At Manchester Grammar, he was already determined to get admitted to Guy's Hospital. On 1 October 1935, he presented himself at the Hospital's Registrar, and signed on as a medical student for the next 6 years. From a Siamese temple school in the provinces to London's leading medical institution, Smarn had made the impossible possible.

At Guy's Hospital, Smarn was an exemplary medical student for the entire period, receiving a Certificate of Honour twice, the first time in 1936, upon completion of his first year, and the second time in 1940 in Bacteriology, receiving the much-vaunted Golding-Bird Gold Medal.

To maintain his connections with the Siamese community, he joined the Siam Students' Association – the *Somaggi Samakhom* – becoming its President in 1939 and 1940, winning its golden award as the best Siamese student in England in 1939. He loved photography and his still-life black and white close-up of a shining droplet of water on a leaf, which he titled "All that glitters is not gold", won him first prize from Guy's Hospital Photographic Society.

Smarn spent the best years of his life at Guy's, participating in all the extracurricular activities of the Hospital and discovered the pleasures of classical music through Guy's Opera Society. He made lifelong friendships with his fellow students and was fortunate to have the opportunity to learn from Britain's finest doctors, such as Sir Arthur Hurst, who developed new ways to cure gastric and duodenal ulcers through analysis of the blood in the patient's stool. Lord Brock, Britain's leading heart surgeon, became Smarn's role-model. Long after the war, in 1973, Lord Brock invited Smarn and his family to dinner at the House of Lords.

He continued to keep up his athletic prowess in track and field, winning 8 championship trophies for Guy's in the 100 metre and steeplechase races, as well as the high jump, and played right wing for the Hospital football team.

Until that fateful night in December 1940, Guy's had largely been spared the brunt of the Blitz. When Neville Chamberlain, the British Prime Minister, informed the nation in September 1939 that Britain was at war with Germany, 250,000 men over the age of twenty were conscripted and Britain was on war alert. Frightening sirens pierced the night, the population was issued with and taught how to use gas masks, and Guy's Hospital, like many public buildings, was fortified with sandbags. A platoon from the Queen's Regiment was posted at the Hospital.

In preparation for an all-out war, Guy's Hospital, and indeed all the other London hospitals, were evacuated to make way for air-raid casualties. Only those patients who were truly immobile – thirty-seven of them – remained. All the other patients were transported to Brighton by train and on special Green Line coaches. Many doctors, nurses, and students, including Smarn, moved out to the country.

The expected German invasion never came. This early phase of the war, when not very much happened on the home front, was called the "Phoney War." By early 1940, the government realised the futility of the evacuation and by mid-1940, the entire staff returned and Guy's went back to normal, at least until the Luftwaffe intensified their air attacks from the end of 1940. Back at Guy's, Smarn immersed himself in his studies, in preparation for the finals in January 1941.

It takes a man with incredible determination like Smarn to face the day of his final exams without his valuable notes, without proper sleep for a whole week, and without clean, decent clothes to wear. He borrowed a razor from a fellow student. At least his face was more presentable to the examiners.

Normally it would have been a relaxed half-an-hour's walk from Lambeth School to Guy's Hospital, but the rubble and mass of ruined masonry from toppled buildings made the streets impassable. Smarn, and indeed none of his fellow classmates, could make the journey safely on foot. London Bridge station was closed and many train services were cancelled. The entire length of the Great Maze Pond Street was gutted and Guy's Hospital itself, ironically short of water the night before, was now "swimming in it."[7] For Londoners, incredibly, that Monday morning was the start of a normal working week. Secretaries, shopkeepers, and office workers stumbled across the debris to their places of work that were still standing. For those whose train services were interrupted, they walked, some taking as long as four hours. The final exams, Smarn discovered, were *not* cancelled. For brave Londoners, it was business as usual.

Smarn had to hitch a lift to the examination venue at the Hospital. The exams took the entire day of Monday, 6 January 1941. The finals at Guy's are still considered to be the most arduous and intellectually demanding in the English medical profession.

7 M.J. Gaskin, *Blitz*, Faber & Faber, 2005.

In his diary, Smarn wrote one single word to describe the results of that gruelling day.

*"Qualified."*

The terrible toll that was taken on both civilian and military lives during the Battle of Britain and the Blitz compelled Britain – and in particular London – to reorganize the country's hospital services. A new centralised state-run Emergency Medical Service (EMS) employed doctors and nurses to care for those injured by enemy action and arrange for their treatment in whichever hospital was available. Their general aim was to establish first-aid and casualty sorting centres in the danger areas and provide enough treatment to the injured for the ambulance journey to the nearest hospital. Doctors and nurses moved freely between hospitals, and like Smarn in early 1942, were continually relocated to where they were most needed, according to their specialities and skills.

Senior members of teaching hospitals' staff, such as those at Guy's, were appointed Medical Sector Officers. There were ten sectors in London to service the Home Counties.[8] Guy's Hospital was in charge of Sector 10, responsible for parts of southeast London and the county of Surrey. One of the Senior Medical Sector Officer's job was to assign the medical staff to various hospitals in his sector.

"Doctor Muntarbhorn, the Senior Medical Sector Officer, will see you now."

Since April 1941, when Smarn received his two medical degrees from London University – his Bachelor of Medicine and his Bachelor of Surgery – he was continually being addressed as Dr. Muntarbhorn. He was still not used to this new title, and was

8 Counties surrounding London that are now suburban areas.

taken by surprise when the Senior Officer's secretary addressed him.

"Could you please step this way, *Doctor*."

Smarn entered the Senior Officer's office. A friendly middle-aged doctor in a black pin-striped suit who Smarn had passed dozens of times in the corridors of Guy's Hospital extended his hand and introduced himself.

"As you know, Dr. Muntarbhorn, we need all the medical help we can get. Like the RAF that is continually recruiting new young pilots, we at the EMS are recruiting new doctors all the time. We've noticed that since July 1942, rather than return to Siam you have decided to remain in England and join the Free Siamese Movement. This of course means you are no longer considered an enemy alien and that you are now at liberty to work for us. You have of course been working unofficially at Guy's as part of our ambulatory EMS team, but now we would like you to officially transfer to the Royal Surrey County Hospital in Guildford, where they have recently been getting more than their fair share of injured soldiers and airmen. You will report to Mr. Sheaf on 1 January 1943, and offer your services as his House Surgeon."

Smarn was pleasantly surprised at how much the Senior Officer knew about him. Well, maybe not surprised, but certainly *impressed*. The officer had obviously been fully briefed by either the Intelligence Service or the Foreign Office about his case. But they needn't have worried. He had already made up his mind since the Blitz, as had many other Siamese students and legation officials,[9] that any regime that authorises wanton bombing of innocent civilians must be an evil one. The Japanese, as it turned out, were just as aggressive as the Germans.

Smarn worked day and night saving lives for two full years, first as a House Surgeon[10] in 1943, and then as Resident Surgical

9 Including the writer's father who was serving at the Siamese Legation at the time.
10 In America, his title would be "Intern."

Officer in 1944. As Surrey was in the line of fire from invading Luftwaffe bombers heading for targets in London and the industrial north, Smarn would often perform surgical operations on downed airmen, some of them German, but mostly British and Canadian RAF pilots. The operations he performed were always under adversity, to be expected under wartime conditions. It is said in the medical profession that the best surgeons are the ones that have worked under the pressures of battle. During peacetime they are the calmest, they work the fastest and are sure of themselves.

It was during his two years at the Royal Surrey that Smarn discovered what he had long suspected, that he had the skilled hands of a surgeon and the exceptional mental discipline to stay focused on difficult tasks for long periods of time. Like all good surgeons, Smarn had high respect for the human body and complete knowledge of the anatomy. He had the surgeon's natural talent for being able to work his mind in perfect synchronization with his hands. Indeed, he would first plan the operation in his mind before performing the actual operation.

The civilian patients that Smarn had to care for were mostly blast victims from enemy bombs. Before he could operate he would often have to clean the patient. After a bomb explosion, the injured were often covered with so much dust, ash and rubble, that they had to be thoroughly cleaned before he could decide what was needed. Sometimes the force of the blast was so great that the dirt was pitted right into the skin, making the wounded look like coal miners.

Often he would see pilots' bodies being brought on a stretcher and parts of their body had been ripped off, exposing their kidneys or their entire stomach. Smarn could do nothing except give them morphine and leave them to die.

But in many cases, Smarn was able to operate successfully and gave much needed hope to his patients. Sometimes many airmen were downed together from one single aircraft, and he had to work on all of them at the same time. His hands would work like magic.

So pleased was Mr. Sheaf with Smarn's contribution that he wrote a glowing testimonial on 30 January 1945, before Smarn left the employ of the EMS. Mr. Sheaf[11] was Smarn's superior, the Honorary Surgeon to the Royal Surrey County Hospital.

It is worth reproducing the contents of Mr. Sheaf's testimonial in its entirety:

> MR. SMARN MUNTARBHORN came to the Royal Surrey County Hospital two years ago as my House Surgeon. At the end of his normal six months time of office, he was re-appointed for another six months, and then as Resident Surgical Officer for one year.
>
> He has a very good knowledge of his work, especially anatomy, which he knows very well. He is keen to learn, careful, and thorough in all he does, and very conscientious. He is completely honest, and never tries to cover up a mistake.
>
> As Resident Surgical Officer he did a great deal of emergency surgery by himself, several cases involving gut resections. He has, as well, been given such operations as for gall stones, and carcinoma of the breast. In all this work he has shown himself a good and careful operator, and his cases have done very well indeed.
>
> He has a pleasant, happy nature, and throws himself with zest into all the activities of the hospital. He gets on well with all those with whom he works.
>
> He is a loyal colleague, and I am sorry to lose his services.

---

11 In England, he is known as *Mister Sheaf* just as much as Smarn was to be officially called *Mister Muntarbhorn*. It is one of the eccentricities of the British medical profession that a full-fledged surgeon is addressed as Mister and not as Doctor. Smarn learned to respect the English people, particularly their sense of fair play, although he was sometimes puzzled by some of their more quirky traditions. This was surely one of them.

Before Smarn returned to Siam in early 1946, he was able to pick up two more English qualifications. He is the first Siamese to pass the difficult Royal College of Surgeons exams, and proudly returned home with the prestigious title of F.R.C.S. (Fellow of the Royal College of Surgeons of England) after his name. In November 1945, he picked up his last qualification before leaving England, the Diploma of Tropical Medicine from Liverpool.

If the dear reader is under the impression that life in Siam would be easy after such a bright academic performance at Manchester Grammar and Guy's, and after such a heroic career in wartime England, you would be mistaken. True, Smarn was to become known as the "Father of Thai Cardiac Surgery", but this accolade came much later. It was hard earned in the peacetime trenches of Thai hospital politics and rivalry.

After returning to his homeland, Smarn had to navigate his way through the complicated bureaucratic corridors of the Thai medical profession, moving back and forth between three medical school institutions, instead of following the conventional career path in one hospital. Chulalongkorn Hospital, institutional, rich and highly politicised; Siriraj Hospital, royally sponsored, never short of surgeons, leaving little space for Smarn to introduce innovative surgical methods; and Phra Mongkut Khlao Hospital, the newest medical school at the time, where he was able to do what he did best – cardiac surgery – right to the end of his career. Here, despite the bureaucracy, he was happier, teaching his surgical skills to new hopefuls.

Smarn *insisted* that both his lectures and exams be given in English. In this, he was way ahead of his time. Today, more and more subjects at Thai universities are taught in English, in all faculties.

He was often accused of being a strict disciplinarian, and many interns were afraid of his sudden outbursts when they did things incorrectly. With Smarn, there were never any half measures. Those who worked with Smarn either loved him or hated him, but he was always highly respected. The work came first and he naively believed that it would speak for itself. It did, but not in the way that Smarn intended. He wanted to be a leader in his field.

The challenge of leadership is to know when to be expedient and practical on the one hand, and when, on the other, to stand firm on principle and be true to one's calling. Smarn was too proud to be anything but the honest, straight-shooting person he had always been. He frequently spoke his mind. A mark of a true politician is to never tell the truth. Smarn could never tell a lie.

Smarn's main problem was his total lack of diplomatic skills. There are ways to get ahead if you disagree with the system. You can pretend to be humble and sympathetic, you can try to be patient, and you can at least be flexible. Importantly, you need to know how to ingratiate yourself with the people who matter, in particular with those in power. Smarn could do none of these things. He reluctantly found himself embroiled in confrontational situations not of his choice, all in the name of principle. He was too self-assured and always believed he was in the right. Unfortunately, *he was*. People who are self-righteous are annoying. There were a lot of annoyed bureaucrats in Smarn's life.

He would frequently act first, then, to the aggravation of his superiors, report back later, not a good way to get ahead. As a result, Smarn would often find himself without the support he would need to do his work efficiently.

Yet despite these habits, he was a pioneer and a trailblazer. He was the first Thai surgeon to perform both closed (1953) and open (1959) heart surgery, and the first to perform an operation carried out under general anaesthetic, replacing the antiquated method of freezing the body to allow the brain to continue functioning. In 1950, he pioneered a surgical procedure to arrest bleeding in cirrhosis; in the same year he performed the first pneumonectomy and lobectomy and heart surgery for patent ductus arteriosus. He was also the first to operate on a newborn infant suffering from congenital postero-lateral diaphragmatic hernia. The baby was cured in 7 days. The list of firsts goes on and on.

Impatient to get on with the job, and especially to perform operations that had never been done before, Smarn often had to work with equipment that was either not working well or hopelessly out-of-date. He could not understand why the bureaucrats running the hospitals could never give him the budget he needed for new equipment, and *immediately*. More often than not, rather than let a patient die, he would advance his own money to pay for the latest medical supplies and surgical machines. On many occasions, he had to assemble the machine himself, repair it and then teach the hospital staff how to work it. Money, or the lack of it, was always a problem. He would frequently perform an operation without getting paid.

On one notable occasion, the Rotary Club of Ipoh in Malaysia sought the assistance of the Rotary Club of Dhonburi in Thailand to help Chia Choon Lam, a frail, tiny wisp of a woman of 23 who weighed only 35 kilos. From a poor family in Ipoh, she had been diagnosed with a congenital heart defect. Choon Lam had a hole about one inch in diameter in the septum (atrio-septal defect/ ASD), which, standing between the two upper chambers of the heart, separates the used and purified blood. Through this hole the purified blood in one chamber passed freely into the other and mixed with the used blood, causing dilation of the right side of the heart. If an operation to close the hole was not performed and performed soon, Choon Lam would die of heart failure.

The Rotary Club of Dhonburi picked her up from Don Muang airport on 30 July 1963, and whisked her off to Chulalongkorn Hospital. She was given a further examination by Smarn who concluded after a full day of tests that, yes, he could close the hole in her heart.

At 8 a.m. on the morning of Wednesday, 7 August, Chia Choon Lam was wheeled into the Hospital's operating theatre. The atmosphere before an operation is always tense, and today it was especially so. The specialists, surgeons and doctors, the heart and lung machine operators – the perfusionists – and the nurses, were nervous. Thanks to Smarn's upbeat tone of voice and reassuring smile, they all relaxed when he entered the theatre. Smarn started to work.

A continuous droning of reports from the various units began.

*"Temperature 36 Centigrade... Venous pressure 10 centimetres of Water... Arterial pressure 100 millimetres of Mercury... Pulse rate 80 per minute"*

*"Heart-lung machine?"*

*"Ready, sir."*

*"Anaesthetic?"*

*"Ready, sir."*

*"Instruments?"*

*"Ready, sir."*

The figures kept changing but Smarn's work went on.

*"I'm now making the skin incision and opening the chest. Now you can start the timer."*

*"Forceps, please. Suction, please..."* said Smarn confidently.

The report continued to drone on. The heart, now laid bare, was pulsating freely. Then Smarn asked the dramatic question that even made his own heart skip a beat.

*"Are the bypass tubes and the pump ready?"*

*"Yes, sir."*

*"All right. One, two, three. Now."*

This was the moment when Smarn used his skilled hands like a sculptor to insert the tubes into the major vessels just before starting the pump.

*"All right. One, two, three. Use the pump now and cool the patient!"*

Five minutes later, a continuous droning of the reports from the various units began.

*"Temperature 33…Venous pressure down to 8… Arterial pressure 70… Heart rate 70… Perfusion OK."*

Smarn took the scalpel and opened the pericardium of the heart. The heart-lung machine had already taken over the function of Choon Lam's heart.

The droning tone of the report suddenly changed after the word *"now!"* rang out.

*"Temperature down to 30…Venous pressure down to 6…Arterial pressure 50…EKG stable…Perfusion OK."*

Then another voice chimed in confidently.

*"Bypass is now ten minutes… Bypass is now twenty minutes…"* reporting the length of time that the heart-lung machine had taken over the function of Choon Lam's heart. Pressure in the veins and arteries started its downward slide.

*"Temperature 29 degrees…Venous pressure 5… Arterial pressure 50… Pump working okay"*

The heart-lung machine operator's voice, equally excited, asked:

*"Are we nearly finished?"*

The confident voice of Smarn boomed back above the drone:

*"Yes. I've repaired the ASD! But there's still more to be done… Perfusionist, warm up the patient…Anaesthetist, ready to ventilate?"*

Soon afterwards, the bypass tubes were removed, the heart-lung machine was switched off, the anaesthetist controlled the respirator and the chest's skin was sutured.

Smarn laid down his instruments and looked at the clock. It was 9.40 a.m.

The hole in Choon Lam's little heart had been closed.

The next step was equally critical and tense. It was now 10.30. The final report came after what seemed an eternity:

*"Temperature 36.5...Venous pressure 10...Blood pressure 115 over 80...Pulse rate 90."*

There were audible sounds of relief throughout the theatre. Smarn took off his glasses and removed his mask, and gave his characteristic smile to all the anxious faces around the operating table.

*"The bypass is terminated. The patient is ready to leave the operation theatre"*. It was 11.15 a.m.

The next day, in the ICU room next to the theatre, where Choon Lam was recovering from the operation, Smarn went to her bedside. He gently took her hand and smiled at her. She smiled feebly back, as tears of gratitude started to well in her eyes.

*Thank you, Thai doctor, for giving me a new life,* she seemed to be saying.

After the success of Choon Lam's operation, Smarn went on to perform heart operations on eleven more Malaysians, one a little boy of four.

Smarn was one of those versatile people who could have excelled in any number of professions requiring the dextrous use of his hands. He was creative and could have been an artist or a sculptor. His love of music was such that he could have easily become a concert pianist or professional violinist. Had he become a musician, his career would have very cruelly come to an end at 50, when he started to have trouble hearing. It was becoming increasingly difficult for him to join in conversation with his friends and colleagues, yet incredibly, he was able to hear the sound of the human heartbeat. As a result of becoming deaf, he was to spend the next 40 years of his life partially shut out from the world that meant so much to him. He would attend international seminars and medical congresses, only being able to understand the visual parts of a presentation. His trusted nurses and his son Kanit were his constant companions, transcribing what was said on paper for him to read. After 1970, he could no longer attend a concert or enjoy the cinema. Yet he was able to continue his lifetime work as a surgeon until the end of his career.

Smarn was by turns charming, obstinate, eloquent and impatient, and unorthodox in his methods. There was streak of rebellion in his dealings with hospital boards, and he was a fighter to the end. He permanently wore his smart double breasted suit and his trademark blue and yellow striped Guy's Hospital tie, even on the hottest day, ever craving for recognition and driven by success, yet frequently short of money. He is now remembered paradoxically as one of the most beloved personalities in the Thai medical profession.

*Mister Smarn Muntarbhorn, FRCS.*

An original Siamese.

# COLONEL VICHA DHITAVADHNA

# 1918 – 1981

A soldier from another time

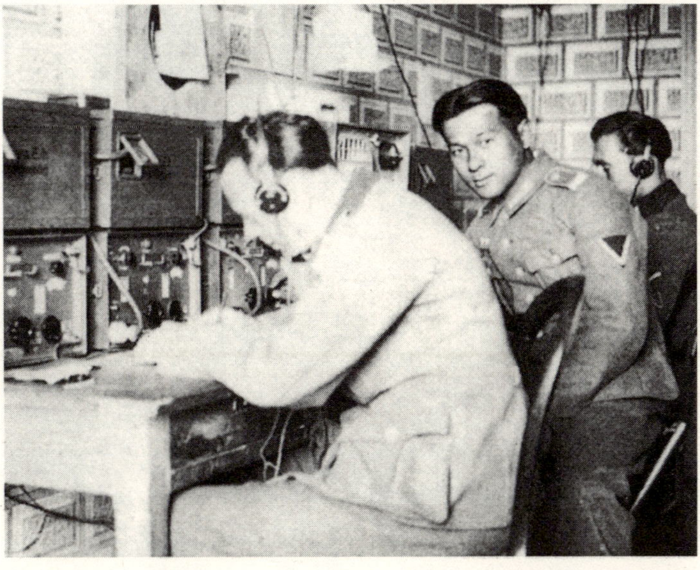

**Previous page:** *Narbonne, France, 1943. Vicha at work at the German 1st Army Radio headquarters.*

**Above:** *Vicha preferred fishing in the French countryside more than urban life in nearby Poitiers in 1940.*

# 9

# An Officer in the Nazi Army

Twenty thousand "Heil Hitler!" salutes reverberated through the colossal hall as the Fuhrer himself stepped up to the huge swastika-draped podium. In front of him, new graduates of Germany's unified armed forces, and among them a most unlikely person, a 25-year-old Siamese army officer named Vicha Dhitavadhna.

Immediately following graduation, the class of '43 to which Vicha had belonged had been confined to their barracks. None were allowed to write letters home or telephone out. They had quietly boarded a train for an unknown destination, stopping for the night at an army camp at Breslau. At 4 a.m. they were herded through the snow to their secret rendezvous and joined 18,500 other new graduates from all three branches of the German armed forces at the Jahrhunderthalle. The 20,000 young officers had been seated in dozens of sections, each with its own entrance door, and as they waited – ordered not to speak – an eerie silence pervaded the hall.

All that changed when Adolf Hitler took the stage. The theme of his speech that morning was his usual political soliloquy – "Defend the Fatherland against the Jews and Communists" – which the German population had been hearing *ad nauseam* for years. But his passionate delivery held his audience of new graduates rapt, and for an astonishing two-and-a-half hours, without notes and without losing his strident voice, he did not stop speaking. Unrelentingly, he attempted to instil fanaticism and loyalty in the new officers by giving them a pep talk to boost their morale. His xenophobic ranting, however, was beginning to flag on a nationwide level, particularly amongst the older population. Indeed, the only person who refused to believe that it was the beginning of the end was Hitler himself.

As the Fuhrer concluded that morning and Vicha Dhitavadhna joined his comrades in offering him a last salute, what had this young Siamese officer come to believe?

## Journey Into War

Four years earlier, on 10 July 1939, two days before he was to depart for Europe, Lieutenant Vicha Dhitavadhna arrived early at Wang Suan Kularb Palace in Bangkok and reported to the senior officer in charge, who told him to wait. It was customary for all Thai army officers who had won scholarships to attend military academies in Europe to formally request permission to leave from the Supreme Commander of the Armed Forces, Field Marshal Pibulsonggram. At precisely 10 a.m. Vicha was ushered into Pibul's office. He saluted to attention and the Field Marshal beckoned him towards a chair in the formal reception area in his office. Pibul got up from behind his desk and joined him. It was a relaxed meeting and Vicha could see from Pibul's smile that the Field Marshal was in a good mood. Pibul told Vicha to do the country proud and wished him success. His years at the *Ecole d'artillerie* in France when Pibul had been a cadet were the best years of his life, he told him.

"But don't go around falling in love with all those beautiful blonde *farang* women!" the Field Marshal joked, noticing that Vicha was a handsome young man.

"And another thing. Don't you dare stage a *coup d'etat* against me either when you get back!"

Vicha respectfully bid his farewell, happy at the impression he had made. He was just 21 years old, the youngest junior officer in the army and one of the most promising.

While Vicha would ultimately end up in Germany, his journey would first take him to Brussels. It was not his ideal choice. He had wanted to study in France, where many of his senior officers graduated, including the Field Marshal himself. But the French he had learned at Assumption College, a Catholic school in Bangkok, was too basic for him to study the principles of warfare. So he was first sent to the Belgian capital where he attended the Institut Michot Monganast to brush up his French. The school no longer exists, but before the start of the war it was exclusively for the offspring of rich business leaders, politicians and diplomats. Vicha fitted well into this new elite environment. A fast learner and a charmer, with a winning smile and clean-cut good looks, he easily made friends with his fellow students.

Vicha survived his first winter in Europe, and despite the bitter cold, he enjoyed his new life in Brussels where he had found a comfortable furnished third floor room in town near some Siamese friends who were also studying there. Like all army officers he was an early riser and by 5 a.m. he was often at work at his desk. On one particularly bright spring morning in May, the weather was so balmy he stepped out on to the balcony outside his room and lingered there for a while to enjoy the sunrise that was slowly appearing above the city's green copper rooftops. The only sounds he heard were the wheels of a milk cart grinding on the cobblestone street, pulled by dogs, and the clinking of glass bottles, as the milkman made his early morning deliveries down the road. On this beautiful dawn, he wanted to savour the early morning stillness to the full before trams, cars and bicycles quickly filled the streets.

But the peace of that morning was interrupted by the buzzing sound of several airplanes in the distance, a noise which intensified as the planes approached, when suddenly, Vicha was awoken from his reverie by the screaming sounds of diving firebombs. Before he could grab his camera to take pictures of the attacking airplanes, he was thrown to the floor by a nearby blast and his room was totally covered with debris. Soon the entire street was ablaze. It was 10 May 1940. Adolf Hitler had just launched operation *"Sichelschnitt"* – Sickle Stroke – with a Blitzkrieg assault against Holland, Luxemburg, France and Belgium with 200,000 troops and 3,000 aircraft. World War II had begun and Vicha was caught in the thick of it.

Brave Belgian troops started to blow up all the bridges over the River Meuse to impede the German advance that day as tiny Belgium became a battlefield. Total chaos reigned in Brussels. As Vicha ran into the street he saw the huge building of the Institut National Belge de Radiodiffusion transmission station opposite his apartment block in flames. A wireless and radio communications enthusiast, he looked sadly at the institution as it started to disintegrate and crumble to the ground. But he had no time to waste. He hurried to the Siamese legation to check whether his friends were safe.

Schools, offices and much of the government were in lock-down. There was general panic in the city as the more well to do got into their cars to flee the advancing Germans. Both the Gare Central and the Gare du Midi railway stations were clogged with people struggling to board the trains. The less fortunate were trying to hitch a ride with the retreating Tommies – British soldiers on lorries passing through Brussels on their way to the coast. Prince Snidvongse, the Siamese military attaché, was busy arranging the evacuation of the legation officials and students to France. He refused to leave Brussels until the last Siamese was evacuated. They jostled with the locals to get a place on the south-bound train. The carriages were crammed with fleeing refugees, mostly standing in the corridors and some even on the train's steps. As the locomotive steamed to the border, Vicha looked out of the window and saw bombed-out buildings, wrecked vehicles, and hundreds of bedraggled families on the country roads, making their way on foot, the more fortunate ones on bicycles. The devastation of the German invasion was in evidence everywhere.

Near the French border, their train was strafed by Messerschmitt 109 fighter planes returning from a raid. They were fortunately defended by a platoon of Tommies near the railway line who fired their machine guns into the air. The cries and screams of the train passengers were more terrifying to Vicha than the attacking planes on their way back to Germany. After two hours the train reached the French frontier. The passengers disembarked to have their passports stamped.

In France, the French were still in a state of denial, believing in their own propaganda of invincibility, that the Germans could not possibly pass through the much vaunted Maginot Line, an impregnable series of concrete fortresses which ran from Switzerland to the Luxemburg and Belgian borders. There was a popular song, "*Nous allons pendre notre linge sur la ligne Siegfried*" – "We're going to hang out our laundry on the Siegfried line" – which gave the French masses a totally false sense of security, and these Siamese wanderers also (wrongly) thought it would be a safe haven. France, they had decided would be a good country to continue their studies. Vicha and his fellow students were sent to Poitiers where they were instructed to remain until the autumn semester, when they would be placed in their respective military school.

The village of Menigoute is near Poitiers in southwestern France. Today it has a population of 875, not much more than when Vicha and a few Siamese students went there to stay at the end of May 1940. The rest of them decided to remain in the town of Poitiers where there was a bit more life and at least some social activity. But Vicha preferred the peaceful atmosphere of this charming village and was welcomed by Madame de Ville, a well-off citizen of Poitiers, who developed a soft spot for him and offered him a small cottage where he was allowed to stay for three francs a month.

In the meadows near the cottage, Vicha would look for a quiet spot under an oak tree and catch up with his French studies.

He was a fishing enthusiast and on a good day he would reel in a trout from one of the streams. In the woods there was an abundance of mushrooms that he happily picked. In this peaceful rural setting, he almost forgot that Europe was at war.

A few weeks later, however, on 14 June, the Nazi swastika flag was flown from the Eiffel Tower. The German army had smashed through the Maginot Line defences and in less than a month had victoriously marched into Paris. France had become a dangerous war zone. The Siamese government advised the Siamese students that it would no longer be safe to remain in France and to either return home or – if they preferred – continue their studies elsewhere, in Switzerland, Italy or Germany, or even further afield in Canada or the United States. As Siam was still neutral, the Siamese would not be considered an enemy in any of these countries.[1]

## At Home with the Schlitts

Vicha thought very carefully about the decision he was about to make. He was young and determined to make a success of his life. He wanted nothing more than to become a good soldier and to serve his country well. So he decided, with three other Siamese students, to go to Germany where they believed the military academies were better than those of Italy or Switzerland.

When Vicha arrived in Berlin on 23 October 1940, however, it was not the gay city of coffee houses and lively theatres, nor the famous city of culture and living arts that he had read about. Neither was it a city bedecked with swastika flags, of Nazi goose-stepping soldiers strutting along the Kurfurstendamm and imperial eagles on

1 Similarly, many American students at the Sorbonne remained in Paris throughout the German occupation until President Roosevelt declared war on Germany on 11th December 1941.

every balcony, that Hollywood likes to depict. When he arrived in the evening at the Lehrter Bahnhof railway station, Berlin was, in fact, a sombre city plunged in total darkness.

Vicha had never seen such a total blackout being enforced like this before and it took him some time getting used to. Although the five-metre pavements were the widest he had ever walked on, he kept bumping into people and lampposts. Sleeping in the hotel's underground bunker, the constant screams of the nightly air raid sirens made his first week in Berlin an unnerving experience.

His new home was not far from the Lichterfelde Military Cadet School on the southern periphery of the capital. Together with three other Siamese cadets, he was placed under the strict supervision of Colonel Schlitt, a veteran of the First World War, and his Frau, a sympathetic and caring woman, who also took a fancy to Vicha and treated him like a son. Vicha later learned that the Schlitts had lost their only son earlier on in the war on the Polish front.

Colonel Schlitt was tall, thin and extremely fit for his 60 years, and he represented the archetype Teutonic blond that was so admired by Hitler. During the First World War, Schiltt had been a captain of the artillery and fought in the trenches of Ypres in Belgium. He was awarded the Iron Cross for climbing a trench ladder above the parapet line, after spotting a British platoon crawling on their bellies towards their battery position and single-handedly wiped them out. This event occurred during the last months of the war, in July 1918, when the Germans were already losing.

A man of few words, Colonel Schlitt had two scars on his forehead, two pink lines, each about three inches long, which he would stroke nervously. Vicha would later discover that these were "honour scars", the result of a *Schlager*[2] duel that had taken place when Schlitt was a young cadet. The scars were not meant to be deep, but in the course of a duel, the students would deliberately inflict and

---

2 Duelling sword.

receive superficial head and face wounds with the objective of leaving permanent scars purely for public admiration. It was the *sine qua non* of a respected Prussian officer.

For the next year, Vicha would attend junior cadet school and live with the Schlitts, who had a *Hausfrau* to help with the domestic chores and her 9-year-old daughter who gave their Siamese guests German lessons every night after they came back from classes. Vicha was learning German at the rate of 100 new words a day. He decided that with three genders (masculine, feminine and neuter) that had to be learned and the declensions that had to be figured out for each sentence, German grammar was far more difficult than French, but the pronunciation in the correct *Hoch Deutsch* manner was easier.

Living in Berlin under wartime conditions during these years were not as academically difficult as they were personally. The Siamese cadets' main concern was for their personal safety during the Allied air raids, which became more frequent and more targeted from the spring of 1942 onwards. By this time, the German population was mobilized for total war and had to accept longer working hours and even more restricted food rations. Rationing was based on a points system to purchase food products and basic household items like soap, clothing and coal. On the rare occasion when a special food item like coffee came on the market, consumers had to wait until their number was announced or written in the shop window. Once, when Vicha missed seeing his number at his corner grocery shop, it was months before that number came up again.

Those who were directly working for the war effort, like coal miners and steelworkers, received extra rations. When fresh fish and vegetables, and especially chocolate, were available, they were reserved for the armed forces. Paradoxically, those with huge appetites like military cadets and school children, were given less. The quality of the food was poor. The Reich was relatively successful in its effort to make sure that the entire population, both military and civilian, were treated equally and never short of food.

When Vicha and his three Siamese colleagues graduated from the junior cadet school in Berlin, they wanted real-life training at an officers' academy; in the case of his three friends, experience in one of Germany's renowned tank corps, and for Vicha, radio communications in the field. They had spent a year learning the academic side of warfare, including history, geography, physics and maths from books and lectures. Now they were eager to put all this knowledge into practice.

But to be admitted to an academy, the equivalent of university, they had to be German. This was a touchy subject, as the particular skills of modern warfare where they wanted training were deemed by the German High Command as highly confidential and as such "secret weapons" not to be passed on to non-German citizens.

By this time, in 1941, the war had become a global one, with land and air battle fronts in both eastern and western Europe, the Soviet Union, North Africa and China. The war on the seas in the Mediterranean and the Atlantic blocked all the sea lanes. While Vicha and his friends were extremely eager to learn, they were also homesick and would have quite happily returned to Siam, still a neutral country, but there was no safe passage home. So the Siamese legation did their level best to persuade the German government to accept them and a German compromise was proposed. Would the four Siamese cadets be prepared to *volunteer* and serve in the Wehrmacht? Vicha and his friends realized that this was indeed a rare and privileged opportunity to learn from the German Army and so they agreed.

# The Making of a German Officer

Before the Siamese cadets could even be admitted they had to satisfy the examiners that they had no Jewish blood whatsoever, that they had successfully graduated from high school, and were physically and mentally sound. This was followed by three days of intensive tests. Day one consisted of physical tests on strength, speed, balance and reaction. Day two examined their co-ordination and mechanical skills, and day three on their aptitude.

While his three friends were assigned to a tank corps training school, Vicha was to spend the next three years training as a German radio communications officer at various officers' academies in Hannover, Leipzig and Halle, interspersed with active duty in southwestern France.

At Hannover, Vicha was put through the toughest military course in Germany. It was boot camp all over again, with weeks on end doing menial duties in the dormitories, kitchens and latrines. The dormitories were spartan, with straw palliasses for the beds, on bare concrete floors. The sergeant major in charge was a manic stickler for cleanliness and perfection, getting the cadets to make and remake their beds, re-polish their boots and brass buttons over and over again, and making sure their lockers were neat and tidy and ready for inspection at all hours. Often the paranoiac sergeant would make spot inspections in the middle of the night in complete darkness. He would also require the cadet officers to repetitively do sit-ups, press-ups and floor exercises at all times of the day.

Vicha's muscles ached continuously. When punished for some minor infraction, they had to crawl under their beds and remain there for hours. Early morning reveille, a bugle call at 4 a.m., required them to shave, wash and dress, polish their boots, make their beds, clean the latrines and sweep the dormitory, followed by breakfast, all in half-an-hour before going on parade for inspection and roll-call. One button out of place, one untied shoelace, and they had to start all over again. One simple communal mistake like not checking that the dormitory door was securely latched and the entire platoon would be punished.

After a month of dormitory and camp duties, they went on to field training: arms and ammunition, the Morse code, combat basics, radio, telegraph and telephone usage, cable installation, horse riding, vehicle driving, skiing downhill and cross-country, trench digging *with only a bayonet* and how to use it in hand-to-hand combat, camouflage, gas masks, geographic surveys of the terrain, swimming and wading in streams, singing patriotic songs on the march – the list of basic warfare skills and military drills were endless. Each activity required its own uniform and punishment was meted out if they were not worn properly. Most tiring and annoying was the order to "hit the ground" at any moment, normally on snow or mud.

Foreign cadets, especially if they were good looking, were frequently the first to be picked upon. "Can you crawl on our hard German soil, Dhitatavadhna?" Vicha would often be asked sarcastically. Crawling all the way to the battle front was very demanding, particularly when it rained. Vicha was so tired that he often fell asleep at his desk during radio lessons. If he was caught napping, he would have to stand up for the rest of the period. If he was caught again he had to crawl under his desk and stay there until he was excused.

When Vicha was learning how to drive, he had to learn how to shift gears quietly. Any loud crunching of the gears and the offender had to run behind the vehicle all the way back to camp.

During the winter months, the cadets were given dancing classes in town. The local *Frauleins* were invited to participate and the cadets were not allowed to ask the same girl to dance more than once. They danced to the waltz and the foxtrot. The Minister of Propaganda, Joseph Goebbels, had banned swing music and the rumba as "degenerate". Vicha learned the Prussian custom of hand-kissing. It was part of their *training* and not meant for their amusement. The girls were accompanied by their mothers and the cadets took them directly home after the last dance.

By the end of 1942, Vicha was ready to graduate. The Graduation Ball in December at the Hannover Stadthaus city hall was the cadets' last rite before graduation. Before they could receive their formal invitation, they were instructed on how to behave in polite society: the correct way to use a knife and fork, how to behave in front of the ladies at the dining table, how to bow properly when asking a girl to dance, and other such formal social graces. Their officers' uniform was of paramount importance. The correct way to wear gloves, the angle of the cap on one's head and the right way to carry their sabre were all part of their final test. On the big day, each cadet drew two numbers to select their partners for the evening. This was to ensure that each girl had the opportunity to dance, even the plainer ones. Vicha had always been lucky with the opposite sex. The two numbers he drew were the belles of the ball. He had also always been lucky with his studies and he graduated with flying colours. He was now a Commissioned Officer in the Wehrmacht. But Vicha's timing could not have been less auspicious.

## Marching Orders

In December 1942, the German defeat at the Battle of Stalingrad cost 120,000 German lives and when General Paulus surrendered to the Russians on 31 January 1943, 91,000 Germans were taken prisoner. It was the beginning of the end of Hitler's Third Reich. The tables were slowly turning and the Red Army was now advancing westwards, and was to attack the Germans for the next two and a half years on the Eastern Front, Germany's most vulnerable line of defence. Vicha's comrades from the academy were all sent to the Eastern Front. None of them returned. Vicha now received his marching orders.

He was saved from serving on the Eastern Front for three reasons. First, High Command discovered that his knowledge of French would serve them better in France. Secondly, they decided that an Asiatic used to warm climates would not perform to the best of his ability in the cold steppes of Eastern Europe. The third reason was a practical one: winter uniforms in Vicha's size were currently unavailable and a new set could not be produced in time. Vicha was ordered to go to southwest France and serve in the Signal Corps at Perpignan.

It was nice being back in France. Beautiful vineyard country, home to the Grand Roussillon muscat and other sweet fortified wines, Perpignan commands the passes of the Eastern Pyrenees and the Mediterranean. Vicha arrived here in July 1943 during the dry hot summer and he enjoyed the high temperatures. But he was shocked to see how much poorer France had become in just three years. They were no longer the jovial farm people he used to know and with whom he would practice his French. All they wanted now was money and food. The cornfields were dry and the once bountiful lands were parched and bare. Not even potatoes were available. He had never witnessed starvation in Germany, but here there were homes that had been without food for days. The German soldiers would often share their meager rations with poor French families who were literally starving to death. The only produce they had was wine which they would barter with German potatoes. There was a lively black market trade with Spain across the border fifty kilometres away. With his small savings of German Marks, Vicha would order chocolate, olive oil, cocoa, biscuits and tinned sardines.

In the oppressive heat, Vicha's principal mission was to supervise the installation of radio and telegraph networks in this newly occupied area of France. With a platoon of twenty German soldiers assisted by a French brigade of African soldiers from the

Cameroons (at that time a French colony) and two trucks, Vicha travelled the length and breadth of the Languedoc-Roussillon region and connected this relatively isolated area with the rest of German occupied France.

Although he was comfortably billeted at a chateau in Perpignan that was commandeered by the Wehrmacht for their officers, the going was rough when he was on the road, which was most of the time. He had never seen so many flies in his life. Despite the annoying bugs and the oppressive heat, the work proceeded smoothly. The Cameroonians would dig the holes and put in the heavy telegraph poles, and the German soldiers, many of whom were post and telegraph workers during peacetime, would install the lines. It was so hot and his men were so tired that he ordered a long lunch break so that the men could have an hours' siesta.[3] Vicha would swap his German black bread for the Cameroonian tubers stewed in a weak tomato sauce and a little bit of chili. It was the best lunch he'd had for a long time.

At the end of his assignment, Vicha took time off in Berlin and went to visit Colonel Schlitt and his wife with a sack of black market food from Spain. They called him *der Weihnachtsmann*[4] and noticed that he was darker than they had ever seen him. Berlin was even sadder than before. Many of the familiar streets where he walked in 1940 were unrecognizable. Allied bombings were now a nightly occurrence.

Vicha quickly left this city of rubble for Vienna before reporting back for duty in France. He was transferred to the Army Radio HQ

3 As a Siamese in the German army, could Vicha command as much respect from the troops as a German officer? At no time during his service in the Wehrmacht was he ever treated any differently from, or by, other German soldiers of any rank. Once an officer in the German army you are in total command of your unit and you command the respect of your peers. On one occasion, on furlough in Vienna with Boonchuey, one of his Siamese friends who became a tank commander, an SS officer of a lower rank walked passed them without saluting in the appropriate manner. Boonchuey called him back to tick him off, ordering him to go back twenty paces, and walk past them again with the correct salute, much to the amusement of the locals.

4 Santa Claus.

of the First Army in nearby Narbonne. On top of getting familiarized with new telex and telegram technology, and making sure that all the radios were set on the right frequency, Vicha discovered that none of the Germans here spoke French, and he was soon requested to liaise with French Vichy officers. His most delicate task, however, was to translate love letters from French girls to their German boyfriends.

In September, Vicha was ordered back to Germany to report to the Military College of Communications in Leipzig where he was to receive further training in the latest wireless telegraphy and telephony equipment and their implementation in the field. He also attended courses in radio intelligence and how to intercept station operations.

Life in Leipzig was certainly better than boot camp in Hannover. Now that Vicha was a commissioned officer, he enjoyed a number of privileges in the town. He was allowed free access to many cultural events and given free theatre tickets. To keep fit he frequently went to the sports gymnasium swimming pool. On one occasion some prankster stole his clothes. He had no time to change and went on parade in his swimming trunks.

"*Someone* among us here likes to sunbathe while standing on parade," the commanding officer, straight-faced, commented without even looking at Vicha.

None of his fellow officers batted an eyelid and stood erect to attention. The only person who almost broke down with laughter was Vicha himself. The inspection was conducted normally, as though there was nothing amiss. The *cameraderie* amongst the officer class was solid.

In the early hours of 4 December 1943, the heaviest raid on Leipzig was carried out by the RAF. Four hundred and forty British bombers, mainly Avro Lancasters and Vickers Wellingtons, dropped 1400 tons of explosives and firebombs on the city. Leipzig was a major trading city and printing centre for the Reich, with more than 200 printing presses. The city was in flames and the printing industry never recovered. The fire raged all night and the concert hall and the theatre that Vicha had so much enjoyed were totally gutted. The Trade Exchange, the railway station, 472 factories and 9 churches were destroyed and several buildings of the Communications College were on fire. Vicha and his comrades spent the next day fighting the fire and saving as much radio equipment as they could.

## The Collapse of the Third Reich

It was at this time when Vicha was sent off to hear Hitler's pep talk. But if Hitler was in denial, Vicha himself was beginning to realize that the Third Reich was starting to crack at the seams. In his position as an itinerant officer, he had seen too many towns that were totally destroyed. He had witnessed too much suffering amongst the brave and misinformed population, and he observed in France that there was no way that the German occupying forces could stay on forever. He had lost too many of his fellow student officers on the Eastern Front. His chief source of information was through the radio communications that he was privy to. The news was generally bad on all fronts. The worst bit of news that slipped through the censors strict control, even worse than the successful Allied invasions in Sicily on 9 July 1943, was the Allies' successful invasion of Normandy on 6 June 1944. The Germans were losing control of all their occupied territories.

Before his next transfer to the Senior Officers Radio Communication Academy in Halle, Vicha decided to take a short furlough and visit Helga, his blonde girlfriend from his time in Hannover. He had met her during his officer training days when he was learning how to dance. When she came to the station to meet him off the train, she greeted him with her beautiful smile. But this was to be a sad reunion.

In the days when they went everywhere together – to the opera, to the theatre and for walks in the park where they would talk for hours – she was vivacious and pretty. Now pale and thin, she had not only lost a lot of weight but also her lively spirit. He had been looking forward to seeing her and although his sentiments towards her were the same, he noticed that she was now a different person.

It was only when they went into town together did he discover how much she had suffered. He could no longer remember the streets where they walked together. The pavements were almost impassable. The few houses that were still standing were roofless. Others were skeletons without walls and floors. They had to step across shards of broken glass, piles of bricks and twisted metal, taking care not to slip on the puddles of water leaking from the burst mains. He was lost in a razed city where he was once so happy.

"Do you know where we are now, *liebe* Vicha?" she asked, leading the way.

Vicha looked at a large pile of charred brickwork and burned-out debris of what seemed to be the remains of a big terraced house. Vicha shook his head. No, he didn't know where they were.

He looked inquisitively at Helga whose large blue eyes were beginning to swell with tears. It finally dawned on him that this was the house on Papenstrasse where he would take her home after a happy evening out together. It was now a waste of ruins.

He was afraid to ask where her parents were, and fortunately they had all survived the terrible night of July 1943, when 40,000 citizens perished in horrific firestorms. They were still alive and were now living a few miles out of town.

They continued their walk and Helga showed him all the places where they used to go together. The splendid opera house, where they saw *Carmen* together for the first time and *Madame Butterfly* on their last date, was now a burned-out skeleton. The cafe where they would meet and decide where they would go next had totally disappeared. Hannover was now a city of rubble.

Helga's parents welcomed him as if nothing had happened. *Such good people, he thought.* They fed him with what he was sure was the last of their rations, so happy were they to see him again. They thought he had been sent to the Russian front and were not sure whether he was still alive. They talked all night of happier times. Nobody in Germany, Vicha noticed, was now talking of the future. He bid them farewell and they wished him good luck for his next posting. Vicha took Helga in his arms and they held each other tightly for a long time in silence. There was nothing they could say to each other. It was the saddest day in Vicha's life. He was never to see her again.

## Final Postings

The Academy for Radio Communications in Halle, not far from Leipzig, was the largest military communications school in Germany and it was to be Vicha's second to last posting.

This was the most exacting school Vicha had ever attended. The German army took both their training procedures and their radio technology seriously. The ability to communicate and command by radio was largely responsible for their early successes in the war. At a time when the French high command was not even equipped with radio, it was a sophisticated system of radio communications in each tank, each aircraft and each unit that allowed German commanders to control their forces so effectively. The piercing Blitzkrieg that punched through the Maginot line with their tanks and easily crossed Holland into Belgium and France, reaching the English Channel in such a short time, was the result of efficient radio communications.

Furthermore, each German regiment controlled its communication links from the front line back to headquarters in Germany. Vicha learned that it was superior radio communications and technology that enabled senior German commanders to effectively control huge mobile forces.

The Signal Corps was one of the most respected units in the Wehrmacht, and Vicha was now under continuous pressure to prepare for exams every week followed by rigorous field exercises immediately afterwards, which was known as the *Harte Ubung* technique. Vicha performed well and after three months was promoted to head the radio command post in Breslau. He then asked for two weeks rest in Vienna before moving to his next post; it was during this furlough that he seriously reconsidered his future and looked for a way to return home.

In Vienna, while walking in the grounds of Schönbrunn Palace, he looked around and saw an elegant middle-aged woman dressed entirely in black silently weeping, sitting on a park bench. Seeing her emotional state, he sat next to her and gently asked her what was wrong. It transpired that she had just lost her youngest son, a cadet, in the Crimea.

"My first son, a captain, was killed in France. My second, a lieutenant, was shot on the Russian front and my third, also a lieutenant, was blown up by grenade. And now Fritz is gone..."

She started to sob uncontrollably. Vicha gently put his arm around her thin, trembling shoulder. It was a difficult moment. Hitler had recently put out a new order that the lone son of families would no longer be required to join the army. The German race was at risk of being wiped out.

"Young man, don't take any chances! I will pray for you."

This event shook Vicha. He had heard nothing from his family in Siam for almost four years and indeed wondered if they were still alive. He knew that Pibul had allowed the Japanese to pass through Siam and he hoped that this wise policy would keep his family and friends safe. He left Vienna with a heavy heart, and for the first time, unsure of the future.

His new position in Breslau required him to train younger radio operators in the field. Because the army had lost so many men in Russia, each training program had to be condensed to three intense days and nights, for each batch of new operators. Replacements were needed quickly. The main thrust of the program was to operate the radio under real battle conditions and in defensive positions, in trench warfare and in anti-tank fighting, with survival courses in the snow and in the pitch dark of night, quite different from Vicha's training in Hannover and Leipzig, which focused on radio communication in offensive situations to attack the enemy.

Now, the army was on the defence of the Fatherland. The new recruits, Vicha noticed, were not the tall, strapping Teutonic blonds that marched down the Champs Elyśees, but smaller men of his height. In terms of learning skills, they were of a much lower calibre. Thanks to his boot camp training, he was able to carry out his new assignment without too much difficulty. On top of teaching them how to operate the radio, he also supervised trench digging in winter without gloves and got his brigade to sleep without heating for weeks on end. They were often forbidden to turn up their collars or cover their ears.

As a commissioned officer, he slept in more comfortable officer's quarters and he now ate in the officers' mess, with a waiter to serve him. He had unlimited supplies of foul-tasting *ersatz* (substitute) coffee[5] and up to three slices of bread with each meal, plus 250 grammes of fruit juice concentrate per month. Vicha now suffered from acute sinus. After an operation he spent 10 days in Bad Gastein recuperating. He then received his new marching orders to proceed to Berlin following his official request to attend the prestigious engineering polytechnic there. Vicha was forever finding new ways for the Siamese government (who was still supporting him) to send him to new courses on subjects where he felt he needed improvement. He was determined to return to Siam as the best trained soldier in the army. But Vicha never started his new engineering course, let alone completed his studies.

5 Coffee made from acorns.

# The Fall of Berlin

Much has been written about the fall of Berlin and the last days of Hitler. The last days of Vicha and indeed of the remaining Siamese citizens in the wake of the Red Army's attack and occupation of Berlin were traumatic.

On the military train back to Berlin, he passed hundreds of German refugees fleeing to the West. Among them were young German deserters, innocent boys called to the Nazi colours, who had fought valiantly on the Russian front, no longer wearing the smart uniform of the Wehrmacht, hoping to surrender to the advancing Americans before being slaughtered by the Russians. But the sight of SS officers shamelessly throwing away their grey-green jackets and trousers and hastily donning civilian clothes sickened him. They were callous and cruel in uniform, and now, like all bullies, cowards in the face of defeat.

The city of Berlin was totally destroyed by Allied bombs and hardly a building was left standing. The people hid in their cellars and waited in terror, hoping and praying that the Americans would reach their city before the Russians. But that was not going to be the case. In mid-April 1945, Stalin had ordered his Generals Zhukov and Konev to take Berlin before the British and Americans could reach the city and he provided over two million Russians troops to do the job.

By the 21 April hundreds of Russian tanks entered the eastern suburbs of Berlin and the next day the city was surrounded by the Soviet 47$^{th}$ Army and the Soviet Fourth Guards Army. The bloody battle for Berlin raged for 10 days. Half a million Russians entered the city. There was house to house fighting, and resistance by a few remnants of the Wehrmacht, the SS and young boys of the Volksturm, the home guard, was fanatically brave, and thousands died before the Russians reached the Reichstag in the centre of the city.

"Everywhere the Soviet victors held sway, they embarked upon an orgy of celebration, rape and destruction on a scale such as Europe had not witnessed since the seventeenth century," one historian wrote.[6] Even at that late stage, SS diehards shot anyone who tried to surrender. On 30 April, Hitler committed suicide in his bunker. The greatest war in the history of man was over.

A German cavalry officer accompanied all the evacuating foreign diplomats to the Austrian border a few days before the Russians took complete control of the city. The Siamese group consisted of the minister, the military attaché, the students and Siamese officers like Vicha who had worked for the Wehrmacht. He was sad to learn that his friend Boonchuey was killed in his tank on the Eastern Front.

After a short spell in an American army prison in Austria, they were released and repatriated. Vicha was back in Thailand, after six years in Germany. At 27, he was looking forward to serving his country and to share his newly acquired skills and unique experience. He wanted to help make the Thai army an efficient fighting force.

Back in Thailand, Vicha's career wasn't brilliant. He was without doubt one of the best-trained officers and one of the most experienced soldiers in the Thai army. But being the best professionally did not guarantee his success.

To climb the political ladder of the Thai army he needed more than just knowledge – he needed the right connections. Vicha was promoted when he returned, but he never made it past Colonel. While he was learning from the German army, "man for man, the greatest fighting force of the Second World War",[7] to be the best professional soldier, he had lost the opportunity to build important connections back home. The cadets who graduated from the Royal Cadet Academy, the *Jor Por Ror* clique, had stuck together and many became generals. Vicha was not one of them.

---

6 Max Hastings, *All Hell let Loose,* Harper Press, 2011.
7 Max Hastings, *Ibid.*

His career also suffered because of his record as a German officer. The Americans were in the ascendance after the war and both the CIA and the Pentagon would certainly have found difficulty working with Vicha had he become a senior Thai general. Vicha was to later write in his memoirs that had he known about the genocidal policy of the Nazis and of the SS towards the Jews, and the cruelty that would be inflicted by the Gestapo on the populations of Europe, he would not have gone to Germany. At the time when he made his decision, Siam was neutral. Later when Siam declared war on Britain and America, he naively thought that he had made the right decision. Vicha was guilty of ignorance.

Vicha left the military and joined the Civil Service Commission in charge of overseas Thai students. Because of his knowledge of German he was appointed to be their supervisor in Bonn, the capital of Germany before reunification. He then joined the Ministry of Foreign Affairs and was appointed ambassador to France in 1974. When the Quai d'Orsay – the French Foreign Office – found out that the Thai Ambassador was a former officer in the German army who had served in occupied France during the war, the French government requested for his immediate recall. [8]

It is ironic that the country he so much admired should reject him just as he was settling into a successful appointment at 8 Rue Greuze, the historic site of one of Siam's oldest diplomatic missions.

Vicha Dhitavadhna's military career was on the wrong side of history. Arguably the nation's ablest soldier, he was continuously passed over and never made general. Yet he continued to serve his country with honour and ended his courageous journey as Thai Ambassador to Denmark before passing away in 1981.

---

8 As related to Prof. Woraphat Arthayukti by Foreign Minister Chatichai Choonhavan.

# BOONPONG SIRIVEJJAPAN
# 1906 – 1982

## Siamese trader on the River Kwae

***Previous page:*** *The Bridge on the River Kwae was destroyed several times by Allied bombing missions between 1943 and 1945.*

***Above:*** *Boonpong accommodating a Japanese officer in his store, with Panee on the right, in 1943.*

# 10
# The Merchant of V.

Thirteen-year-old Panee Sirivejjapan strolled calmly past the Japanese guardhouse into the Tha Makham[1] prisoners-of-war camp in Thailand's Kanchanaburi province. The guard smiled in recognition and Panee smiled back sweetly. She was one of only a few Siamese who could go in and out of the prison camps along the River Kwae[2] without being searched.

*"Kyo wa gokigen ikadadesuka, Panee San*. How are you today?" the guard asked her. "I'm very well, Keicho San," Panee replied politely in perfect Japanese.[3]

Panee was bright-eyed, and unlike her gangling teenage friends, straight-backed and slender. She had done well at school but the Second World War had interrupted her education. At school they didn't teach her how to be street-smart. Neither did they tell her that she had a natural gift for languages – so she was quickly able to learn Japanese. Least of all did her teachers tell her that she not only had the instinctive intelligence that goes with her sex, but an inquisitive mind as well. She was also a pretty girl and she charmed everyone with her good looks. Concealed behind her innocent face and demeanour was also a determination to do the right thing, and

---

1 What the POWs mispronounced as Tamarkan.
2 Also mispronounced and miswritten as Kwai.
3 Keicho, Japanese for rank of lance corporal.

what she was now learning to do in the real world – an adult world at war – was to become useful to the Allied cause. Panee was a secret courier agent.

Five British prisoners-of-war (POWs) unloaded several large panniers of fresh food from the river barge and, following Panee up the muddy river embankment, carried the heavy cargo on their backs to the prison camp's cookhouse. For the prisoners and the Japanese soldiers, Panee's visit appeared to be a routine delivery of provisions to the camp. But for Panee and Colonel Philip Toosey, the British officer in charge of supervising the prisoners who were building the bridge on the River Kwae, Panee's visit was far from routine. Hidden under Panee's clothing were pieces of paper that she would smuggle in and out of the camp, containing intelligence reports that could change the course of the war. Sometimes she would secretly carry torch batteries into the camp so that the prisoners could operate a hidden wireless receiver. Other times, she would "carelessly" leave an empty Ovaltine can containing a map or other small item at a pre-arranged location.

On this visit, Colonel Toosey gave Panee a tiny piece of paper shaped into a small triangle that fitted neatly into the folds of her sarong and pinpointed the exact location of the bridge. Thanks to Panee's help, the bridge was targeted accurately and bombed by Allied aircraft several times during the war.[4] How did such a young girl become involved in such a dangerous operation?

Panee's father was Boonpong Sirivejjapan. Boonpong was born in 1906 in Kanburi, as Kanchanaburi was called back then, and one of its leading citizens. Son of the town's only doctor, he preferred the hustle and bustle of commerce and decided not to follow in his father's footsteps after graduating from the prestigious Suan Khularb College in Bangkok. Instead he set up business as a retail merchant

---

4 All the characters and events in the film *The Bridge on the River Kwai* were pure fiction. British engineers did not build the bridge under the command of Col. Nicholson (played by Alec Guinness) nor was the bridge blown up by Force 136 on the ground.

in a three storied shop-house, called Boonpong & Brothers, that still stands today on Phak Praek Road, Kanburi's main street. He was the town's mayor for several years in the 1930s. By 1940 he had expanded his retail business to a successful wholesale operation and set up a buying agency in Bangkok.

Before the Second World War, Kanburi was a sleepy river town with less than 2800 residents. By June 1942, the victorious Japanese were planning to build a 415-kilometre-long railway from Siam to Burma, starting at Kanburi, in preparation for an invasion of India. Japanese engineers, employing conventional building contractors, had originally planned to complete the railway line in five years.

After the surrender of the British Commonwealth troops to the Japanese in February 1942, and the defeat of the Dutch East Indies the following month, Changi prison in Singapore became the largest POW camp in the Asia-Pacific region, holding some 120,000 men. When the Imperial High Command realized they could use Australian, British and Dutch POWs, and a hundred thousand Chinese, Indian, Javanese, Malay and Tamil coolies from the European colonies, they aimed to complete construction in half the time. Between November 1942 and October 1943 about half the denizens of Changi were brought to Siam and many to Kanburi. They were to become slave labourers on the construction of what was to become known as the "Death Railway".

After the Japanese had bought land for a cemetery for their dead from Boonpong's family up-river in Chong Kai,[5] Boonpong was able to get a contract to supply food and groceries to the prison camp canteens. During this time, Boonpong & Brothers was "a clutter with an amazing range of goods and clouds of spicy aromas".[6] The store backed on to the river and its yards ran down to the banks where a delivery barge was moored. Next to Boonpong's store was a Japanese

5 Chong Kai was renamed Chungkai by the POWs.
6 *Hellfire,* Cameron Forbes, Macmillan, 2005.

restaurant, where Korean "comfort women" were housed on the upper floors. Boonpong's establishment was the most frequented address in town by the Japanese occupying forces, and amazingly, the centre of a clandestine operation against them.

A Japanese sergeant was viciously chopping up a bunch of bananas into little pieces with his samurai sword and aggressively grinding them into the dusty earth with the heel of his boot. He angrily shouted at the Siamese passenger[7] who had tossed the bananas from the stationary Bangkok-bound train to a hungry group of British prisoners-of-war forced to march under the punishing sun. The prisoners were totally naked and their emaciated bodies were barely covered by a small piece of loincloth. Their skins were burned to a bright red texture and their feet were raw and bloody.

Boonpong was on his way to Bangkok and looked at this scene with disgust. He had never witnessed such inhuman behaviour. The prisoners were treated even worse than animals. Although he was not part of the growing anti-Japanese resistance movement, he decided there and then that he was not going to complacently stand by and ignore what was happening in his province. He'd seen that the prisoners were desperately in need of food and medicines. He'd also heard that they were tortured and starved, and plagued with malaria, dysentery, beriberi, pellagra and the stinking tropical ulcers that wasted their legs to the bone. As a prominent merchant in Kanburi, he would continue to pretend to collaborate with the Japanese. He was already a major supplier to the occupying forces in charge of the prison camps along the River Kwae, and he now needed to find a suitable way to get to the prisoners stealthily and help them obtain essential food and medicines.

7 This writer's aunt.

His first task was to establish contact with the secret "V"[8] organisation. He'd learned about the "V" group, a clandestine organisation operating out of Bangkok that helped the POWs in the River Kwae camps, from Corporal "Johnny" Johnson. Johnny was a Thai-speaking soldier who once worked with the Anglo-Siam Corporation in Bangkok and did business with Boonpong before the war. They renewed their relationship when they met again in early 1943 when Boonpong was making a delivery of groceries at the Chong Kai camp where Johnson was a prisoner. He recognised Boonpong right away and asked him if he could get medicine for men dying of diphtheria. It was a dangerous request for both parties. For Johnson, it was a test – he was not sure whether Boonpong could be trusted. For Boonpong, it was even more dangerous. Helping prisoners-of-war was punishable by death.

Boonpong was a most unlikely hero. He was small, round-faced, bespectacled and tended on the podgy side. Like many Siamese, he was neat and tidy, and wore starched white shirts. His trousers were always well-pressed. He had learned how to read and write English at school and communicated well in that language. Except for the occasional beer, he didn't drink alcohol and he never smoked. He was a clean living person with high moral standards. A soft-spoken man, he was also extremely polite and admired this quality in others. In an interview with the *Bangkok Post* in 1967 he said that, "most Thais see Europeans as polite and were very disturbed to see them tortured by the Japanese" who were "so hard and impolite. For this reason many tried to help the POWs."

"When my friend Mr. Johnson asked me for help, how could I refuse?" Boonpong recalled.

8 Originally "V" was the acronym for "voluntary". As the tide of war began to change, so did the meaning of the acronym to "victory".

Unlike captured Allied prisoners in Japanese POW camps, who suffered great brutality and torture at the hands of their cruel captors, British civilian internees in Bangkok were under the control of the Siamese authorities, and were allowed relative freedom within the Ta Prachan camp in the compound of Thammasat University, provided they confined their activities to social, non-military matters. They were even allowed to listen to the radio, provided it was kept out of sight.

Two of them, former employees of British trading houses before the war, Kenneth Gairdner and Peter Heath, had started the clandestine "V" organisation.[9] Gairdner's Siamese wife Millie and his Chinese employee K.S. Hong were able to travel to Kanburi and make direct contact with the POW officers. A chain of communication between the camps along the river with the "V" organisation was gradually established. Quite soon afterwards small packets of drugs and money started to reach the prisoners and intelligence reports about conditions in the camps and enemy troop movements along the River Kwae slowly began to filter through to Allied headquarters in India.

Heath and Gairdner later disagreed on matters of security and Heath branched out on his own, founding a new aid organization with French, Danish and Swiss nationals in Bangkok. Being a Catholic, he also engaged the help of Italian priests, who helped collect money from European sympathizers. Fortunately, both organizations used the letter "V" as their code name.

Although the two-way traffic of medicines and intelligence reports was well managed by the "V" organization, it was slow and sporadic. The "V" organizers were not able to find a reliable merchant in town through whom goods could secretly be passed into the camps on a more regular basis. It was only after Boonpong's credentials were accepted by both the "V" organization and senior British and Australian officers, that the deliveries of essential drugs hidden

---

9 Incredibly, out of four hundred and fifty British, American and Dutch internees, only a handful knew of the "V" organization.

in ration bags of tapioca and in baskets of cabbages and tobacco increased from less than once a fortnight to as much as twice a week.

Boonpong's daughter Panee would always accompany her father on his tours to the camps, and while the Japanese guards were flirting with her, Boonpong would approach the Allied officer in charge to either inform him on the latest news of the war or obtain intelligence reports on the progress of the railway's construction, as well as to receive a new shopping list of essential medicines. When Boonpong was not able to leave his store, Panee was sent out on her own.

The handover of intelligence information and written requests for medicines at the camp sites right there in the open under the very noses of the Japanese soldiers was risky business. Boonpong did not want to linger too long with the Allied officers to avoid arousing suspicion, and on several occasions when they got too close, they were told to break up their "meeting" and "move on".

At the Ban Kao camp near Wang Po, an over-vigilant Japanese guard once decided that Boonpong and Captain Angier, the British officer in charge of the canteen, were getting too familiar with each other and hauled them off to the prison headquarters for interrogation. He accused them of speaking "in secret" and that a letter had passed between them. Their pockets were searched but nothing was found. The guard was embarrassed and another Japanese soldier spoke up for them, proclaiming their innocence. There were many other close calls and Boonpong was pulled in for questioning on two other occasions. But he was always able to extricate himself.

Over time, number 56 Phak Praek Road became the unofficial branch office of the "V" organisation in Kanburi. Almost every clandestine undertaking between the prison camps and the "V" operatives in Bangkok were channelled through Boonpong's store. Everyone along the chain took extraordinary risks but it was the lives of Boonpong's family that were put on the line everyday. His wife had forced herself to be civil to the Japanese when they came to the store, to make sure that no one would suspect any member of the Boonpong family of helping the prisoners. His daughter was to be used as a decoy for more than two years, a long time for a young girl to take part in such a dangerous game.

Long before Boonpong had joined the "V" organization, Japanese soldiers made regular visits to the store – and to the restaurant next door. Panee helped her parents as a sales assistant and started to learn the language of her new customers. At first, Panee liked the Japanese soldiers. They were kind and always brought her little gifts. She had a weakness for colourful trinkets and little key chains. Even after the war, she loved to collect Rising Sun badges, penny pieces and war medals.

When young Japanese soldiers – those who did not frequent the establishment next door – came to the shop to order new provisions for the camp, they really came just to be with Panee. It was always the same excuse. They simply wanted to practice their Siamese language skills. She was thrilled. She'd never been courted before and she found their attentions flattering. She enjoyed their innocent flirtations and found the boys attractive, with their smooth pale complexions and smart military uniforms. Private Kanaya even proposed marriage and invited her to meet his parents, rice farmers from Kyushu, in southern Japan. But she preferred Corporal Miyoshi, who was taller and better looking, and regaled her with amusing Japanese folk stories. He was the charmer of the two.

But these romantic episodes were not to last. Panee instinctively knew that it was not her job to get involved. Her job was to flirt and keep the Japanese guards at bay while the Allied officers conducted their business in secret with her father, slipping him their special shopping lists of medicines. In the beginning, she even felt guilty for betraying her new Japanese friends, but then she saw for herself the extent of their cruelty that they wrought on their prisoners.

Two experiences in particular would ultimately steel her against the Japanese. One day, Panee saw eight wretched POWs standing on parade, covered only in their loin cloths, and virtually stark naked in the boiling midday sun. When one of them fell to the ground, he was kicked by a Japanese soldier and forced back on his feet. But it was too late. He was already dead. She found out that they had been punished for attempting to escape. Forced to stand in place since 6 a.m. that morning, they were expected to continue to stand there for another 24 hours. If they failed to admit their guilt, they would be executed.

On another occasion, she saw an ill prisoner working on the bridge construction, so weak that he was not able to do his job properly. He was pushed off the scaffolding into the river below to his death.

Boonpong's fame as the "canteen man" spread upriver and he was always well received by the malnourished prisoners who were weak from overwork and desperately hungry. The sight of his barge on the river gave them hope that maybe they were not going to starve to death after all, although many did. The abler ones eagerly ran down the embankment to the ramshackle wooden landing to unload the panniers off the barge and carry them back to the cookhouse. At certain times of the year, especially during the height of the monsoon when the river was unnavigable, a smiling Boonpong would arrive with his deliveries by elephant.

On one occasion Boonpong presented himself to the Japanese guardhouse at Wampo and brazenly asked to see Captain Pavillard, the camp's senior British officer. This is how Pavillard described the incident: "The Japanese could not imagine how a well dressed Siamese civilian knew my name or the fact that I was at Wampo; they seemed very angry. But Boonpong saved the situation by saying that he had ten thousand duck eggs for sale; he gave each guard a dozen eggs, and after that it was a very simple matter to arrange with the administration that he would sell the rest of them to us at five cents each."[10]

---

10 *Bamboo Doctor,* Capt. Stanley Pavillard, London, Macmillan, 1960.

The quality of Boonpong's produce was always good and "his prices were always the lowest and his profits the slightest."[11] Boonpong's reputation for honesty was legendary. In the prison camps there were too many unscrupulous soldiers who cheated their fellow prisoners. In one case, a British colonel had bought pound notes at six baht apiece and sold them on the open market at thirty. With the profits he cashed cheques for his fellow officers at the rate of one dollar to the pound. He bought special food delicacies and sold them to hungry prisoners at exorbitantly high prices.

Boonpong noticed that not all the officers were supportive of their men. Some junior officers were more concerned with their own survival and were totally disinterested in the welfare of their unit. One Denys Peek, an Australian private who spent three years on the railway and refused to give in and die, referred to some of his senior officers as "a mass of layabouts" who were "an invisible presence" in the camps.[12] It is interesting to note that the majority of soldiers buried at the Kanchanaburi War Cemetery are conscripts, with very few officers laying beside them. On the other hand, the courageous British and Australian doctors and surgeons bravely fought on to combat disease and alleviate suffering. They endured the beatings and torture by their Japanese and Korean guards and defied their orders for the sick and wounded to work on the line.

Nearly a quarter of all the POWs who were forced to work on the railway died or were killed. But many more would have died had it not been for the supply of essential drugs and medical supplies secretly hidden in Boonpong's food deliveries. To surgeons like Lt. Colonel Edward "Weary" Dunlop (who was the commander of the Australian POWs), Dr. Robert Hardie and Captain Stanley Pavillard (both British medical officers from Malaya) who saved countless lives by performing incredibly difficult operations using surgical instruments crudely

11 *Railroad of Death,* J. Coast, London, Commodore Press, 1946.
12 *One Fourteenth of an Elephant,* Ian Denys Peek, Macmillan, 2003.

made from scrap metal under the most trying conditions in the jungle, Boonpong was more than "the canteen man". He was their reliable and trustworthy connection with the outside world.

Captain R.R. Fewell, an ex POW serving The Suffolk Regiment, gratefully remembered Boonpong in his memoirs: "From the small town of Kanburi came our supply of drugs to combat the serious diseases, which were smuggled to us by the Thais such as Mr Boonpong. Many of us owed our lives to the resourcefulness of this Thai gentleman, who, if found out by the Japanese would surely have lost his head."

By March 1943, however, the tide of the war was starting to turn against the Japanese. After the American fleet's success at the Battle of Midway in the Pacific, the seas of the Gulf of Siam and the Indian Ocean were dominated by US submarines, making it impossible for the Japanese navy to supply their forces in Burma with fuel, armaments and materiel by sea. The only way to transport supplies and reinforcements to Burma was by railway – the Siam-Burma railway.

Thus, the Japanese Imperial Army ordered that the completion date of the railway be brought forward, from December to August 1943. At that time only twenty percent of the line had been completed. To meet the new deadline, another 19,000 POWs and tens of thousands of Asian coolie labourers were brought in, just in time for the heavy rains of the 1943 monsoon and the resulting cholera that came with it.

Over the next sixteen weeks the prisoners would hack their way through hundreds of kilometres of dense jungle, gouge passes through mountains of rock, build bridges and viaducts across steep river chasms, and move 20,000 cubic metres of muddy earth a day, using the most rudimentary tools, like picks, shovels and axes. They worked day and night for 30 hours at a stretch, and hundreds would die of disease and exhaustion along the way. It was during this period when this huge civil engineering project came to be known as the "Death Railway".

The biggest cutting through the rocky mountain was at Kannyu, a massive rock face 73 metres long and 25 metres high, that came to be known as "Hellfire Pass" because the prisoners were forced to work at night under the light from bonfires, oil lamps and the occasional generator, casting an eerie shadow on their bony, sweaty bodies and haggard faces. Many suffered from hallucinations, thinking that they were dead and already in hell.

As the lines of communication and transport between Kanburi and the upper reaches of the railway near the Three Pagodas Pass on the Burmese border became longer and longer, it became more difficult to deliver essential supplies, not just food and medicines, but building tools and materials as well. At this end of the line the working hours were at their longest and the work their heaviest. The Japanese soldiers on the railway were under pressure themselves to complete the project on time and every morning they would beat the sleeping prisoners with wet bamboo sticks and order them to start "worko speedo". "Light sick" prisoners, those who were suffering from malaria, dysentery and tropical ulcers, were considered fit enough to work and forced out of the wards to augment the "speedo" teams. A high-ranking Japanese staff officer in charge of the railway told a junior officer in the POW camp, "I don't care if they all die, so long as the railway is finished."[13] The completion of the railway resulted in one death for every railroad tie that was laid. Some 12,000 POWs and 30,000 Asian workers died.

Boonpong ended up working full-time for both "V" organisations and spending more time operating as an Allied agent than a provision supplier. He was now making fortnightly trips to Bangkok trying to cash the POWs' IOU cheques in the open market

---

13 *Prisoners of War in the Pacific: Japan's Policy,* Aiko Utsumi, translated by Gavin McCormack. *The Burma-Thailand Railway,* Silkworm Books, 1993.

for redemption after the war. The prisoners were more in need of money than ever before and Boonpong became their banker and pawn-broker. The POWs would entrust Boonpong with personal valuables, such as their gold rings, silver cigarette cases and watches, and if he was unable to redeem them, he would advance the cash himself. He kept a record of each item that was not pawned and they were diligently returned to their rightful owners in 1945. He would lend his own money to the prisoners to purchase food and clothing, certain that the British government would reimburse him. Boonpong was always out of pocket and after the war his firm was almost bankrupt.

Boonpong was also in touch with Herr Singenthaler, the Swiss Consul in Bangkok, and he was able to give a firsthand account to the Swiss unit of the "V" organization on the appalling conditions that were suffered by the POWs and the Japanese atrocities. The Swiss Red Cross knew that their medicines and parcels of food were sometimes intercepted and confiscated by the Japanese and resold to the POWs, clearly in breach of international law. A lot of the medicines also ended up on the black market. More often than not, Red Cross supplies were held in Japanese stores adjacent to the camps and put to their own use. The consul and Boonpong coordinated their efforts to ensure that future medicines arrived directly in the hands of the camp leaders.

The Japanese prison camp authorities had begun to notice Boonpong's frequent absences from his store. He was in Bangkok, walking from company to company, trying to sell the prisoners' cheques and IOUs, and pawn their valuables. Before the *kempeitai* – the Japanese secret police – could discover him, Mr. Tanner, a Swiss diplomat and one of the chief "V" organisers, advised Boonpong to return to Kanburi and took over the task himself. Boonpong said that he passed "everything to him – cheques, rings, diamonds, and so on, and the names of their owners. Everything centralized with Mr Tanner. It was necessary to be very strict about the accounting and a proper check on things. On occasion, this caused me a great worry."[14]

During his absences in Bangkok, Boonpong's wife Surat looked after the store, while Panee supervised the provisions on the barge and delivered them to the camps on her own. She had blossomed into a beautiful fifteen-year-old. More mature, she now became aware of the futility of war and no longer wanted to see her family in danger. For the first time, she was missing her school friends and young people of her own age. She had become a reluctant courier agent.

When the prisoners heard the faint sounds of aircraft engines in the distance, followed by the rumble of exploding bombs, they knew that the war was not going well for the Japanese. These Allied attacks were not the bombing sorties on the River Kwae of the past, but daily occurrences. This was followed by spreading rumours that two huge American bombs had devastated two Japanese cities.[15] When these reports were confirmed by the secret radios in the camps, the prisoners renewed their hopes for rescue.

But peace did not come to the POW camps right away. Until the Japanese received orders from their high command to surrender, the war was not over. After 3½ years in captivity, even the prisoners themselves were not able to believe that the war had ended. Many Japanese units at the end of the line ignored the Imperial command to surrender to the Allies and continued to fight on to the death. Incredibly, the prisoners were still forced to work on the railway. It was several weeks after the Japanese surrender before freedom came to some of the camps further up-river from Kanburi.

"War finish! War finish!" shouted Boonpong, as he cycled by

14 *Bangkok Post,* interview with Rafael Grant, 1967.

15 *The Bangkok Chronicle,* 7 August 1945, reported "Yesterday an American aircraft dropped a single bomb on the Japanese city of Hiroshima. The bomb, said to have been manufactured on a new principle, caused great destruction."

the Ta Makham camp several times, waving V signs in jubilation. It was 15 August 1945, the day after Japan accepted Allied terms for unconditional surrender.

The war was over, but for Boonpong a different sort of battle was yet to be fought. Only a few weeks later, someone tried to assassinate him. A lone gunman in a passing car shot him in front of his store. The bullets lodged in his left arm, left shoulder and left lung. There was a large hole in his chest where a bullet had emerged and spent itself. Captain Newell of Force 136 rushed Boonpong to the British Army hospital where he was given blood transfusions and a surgeon operated on the wounds. He received treatment at the hospital for several months and within a year Boonpong had put back the weight that he had lost during his recuperation and returned to his normal, cheerful self. His left hand though, was to bother him for the rest of his life. He could no longer hold a fork or spoon without trembling and he could never drive his car properly again without suffering excruciating pain in his wrist.

While he was confined to the hospital he was provided with maximum security and the British army supplied him with an armed escort wherever he went. On one occasion, his trusted fortune-teller told him that his life was not in danger and that he no longer required military protection. It took a lot of persuasion from his British friends to convince him otherwise and that he should never leave home without an armed escort. He carried a Luger pistol in his pocket for years afterwards.

It was an honour for British officers to serve on the platoon assigned to protect him. They were also well compensated in kind by Boonpong who rewarded his bodyguards with complementary massage and hairdressing services, the best meals in Bangkok, passes to all the best night clubs in town and free hotel accommodation wherever they went. When the soldiers insisted on paying, he would say something in Thai to the service staff at wherever they happened to be to the effect that they were his guests, and that was that.

Nearly 70 years have passed and Boonpong's descendants would prefer to lay the assassination attempt to rest, and put it simply down to jealousy. No one knows who was responsible. Certainly, the citizens of Kanburi were proud of him, but there must have been some envious elements in town, particularly other wholesalers, who may have lost out when Boonpong became the main supplier to the camps.

And why was Boonpong suddenly treated as some kind of celebrity by the Allies after the Japanese capitulated, they must have wondered? Nobody in Kanburi were aware of his heroic "V" activities. Only a handful of Allied officers knew of Boonpong's involvement, mainly camp commandants and senior medical officers who dealt with him directly. The rank and file of the POWs did not learn of Boonpong's role until well after the war.

There were other more sinister and politically motivated theories about the attempt on Boonpong's life. One was that there was a conspiracy to assassinate him by the Thai authorities or police. To those Thai officials who had collaborated with the Japanese, Boonpong may have been guilty of knowing just a little bit too much. But Boonpong was never involved politically and his acts of kindness to the prisoners were purely humanitarian. In an interview with *Newsweek* in 1973, Boonpong recalled with sadness: "I would see fourteen or fifteen prisoners die in the camps each day, but I was almost helpless. It was terrible."

Or was it part of an anti-Chinese backlash that was taking place in 1945? After all, Boonpong's family *did* descend from the Chinese, although his mother was Thai. Most successful merchants were of Chinese descent, although he never thought about his Chinese origins very much. He went to an elite Thai school, he did not know how to speak Chinese, and he never celebrated Chinese New Year.

We may never know the motive behind the assassination attempt. But at least his life was never threatened again. Perhaps it was simply due to the absence of law and order at a time when the country was in a state of uncertainty, like many countries that were emerging from the vicissitudes of war.

Boonpong now went back to what he wanted to do most, and that was to be a successful businessman. But the war had not made him rich. Instead, he found himself short of cash. He contacted the British and Australian governments for reimbursement for the monies he had advanced to the prisoners. Both governments disclaimed responsibility on the grounds that members of the "V" organization had no authority to raise funds on the prisoners' behalf and neither did the commanding officers of the prison camps have the authority to sign for money and goods on behalf of their respective governments. His "battle" to recover the money that was owed to him lasted longer than his "battle" with the Japanese. In the end he received partial payment, but not quite enough to cover all his expenses. The Australian government reluctantly granted him a sum of £1,000 as recompense. Lt. Jack Leemon, author of *War Graves Digger,* wrote: "I would never have run the risks he ran for a hundred times that miserable sum."[16] As for the money he lent to the prisoners, he hardly got any of it back.

By 1948 Boonpong was heavily in debt. The bus company that he had launched was in deep financial trouble. When three senior British officers who had been involved with the "V" scheme in 1943 learned about Boonpong's financial difficulties, they got in touch with the British National Federation of Far Eastern Prisoners of War in Britain and together they wrote a letter of appeal to all the ex-POWs asking them for a contribution to help out "this foreign trader who risked his life and did so much to help us."[17] A total of £38,000[18] was raised and transferred to Boonpong. His bus company was saved.

---

16 *War Graves Digger,* Jack Leemon, 2010.
17 *The Colonel of Tamarkan,* Julie Summers, Simon & Schuster, 2005.
18 Three million baht at the rate of exchange in 1950.

The British government awarded Boonpong the George Cross Medal for Courage and an MBE for his services and bravery. The Dutch royal family made him an Officer of the Order of Orange-Nassau. In 1972, Boonpong was invited by Queen Elizabeth and Prince Philip to a reception on board the Royal Yacht *Brittania* during Their Majesties State Visit to Thailand. In 1986, the Dunlop-Boonpong Exchange Fellowship program was created in his honour to grant scholarships to help young Thai surgeons study in Australia. In a commemoration ceremony in April 1994, the Australian Prime Minister, Paul Keating, laid a wreath at the Kanchanaburi War Cemetery and mentioned in a speech that "thousands of Allied prisoners survived captivity here because many heroic Thais like Boonpong gave Dunlop and other doctors invaluable food and medical supplies." In 1998, Australian Prime Minister John Howard, awarded Boonpong's descendants a Certificate of Honour from the government and people of Australia.

*The Bridge on the River Kwai,* a popular and award-winning Hollywood film released in 1957, was an inaccurate and fictionalized account of the construction (and destruction) of the bridge. The dramatic film totally obscured the real events that Boonpong had witnessed on the Death Railway. Before he died in 1982, he said that he had never seen the film because, in his own words, "I am trying to forget and trying to forgive."

# HIS ROYAL HIGHNESS PRINCE BIRABONGSE BHANUBANDH

a.k.a. B. Bira

1914 – 1985

The Prince of Speed

***Previous page:*** *Prince Bira's trusted Hanuman, his ERA racing car, in 1937. Bira always wore lensed goggles on the track.*

***Above:*** *Prince Bira married Chelita at the Royal Thai Embassy in Paris in 1951.*

# 11

# The Three Lives of a Champion

## First Life: Racing Champion

Prince Bira gripped the wheel of his trusted English Racing Automobile six-cylinder supercharged racing car "Romulus" as it reached one hundred and twenty miles (192km) an hour. Each piston of his E.R.A.'s screaming engine was turning at more than eight thousand revolutions per minute, vibrating his whole body, and his pulse had spiked to 180 beats per minute. Maintaining the same speed, he shifted down to third and confidently took a sharp corner. The g-force was so great that every time he changed gears and accelerated, his body was smashed a second later into the back of his seat followed by what seemed like the insides of his body.[1] A split second in a Grand Prix racing lap can seem like an eternity, the difference between winning and losing.

His Royal Highness Prince Birabongse Bhanutej Bhanubandh, or B. Bira as he was known on the circuit, was participating in the

1 G-force is the outside force that pushes hard on the body three or four times greater than the force of gravity. Test pilots and Formula One drivers have to contend with g-force when speeds of one hundred miles an hour and more are reached in a few seconds. Today's Formula One (F-1) drivers' necks are securely harnessed to the back of the cockpit's seat so that the head is no longer pushed by g-force pressure.

Coupe du Prince Rainier de Monaco championship, and he still had 40 laps to go. At one hundred miles, the Monaco Circuit was narrow and twisty, and considered one of the most challenging in Europe. At the top of the hill of the Casino de Monte Carlo, Bira narrowly avoided a collision of Maseratis and E.R.A.s by deftly negotiating a gap of pavement three yards wide and safely carved a path through the pile-up. Twenty laps later he was in second place. Only Tomasso Tenni's Maserati was ahead by two or three seconds per lap. On the 30th lap Tenni was given the "faster" signal from the pit but his car started to spin uncontrollably.

This was the opportunity that Bira had been waiting for. He shifted down to second and opened up the throttle. After overtaking Tenni's Maserati, he shifted back and found himself in first position. In a letter after the race to his fiancée Ceril he told her how proud he was of his car. "Romulus was running like an angel with wings," he wrote. Indeed, it was a momentous day for the Siamese prince. At only 22 years of age, he had won the world's most important small car race.

It is often assumed that a footballer or a tennis player, on his feet for the entire match, is in much better physical condition than a racing driver who is "comfortably" seated throughout the race. But such a comparison ignores the physical strain the driver is under, so great that the heart, the lungs and the muscles must work overtime under extreme pressure for the duration of a two- to three-hour race. On average a racing driver changes gears two thousand five hundred times in one hour,[2] allowing no time for the body to rest.

But physical endurance is only half the story. First, the driver must memorize the circuit, and consider the surface and the length of the *piste* that has to be negotiated before each hairpin bend. Inside the car, at average speeds of one hundred miles an hour, the

2 In Bira's day, gears were floor-mounted and shifting was a tiring process. Today's F-1 cars have paddle gears on the steering wheel, which are much easier to manipulate.

brain must process new information like a computer. Strategic, split-second decisions must be made continuously – when to shift, when to brake and when to accelerate. The driver also needs to calculate overtaking points well in advance and keep an eye on the signals coming from his pit manager for any number of strategic or technical reasons.[3] During a pit-stop, each second is critical. In those days, a change of tyres that took more than one hundred seconds could cost the driver his victory. The engine oil would be at boiling point and combustion would be put under such fierce pressure that twelve new spark plugs were required every five laps.[4] On the other hand, on a rainy day, wet spark plugs could cause the car to stall and the race would be lost.

Time, machine and terrain, these then, were the three disciplines that a Grand Prix driver had to master all at once. The price for mistakes was not simply a poor placing. A bad mental error could be punishable by death. Indeed, Prince Bira always bore in mind the famous French racing maxim: "It takes all of man's ingenuity and all of man's courage to produce and race the perfect machine. Thanks to her, a man can ride to victory. Thanks to her too, he can also ride to his death."

It is no wonder then, that racing drivers have a devil-may-care attitude towards life. Prince Birabongse Bhanudej was no exception. But Prince Bira, as we shall see, was to be blessed with three lives – as a driver, a romantic and a yachtsman – and he threw his heart into all three. But it was his racing championship years from 1935 to 1955 that were certainly his most illustrious.

In his twenty-year racing career, Bira competed on almost every single circuit in Europe and participated in hundreds of

3 To confuse the other contestants, the signals that Bira received from his pit manager were written in Thai letters.

4 Electronic injection on F-1 machines now obviates the need for spark plugs.

championships. As he was achieving international fame in the last years before the Second World War, he had participated in 68 long-distance events, out of which he won 20, placed second 14 times and third 5 times. In 1936 he won the JCC International Trophy and three International Car Races, at Monaco (as described above), at Peronne and at Albi, in France. In 1937 he won the Campbell Trophy, the Light Car Race at the Isle of Man, the London Grand Prix, the 12-hour Race at Donnington Park and the Imperial Trophy. In 1938 he won seven major races, including the Coronation Trophy, the Light Car Race at Cork, the Nuffield Trophy, the BRDC (British Racing Driver's Club) Road Race, the Siam Trophy and, once again, the Campbell Trophy and the London Grand Prix. He was the first driver in Britain to be awarded the prestigious BRDC Road Racing Gold Star three years in succession, in 1936, 1937, and 1938. He was also the first driver to cover a lap of Dublin's Phoenix Park Circuit at over 100 mph. His particular strength was the rare ability to maintain the exact lap time, lap after lap.

Unlike other drivers, employed by a car manufacturer's "works team" to race their new models and promote their marques, Bira had entered these races as the representative of the privately run and independent White Mouse team, founded and sponsored by his cousin Prince Chula Chakrabongse, grandson of King Chulalongkorn, Rama V.

In 1935, having watched Bira successfully drive a Riley Imp and an MG Magnette in a number of short handicap races at Brooklands, a 2.75-mile racing circuit near Weybridge in Surrey, England, Prince Chula purchased an E.R.A. car for Bira's 21st birthday. Prince Chula became Bira's manager, and together they would make motor-racing history, with three E.R.A. cars named Romulus, Remus and Hanuman, all of which they painted hyacinth blue, or "Bira Blue" as it became known.[5]

---

5 The blue colour was Chula's mother's favourite colour.

One event stood out in Bira's memory[6] as the best race of his career. The RAC International Light Car Race at the Isle of Man circuit was the main 1500cc race held in Great Britain and therefore considered the most important British race in 1937. The track was wet and slippery. Just minutes before the race began, a storm brought down sheets of torrential rain onto the circuit. As he looked up into the sky, Bira was reminded of the tropical rain of Siam, and he suddenly felt confidently at home.

During the race, sprays of water blurred his vision and he had to continuously wipe his wet goggles, a difficult task considering both his hands were supposed to be in control of the car. Still, Bira was able to gain an early lead on Raymond Mays and Pat Fairfield, both famous British drivers in their "works" E.R.A.s, and also the European champions Baron de Graffenreid and Luigi Villoresi in their "works" Maseratis.

By lap 31, however, Bira found himself in third place. Through sheer determination he was able to track his opponents like a hound until an opportunity presented itself. With help from Prince Chula's precise signals from the pit, he was ultimately able to control both his skidding car over the glassy road surface, as well as his nerves. The next day *The Times* wrote that, "Bira drove a superb race throughout. He thoroughly deserved his victory, having driven a grand race under such very difficult conditions."

Such competitions in all sports would soon be interrupted throughout Europe when the Second World War broke out in 1939, temporarily putting an end to Bira's racing career. During the war, Bira became a Free Thai and volunteered to become a pilot for the RAF. Because he was short-sighted – he'd always worn lensed-goggles for racing – he was, to his chagrin, turned down. Instead, he joined the Air Training Corps and became a gliding instructor with

---

6 As related in *"Bits and Pieces Being Motor Racing Recollections of 'B. Bira'"*, GT Foulis & Co Ltd, 1972.

the rank of lieutenant at the St Merryn Royal Naval Air Station, North Cornwall, and was eventually promoted to running the gliding school there. He would retain a passion for gliding for the rest of his life.

After the war he returned to racing and in 1947 the prince had his closest brush with death.

It was a clear autumn's day at the Brno Circuit in Czechoslovakia and the race started well. In the very first lap three drivers suddenly left the track one after the other and ploughed through screaming spectators packed inside a hairpin bend. Four people died immediately and 54 were hurt. Soon after Giuseppe Farina's heavy Maserati came roaring up to another hairpin bend and as he began to corner, his car skidded and smashed through the concrete posts guarding the bend. More bodies piled up and as Bira reached the very same bend, he skidded, knocked down five concrete posts and plunged towards the crowd, but pulled up just in time.

The prince's leg was severely cut and he was losing blood rapidly. After he was bandaged up, he was rushed to a hospital in Prague. In the ambulance he begged his wife Ceril, who was with him at the time, to get him out of Czechoslovakia at any cost. Prince Bira had learned from his cousin Prince Chula, who was half Russian, that the Czar's entire family had been brutally murdered by the Bolsheviks decades before and Bira was terrified of remaining in communist Czechoslovakia. When Ceril told him that he needed serious medical attention and should remain in hospital for several days, he panicked. "Don't you see," he told her "they are taking me to a *communist* hospital, and I am a prince – think what they did to royalty during the revolution!"

Bira was more in fear for his life from the communist doctors than from the effect of his car accident. He reluctantly spent the night in hospital. The next day, Ceril drove him through the Iron Curtain to Austria.

Bira had four wins in 1947, but, in general, the newer competitive "works" cars from Maserati and Alfa Romeo had surpassed their beloved Romulus, Remus and Hanuman cars. After a series of losses in 1948, Bira almost gave up racing altogether, before joining a number of "works" teams. With Simca-Gordini he started to win again, at Rheims, the Isle of Man and Lausanne. By 1948 he became a regular on continental European circuits, and raced regularly at Pau, Monte Carlo, San Remo and Albi. In 1949 and 1950 he participated in a number of Argentine Grand Prix races. At the Mar del Plata Grand Prix in Argentina on 27 February, 1949, Juan Manuel Fangio, the greatest Formula 1 driver in the last century,[7] won both heats over several laps to take the aggregate win by almost a minute over Prince Bira. Bira was never able to beat Fangio. The second time he raced him, in April 1949, for the Grand Prix de Roussillon in Perpignan,[8] Bira again came second, and again he was beaten, this time by less than one second. Between 1950 and 1954 he took part in 19 world championship Grand Prix events. He came in second in the Swiss Grand Prix in 1950 and fourth in the French Grand Prix in 1954. In that year, he made his most spectacular post-war victory with a Maserati 250F at the Grand Prix des Frontieres on the Chimay road circuit in Belgium.

In January 1955, he won the New Zealand Grand Prix at Ardmore then promptly retired. "I woke up the next morning and said to myself, well, what are we doing here? Cups, girls, cars... maybe you're dead the next day. And I quit."

Bira was 41 years old.

## Second Life: The Romantic

Throughout his racing career, a pretty English girl was not only Prince Bira's lover and wife but also part of his pit crew. Her name

---

7 In 2007, Michael Schumacher became the first race driver to beat Fangio's record of five F-1 World Driver Championship titles.

8 The very same town where Colonel Vicha was posted with the German army in 1943. (See Chapter 9).

was Ceril Heycock.[9] They first met during drawing classes at the Byam Shaw School of Art in London in 1934 when Bira was 20 and Ceril 17, just before Bira started racing. Bira, who was studying to be a sculptor, fell head over heels in love with her, and three weeks later he proposed. Ceril's parents, however, thought she was far too young to go out with him without a chaperone, let alone get married, so they told her that if she could wait three years until she was 21 and still felt the same about Bira, they would not stand in her way. In 1934, marrying a person of a different race, for both Bira and Ceril, was a serious matter, and even more so for Bira, who was a high-ranking Siamese prince.[10]

Bira hadn't been back to Siam in 13 years,[11] so Prince Chula, his racing manager as well as his guardian, advised him to return for a short visit and think things over. Chula also encouraged him to meet some Siamese girls and perhaps even get over this infatuation. But Bira's visit to Siam had the opposite effect. He wrote to Ceril almost every day, calling her "my darlingest future wife", and missed her terribly.

When he had asked him for her hand in 1934, Bira told Ceril's father that sculpture was his work and that car racing was his hobby, but the reverse ended up being true. Bira's racing career was taking off and Ceril attended many of the races, helping Chula record lap times, and learning about professional pit management. In time Ceril became an asset to the team. Keeping the lap chart that recorded the position of all the cars in the race as well as their lap times was not an easy task, especially when two or three cars came roaring past at the

---

9 Ceril's life with Bira is from her poignant memoirs: *The Prince & I,* Princess Ceril Birabongse, Veloce Publishing, 1992

10 Prince Bira was a grandson of King Mongut (Rama IV) who reigned from 1851 to 1868. He had to receive permission from the Siamese Council of Regency to get married and for Ceril to be accepted as a Siamese princess with the title of Mom (Princess).

11 Bira had always felt like an orphan, having lost his mother when he was 4 and his father when he was 14. When Prince Chula became his legal guardian when he was still at Eton school, he had no reason to return to Siam. Besides the sea voyage home in those days took a month.

same time, nor in wet weather when a blinding spray made it difficult to identify the car. Ceril quickly learned at an early age what it would be like to live with a racing driver. After three years the infatuation had developed into true love. Four years after they met, on 12 January, 1938, they were married at the Siamese Legation in London,[12] and for the next twenty years, Ceril was to be at Bira's side at almost every race.

But first she had to learn how to be the wife of a Siamese prince. In November 1938, Bira and Ceril, together with Chula and his new English bride Lisba, decided to return to Siam to see whether their respective wives could be happy there. The first few weeks of official parties and ceremonial activities expected from the two royal couples were hectic. Both Ceril and Lisba were overwhelmed by the crowds that came out to greet them wherever they went. They became the main event of the season and the foursome were the most talked about couples in Siam. Chula had not only been the White Mouse team manager and Bira's mentor, he was also a famous writer and broadcaster. But it was Bira who drew the crowds. Everywhere he went he was greeted with enthusiasm and surrounded by adoring fans. Siamese women wore dresses in Bira Blue colours, and had it not been for Ceril's presence, they would have unabashedly thrown themselves at him.

Bira took it all in with modesty and without affectation. Ceril was happy for him and never showed any signs of jealousy. On the contrary, she loved Siam and it took her very little time and effort to get used to the court customs, the new culture, and even the weather. She comported herself well in court and Bira's family and senior members of the royal household soon came to love and respect her. She had only one complaint. Even away from formal activities at the palace, she had almost no privacy; in her own room there were always two or three maids in attendance. Most of all, she wanted

12 The writer's father was present at the wedding ceremony.

to be alone with Bira. Bira himself was not fond of the interminable receptions and formal dinners that he had to attend, and the couple eventually decided to escape from Chula and Lisba and the serious life they were living in Bangkok.

Chula was concerned about the country's political situation at the time and was forever meeting important people. Bira was totally apolitical and wanted to play golf or sail. He complained to Ceril that since his return to Siam he never had time to sculpt. In the end, they fled to Hua Hin where Chula's uncle had a beach house, and this was where Ceril was at her happiest. In a letter home, her description was of a Hua Hin that was a far cry from today's crowded beach resort:

"There are miles and miles of white sand and wonderful shells. The place is just a little fishing village. The country there is a little like Connemara in Ireland, with a touch of Biarritz: surf bathing with huge waves. The house is right on the beach with a large garden and is built off the ground on white pillars."

Each time they returned to Bangkok by train to attend yet another round of official functions they could not decline, Ceril was understandably sad.

In April 1939, they returned to England. Ceril was convinced that she could well live the rest of her life in Siam, and Bira was happy that their visit to Siam had proven that they could love each other wherever they went. Ceril had learned how to be the wife of a Siamese prince, while Chula had taught her how to be the wife of a racing driver. What she was totally unprepared for, however, was to be the wife of an incurable romantic. Bira was to fall in love again… and again.

The ensuing war years were not easy. When Siam was forced into an alliance with Japan, all the Siamese residents in Britain received a letter from the Siamese Legation on 14 July 1942, instructing them to return home. Like this writer's father, Bira and Chula chose not to return to Siam and they were immediately classified as enemy aliens. For a short while they suffered the indignity of being under the scrutiny of the British Home Office. Both Ceril and Lisba had become Siamese citizens through their marriage and ironically they too came under the same restrictions. When Bira's beloved radio set was confiscated by the local police, he immediately rang up Sir Anthony Eden, the Foreign Secretary, to complain, and, to his surprise, got through to him. The next day his radio was returned and after the princes became Free Thais they were no longer bothered by the Home Office throughout the duration of the war.

Although Bira was to become a gliding enthusiast and the first flying trainee to obtain an "A" license from Marshall's Flying School immediately after the war, it was car racing that was his true passion. Chula had decided to leave the racing business, so Ceril faithfully took over as pit manager. They were now together for longer periods than they had ever been in the past and although they led an exciting life together, Bira was starting to have affairs with other women. They were beginning to emotionally drift apart and their differences became so serious that they no longer lived together after November 1949.

Celebrity is a major aphrodisiac and Bira received the attentions of young, immature women, who enjoyed having liaisons with famous people. During the war, he had forgotten what it was like being a racing champion and the object of adulation. Bira did not want a divorce and asked Ceril if he could be free to have affairs with anyone he fancied. She responded that "to have his cake and eat it too" wouldn't make anyone happy. In a touching letter to her on the 14 November 1949, he wrote: "Through many circumstances we came to where we are now, but I do feel that life has not ended for either of us. I have had a really happy time with you – what with racing and travels and so forth. You have been more tolerant and forgiving than anyone I know – and I love you for that. I am what I am today and deserve anything that comes along and fate will deal with me as she wants – but I should like to tell you that I have never loved anyone like you before or will ever again. Take care of our sweet memories."

A short while afterwards, in May 1950, they were divorced. Bira spent the next few months with grave self-doubts. He had met a young Argentinian girl of 24 named Chelita Howard in Buenos Aires that same year. She had moved in with him to his hotel and he wasn't quite sure whether he was in love with her or just obsessed with her sexually. She was attractive and vivacious and like many Argentinians, spoke excellent English. When he returned to England he brought her home with him.

Chelita felt that coming back to England reminded Bira too much of his young love with Ceril. They argued a lot on this point. Chelita's fears were well-grounded. Bira made a last-ditch attempt before the divorce decree became final and asked Ceril to return to him, in which case he was prepared to send Chelita packing, but it was too late. Ceril knew that Bira would not be totally faithful to her if they got back together again. So she said no. It was one of the saddest days in Bira's life. Yet they were to remain lifelong friends and in contact with each other until 1975.

Bira needed a change of scenery and moved to France. He bought Les Faunes, a small secluded villa on a hill above La Napoule with a beautiful view on the Mediterranean in Mandelieu, near Cannes where his sailing yacht was berthed. Ceril moved to Lake Garda in Italy to live with Bruno Tomasoni, captain of the Riva yacht club, who had long been in love with her. It wasn't long before Bira started "bursting in", as he put it, into Ceril's life in Italy, taking Chelita with him. Chelita was terrified that Bira would return to her, but Ceril assured the young Argentine that she was now happily settled in Italy with Bruno and there was no going back. Chelita complained to Ceril that Bira was difficult to live with and was showing no signs of marrying her. On top of it all she found out that he was being unfaithful to her. Ceril assured her that Bira was a man of his word, and if he said he was going to marry her, he would. On the 18 December 1951, they were married at the Thai Embassy in Paris.

By the end of 1952, Bira admitted that he'd had a series of rather disappointing racing seasons, so he decided to take a break for a while. He'd recently acquired a new twin-prop airplane, a Miles Gemini, and he was excited by the idea of becoming the first Siamese to fly single-handedly from England to Siam. In October he landed at Don Muang Airport with Chelita and their little terrier, Tich. The news had apparently gone ahead of their arrival and hundreds of admirers gave him a hero's welcome on the tarmac. To Bira's delight many young female fans were dolled up in Bira Blue and surrounded him for his autograph as if he was a movie star. Chelita was proud of her new husband's fame but was somewhat daunted by the adulation that he was receiving. It was her first day in Siam and already she wondered whether she was going to like living in this country. They stayed until April 1953.

Bira was now planning his comeback. He still wanted the fame and fortune that come with Grand Prix racing, but Chula was no longer his sponsor. One of Bira's missions on this visit to Siam was to find a new financier for his racing and now that Ceril was no longer there to help him on the circuit, he would also look around for a new pit manager. Chelita was a decorative companion, but hardly qualified to keep records of his lap times, let alone the lap times of other contestants. She did her best, but Bira was always comparing her with Ceril. She just didn't understand car racing. On the strength of her beauty and her enthusiasm, Chelita was popular and together they made a handsome couple. Indeed, Bira was frequently complemented on her looks by his friends. But it was the simple, even innocent things she would say that would annoy him, and he would openly show his frustration with her. And of course, he was continuously surrounded by beautiful Siamese girls, good for his ego but terribly bad for her morale. The physical chemistry between them, however, continued to be strong.

Driving back one day to join Chelita for lunch at Ta Tien, Chula's villa on the river in Bangkok where they were living, Bira noticed a water sports shop on Rajdamnern Avenue called Charn Brothers. In the window, displayed amongst the diving gear, flippers, rubber dinghies and other equipment, was a white pair of water skis. Bira parked in front of the shop and went inside to ask how much they cost. When he was told by the shopkeeper that they were lent to him to decorate his window by his friend Prasom Yuangtrakul and were not for sale, Bira immediately wanted to meet Prasom. Two days later they met at the shop and Bira invited him back to Ta Tien for a meal, where they hit it off immediately. Both keen sportsmen, they instructed Charn to order a new pair of skis from Europe, and after they arrived they went to Hua Hin together. Soon, Bira became a first-rate water skier, and even gave a public performance on the lake of Lumpini Park. The next day's morning newspaper *Siam Rath* carried a front page picture of Bira skiing with the headline,"HRH Prince Bira, the first Thai water-skier." Prasom wryly told this writer that it was really he who was the country's first water-skier, but he was happy to let Bira take the credit.

The two became fast and firm friends. Prasom, Bira discovered, was also a competent ship's pilot, a motor engine mechanic, an outboard motor boat enthusiast, and he had a licence to fly airplanes. He also owned a small yacht. In the evening they enjoyed going to the cinema together to see Esther Williams, the Hollywood film star of swimming musical extravaganzas. They became inseparable for the rest of Bira's stay in Siam. Prasom, who was ten years younger than Bira, was proud to be seen in the company of the illustrious Grand Prix driver.

When Bira returned to France in May, he offered Prasom a job as his pit manager, co-driver and secretary. As "secretary" Prasom found himself being nursemaid to Chelita, looking after her when

Bira was away, often on dates with other women. Prasom told this writer that he found Chelita not just incredibly beautiful, but a kind and generous person. He could see that she was unhappy and he felt sorry for her. Partly due to Bira's infidelities and partly because she was unsure of herself, Chelita would, Prasom noticed, try to prove her worth by being flirtatious with other men when Bira had friends over. It was not a happy marriage.

In France, Bira was in his element. Everybody loves a lover, as the old song goes, and for the French even more so. They admire their presidents, film stars and sports champions who have lovers on the side. Bira was a local hero on the French Riviera and women in his presence were either enchanted by his magnetism or they turned on their sexual charm. Either way, they invariably ended up in bed. The word got around that he was a generous and exciting lover. Bira, already 39, began sowing his wild oats like a teenager. Perhaps it was because he had met Ceril when they were both so young and innocent, and he loved her so much, that the thought of going out with other girls at that time never entered his mind. Now it was as if he had just discovered sex. His libido took over from his normal common-sense self and during this period of his life, he became a compulsive lover.

Prasom ended up being chauffeur, driving Bira's romantic conquests back and forth from Les Faunes to where they lived. Bira had two cars, a Buick eight-cylinder saloon car and an open-topped supercharged Aston Martin. He would instruct Prasom to collect his girlfriends in the Aston Martin, presumedly to get them all excited, and to drive them back afterwards in the more sedate Buick. The local gendarmes always waved his cars on and gave him special parking and speeding privileges. He was never stopped. They were proud of their famous royal guest.

In the course of his duties as friend, confidante and employee, Prasom often found himself making excuses for Bira and picking up the pieces. He made calls, booked his appointments and even sent flowers the next morning to girls he spent the night with. On one occasion, Prasom was instructed to fetch two English girls that Bira had picked up at the Hotel de Paris in Monte Carlo. The two girls sat in the back of the Aston Martin and innocently asked Prasom if this was a racing car, and when Prasom said no, they looked disappointed. Prasom then asked them whether they would like him to drive it like a racing car? "Ooh, yes pleeease!" they said in unison. Prasom, who was Bira's co-driver on many circuits, drove through the hairpin bends of La Grande Corniche at breakneck speeds, well above the limit without being stopped. When they arrived at the villa, he looked in the back seat and saw that both girls had fainted. It was just as well, because Bira had forgotten that he had made a date with them and had somebody else in his room. Prasom drove the two girls back to Monte Carlo and deposited them safely at their hotel.

Now, for the first time in his life, Bira was becoming aware of his mortality. He still participated in the occasional Grand Prix event because he enjoyed the sheer thrill of driving competitively and basking in the fame and adulation of his fans, but he also considered himself lucky to be still alive after having survived several serious accidents on the track. The loss of Dick Seaman in 1939, winner of the German Grand Prix in a Mercedes in 1936 and a valued friend, cut him up very badly. Over the years Bira would lose many of his racing colleagues and each year he vowed to quit while he was still ahead. Not surprisingly, he had become very superstitious, avoiding walking under ladders and other symbols of bad luck, like black cats crossing his path. Whenever he heard the thumping oompah sound of a brass band leading a Catholic funeral procession down the road, he would instruct Prasom to turn back immediately.

During his French Riviera days, Bira was spending more than the income he received from his inheritance in Siam. Chula had stopped supporting him and his funds were starting to run low. Once, when Prasom casually mentioned to Bira that with his reputation it would be so easy for His Highness to find a job, Bira exploded,

"What? How can I, a *Pra-Ong Chao,* a royal prince, be expected to work? A *Pra-Ong Chao* never works!" he retorted. Bira was quite right, of course. He had never worked in his life, and as a result he was not brought up to appreciate the value of money. He spent on anything that took his fancy. Unfortunately, they tended to be high-ticket items like cars, boats and planes. For example, he bought a 73-foot three-masted schooner, the *Lelanta,* which became his pride and joy. Like many rich people, he had a curious way of economising. He bought an airplane, he once said, to save money on expensive air fares. By the time he was fifty, he was totally bankrupt, and when he finally decided to work he didn't know how. It was sadly too late.

In August 1955, Chelita gave birth to his first son Biradej. Bira was overjoyed and hoped that the little boy's arrival would save his marriage. But it didn't. They were now both having extra-marital affairs and they were often seen bickering in public. During one of his visits to Siam on his own, he met a pretty Siamese air hostess, Salika Kalantanonda, known to her friends as Salee,[13] who would soon become his third wife, and Bira brought her to Europe to live with him at Les Faunes. He was a master at managing this *ménage-à-trois.* On one occasion, barging in on Ceril and Bruno at La Compagnola, their villa on Lake Garda, he brought Salee. On another, he brought Chelita. Once he brought them both together. Only Bira could carry off such a feat, and entertain one ex-wife, one present wife, and one future wife all together under the same roof.

But the situation was not tenable. Bira and Chelita were divorced at the Thai Embassy in Paris on the 29 September 1956. Chelita was given custody of Biradej, and she married her Dominican lover soon afterwards and returned to live in the Argentine. Biradej tragically died of cancer in Buenos Aires when he was only sixteen. It was a blow to Bira, whose life was now at a low point.

Running short of money, Bira returned to Thailand. Prime

13 *The Prince & I,* Princess Ceril Birabongse, Veloce Publishing, 1992

Minister Pibulsonggram was supportive when he learned that Bira wanted to set up a company to import European cars. In early 1957, he launched Bira Sport Ltd, which imported Neckar cars from Germany and other vehicles for individual customers, but it was not at all profitable. Salee gave up her air hostess job to marry him, but when Bira brought another girl, Lom, to live in the same house in 1958, she promptly divorced him and married her first love before she met Bira, a Thai Airways pilot[14].

"It's me, darling." Ceril immediately recognized Bira's familiar voice as he stepped out of the car he had parked in the driveway of her Lake Garda villa in Italy.

It was the hot, dry summer of 1971. Twenty-two years had passed since he'd divorced her, but he still loved her. Indeed, Bira had slept with hundreds of women since then, and had already re-married twice. But his love for Ceril, who was now happily married to Bruno Tomasoni in Italy, had become platonic and if there was any attraction left, it was a romantic one based on fond memories and a caring friendship that had lasted since 1934 when they first met.

Bira's car was parked under the olive trees and she invited Bira and Lom, his new Thai companion, inside. There was also a child and another Thai woman in the back, and Ceril assumed the child was Lom's[15]. Lom replied that she was unable to have children and that the little girl was "Bira's and Lek's,[16]" pointing to the other woman, who couldn't speak English, but immediately smiled at her. Curiously, Bee[17], the little girl, called Lom "mother" and Lek "auntie". Bira told her that he was married to neither. He had tried three times and that was enough, he said[18].

14 *ThePrince & I*, Op.Cit.
15 Arunee Chuladakoson.
16 Chuanchom Chaiyananda.
17 M.R. Rabibara Bhanubandh.
18 *ThePrince & I*, Op.Cit.

Over the years since their divorce, Bira has dropped in and out of Ceril's life at irregular intervals, and they would be reunited for an hour or so, or for a day. Ceril herself always had time for Bira and their sporadic reunions were always the same. There was no question of rekindling the fires. It was just for old time's sake, a traditional English roast perhaps, and a lot of catching up to do. Ceril was simply the best friend that Bira ever had. They would sit down and talk for hours. Often, Bira would seek her advice. But today, it was Bruno he wanted to talk to. Once a sailing champion and former president of the Riva yacht club, Bruno was now a ship's chandler, a dealer in sailing boats and a regatta expert, and was able to give Bira advice on sailing, the third passion of his life. Bira was preparing to participate in the 1972 Olympics in Munich, Germany, and needed some technical advice. Bira and Bruno chatted throughout the night and the next morning he was gone.

## Third Life: The Yachtsman

"Life begins at sixty," Bira would often tell his friends at the Royal Varuna Yacht Club in the coastal Thai town of Pattaya, where he spent most of his time when he was not on short business trips to Europe. It was 1974 and Bira was happy. He adored his second son Bird[19] who was born the year before and he wanted to be a good father to him. He was happy because he was at last finding peace of mind in his life's new third phase. His testosterone was no longer a driving force and he was content with his current domestic arrangement. He adored Lom, who kindly allowed Lek to share their home, when she was thrown out by her partner and had no place to live. Bira took pity on her and loved her as much as he loved Lom. Lek was the biological

19 M.R. Biranubongse Bhanubandh.

mother of his daughter Bee and his baby son Bird. All five of them lived very happily together without conflict or embarrassment. It was the perfect Thai arrangement, totally devoid of stress and based on love and tolerance. Neither Ceril nor Chelita, and not even Salee, would have understood this, he thought.

At this point in his life, he was not quite ready to live off his laurels, nor was he content to be known as a retired "has been" either. His years as a Grand Prix champion were well behind him, yet he never boasted, nor gave talks, about his victories or past glories on the race track. The last motor racing event that he took part in, purely for fun, was the Vientiane to Singapore Rally in 1969. If he could help it, he also tried to avoid driving his battered old Toyota Corona, even for the short journey from Bangkok to Pattaya. He was quite content to get a lift from his friend Bob Kennett who drove him to the yacht club while he slept peacefully in the back for two hours. In this third phase of his life as a yachtsman, Lom became his driver.

Now, in his autumn years, he preferred to have the respect of his peers as a yachtsman. Bira was proud of his sailing skills, which had allowed him to be part of the national yachting team that competed in the 1956 Melbourne, the 1960 Rome, the 1964 Tokyo and the 1972 Munich Olympic Games. In 1970 he won the club's inaugural Firebird Trophy, a long-distance race in Pattaya Bay for Fireball class sailing boats. He personally sculpted the 200-kilogramme Varuna trophy cast in bronze, making it so heavy that it would never leave the club's premises. Otherwise, the winners would, as they always did, take it home, he said. The trophy is proudly on display at the entrance of the club, reminding new members that Bira was a talented sculptor as well as a great yachtsman. He was also instrumental in getting the Royal Varuna Yacht Club to play host to the 1978 World Championship Race.

Talk to anyone at the Varuna and you will find that Bira was something of a legend. He made friends with every single member of the club and, even today, older members remember him with great fondness. As a sailor he was a formidable opponent. Like car racing, starting at pole position and getting off to a good start could make the difference between winning and losing. Although he was a good loser he preferred to win, and he did consistently. His competitors always hoped and prayed that they didn't have to race him downwind, because downwind Bira was unbeatable. He was a clever tactician, and he was known by members as that "wily old fox". On many occasions out at sea, his competitors thought that they were well ahead when the "old fox" would suddenly appear from nowhere, a big grin on his face. Bira is famous for winning the first National Sailing Championship of Thailand in his Enterprise class boat in 1976.

He always came to the club with both Lom and Lek in tow. The story goes that before going out to sea Bira would first assess the wind strength. If the wind was strong he took Mom Lom on board for the necessary ballast, and if the wind was weak and he needed lighter ballast, then he would take Mom Lek. Later, when Bird was in his early teens he would take him out and teach him how to sail. These were the happiest days of his life.

Bira knew that he would never again experience the glitzy lifestyle of his youth. He was always broke and he hated living off the generosity of his friends, who were always advancing him money for his scatterbrained projects. In his heart of hearts he still wanted to be a business success. But it was not to be.

His new company, Bira Air Transport, continually needed new injections of cash. The company folded in 1974 when he was no longer able to pay the servicing costs of his plane and the staff salaries. Again, he was declared bankrupt. In 1975, he moved with Lom to Geneva and started a finance company. He now dreamed of selling gliders and to promote the sport he was laying plans to be the first person to fly the Atlantic in a glider, starting from Brazil.[20]

20 This was yet another one of Bira's prodigal schemes, told to Ceril on one of his visits to her villa in Italy. She was not informed about the *mechanics* of gliding across the ocean, an improbable feat!

Bira was busily drawing up a business proposal complete with maps and a report of the prevailing winds at different times of the year. His objective was to find a sponsor and underwrite the cost of the project, which included a ship with a television crew on board to follow him. Bira spent the whole of 1975 looking for sponsors for this costly investment in Paris, Amsterdam, Dijon, Bergen and Italy.

Indeed, throughout the 70s and early 80s, Bira travelled the world looking for partnerships and sponsors for various business projects that never got off the ground. He would describe his latest project with enthusiasm and conviction, but as soon as prospective financiers and backers started talking about balance sheets and profit and loss accounts, he would say, "Don't bother me with the details!" Whenever he "burst in" upon Ceril he would tell her he was on the verge of making an immense fortune. Writing in her memoirs, Ceril said, "His plans for getting rich never materialized, but he went on trying, certain of success."

Two days before Christmas 1985, an old, rotund Asian man with thinning white hair was found slumped on a platform bench of Barons Court underground station in London. He had died peacefully, apparently of a heart attack. When the London Metropolitan Police went through his suit pockets in search of identification, they only found a letter written in a mysterious foreign script. Analysts at the School of Asian and African Studies told police the letter was in Thai, and was addressed to none other than His Royal Highness Prince Birabongse Bhanubandh, world champion driver, enthusiastic Olympic sailor and incurable romantic. It was a humble and ordinary ending to a remarkable and exceptional life.

# KHAMSING SRINAWK

## a.k.a. Lao Khamhom

## Born 1930

An Isan farm boy who discovered the power of writing and became a national treasure

**Previous page:** *Ett dammkorn under dina fotter, or Dust under one's feet, the Swedish translation of Khamsing's best seller, Fah Bo Kan, launched in March 1980.*

**Above:** *A summer's day in Stockholm, 1979.*

# 12

# An Isan in Stockholm

Prawee peered anxiously out of the frosty kitchen window of her $2^{nd}$ floor apartment as if she was expecting someone at any moment. She had developed this nervous, futile habit, but nobody ever came.

In the dim, grey light of a Swedish winter, all she could see was half a metre of snow covering the entire square of Vallingby Torg. It was November, one of the coldest months in Stockholm. The temperature that night had dropped to almost ten below zero. Prawee had been away from Thailand for almost nine months, waiting for news from her husband Khamsing, who was hiding somewhere in the Thai jungle. She wasn't even sure if her husband was still alive. No letter had come in the post.

While Prawee was now well past breaking down into silent fits of sobbing, alone in the middle of the night, when the children were fast asleep, she would still shed the occasional tear or two, as she did on this gloomy morning.

Drying her eyes, she noticed that despite the bitter cold, the locals were in a festive mood. She saw people outside energetically trudging through the snow, merrily carrying home Christmas trees on their shoulders, and children noisily throwing snowballs at each other. It was going to be her first Christmas in Sweden.

Her thoughts wandered back to that unforgettable day in Bangkok on 5 March 1977, when she sought refuge in Sweden. With the help of Jean-Christophe Oberg, the Swedish ambassador in Thailand, and his wife Birgit, Prawee was able to safely board the SAS flight for Stockholm with her children. Ambassador Oberg had issued four Swedish passports to Prawee and her three little daughters.

Birgit had gone ahead the week before, to see that Prawee's accommodation arrangements were in order, and find a suitable school and day-care centre for the children. To make sure that Prawee was able to board and deplane without any mishap, Jean-Christophe had personally accompanied her all the way to Stockholm.

Ever since 1944, when Raoul Wallenberg, the Swedish diplomat in Nazi-occupied Budapest, helped some 100,000 Jewish Hungarians escape to freedom at considerable danger to himself, by issuing Swedish 'protective passports', it had become Sweden's historic mission to champion the plight of oppressed dissidents around the world by giving them political asylum and a safe sanctuary in Sweden. Jean-Christophe Oberg himself had been brought up in a similar environment, with the same ideals and principles. His father had been a diplomat in France during the Second World War and, like Wallenberg, helped Jews escape from the clutches of the pro-Nazi French Vichy government.

Prawee had never travelled by plane in her life. She was more apprehensive about the children than for herself, but she needn't have worried. The two elder daughters, Tuensiri, four, and Khamhom, three, wide-eyed and excited, kept her – and the bemused ambassador – entertained throughout the journey, with their barrage of questions and interminable chatter. Meanwhile, the little one, Phupian, barely five months old, slept all the way.

After arriving at Arlanda airport, Prawee and the children were whisked away to a waiting Volvo. As Jean-Christophe and a foreign office aide gave instructions to the driver, the piercing cold wind slapped Prawee's face like a dry ice pack, and the dark grey sky made her nervous. The children's enthusiasm lifted her spirits though. They were still fully alert despite the twelve-hour flight.

'Oh, look at all that coconut ice cream on the streets and trees. It's *everywhere*,' exclaimed Khamhom, as she looked out of the car window in awe.

'It's called *heema*[1], you silly,' Tuensiri retorted.

'How do you know that?'

'*Everyone* knows what snow is, except you!'

It was an amazing sight, even for Prawee, who had never seen anything like it in her 30 years. It was quite different from the snow she had seen in Hollywood films like *White Christmas* and *Dr. Zhivago*. The car headed northwest to the satellite town of Vallingby, built in the fifties, a concrete development for the new rising working class, and now a suburb of Stockholm.

Life in their two-room apartment was not easy. On some days, weak and feverish from the cold, Prawee had to force herself to get out of bed. With three hungry children in tow, she simply *had* to do the shopping and prepare the meals all by herself. No one was there to help her.

The local *kommun*[2] provided her with an allowance, the same amount that was given to some of her neighbours, political refugees like herself, from military dictator Pinochet's Chile and war-torn Lebanon. Grateful though she was, she vowed that one day she would work and not depend forever on the charitable benevolence of the Swedish government. But first she had to learn the language, which she found even more difficult than English, which was hard enough.

When Birgit had come to her apartment to say goodbye before her return to Thailand, Prawee had a moment of panic. She was going to miss her first, and at that time, her only friend in Sweden. Birgit had been so kind, showing her around the shops and introducing her to the schools and day-care centres. Now Prawee would be on

---

1 Snow.
2 Municipality.

her own, having to fend for herself. She was also slightly envious, knowing that Birgit was returning to the warmth of her country, far from the punishing cold.

But most of all, Prawee had become lonely. As she put *khao tom*[3] on the stove and started to prepare breakfast for the children on that cold November morning, she heard the doorbell ring.

"Children, go and see who it is at the door, will you? *Mae* [4] is busy in the kitchen."

There was a shriek from the two girls, and Prawee's heart skipped a beat.

"*Mae, mae*! There's a black man at the door!"

Khamhom ran back to the kitchen to hide behind Prawee's thick woollen-stockinged legs. Tuensiri stood in defiance in front of her mother, as the "black" man, dirty and dishevelled, entered the kitchen. When Tuensri saw her mother's relieved face, she immediately realised that this stranger was Khamsing, her father. She ran into his outstretched arms.

"It's *poh*[5], you silly! I *knew* it was daddy right away," shouted Tuensiri boastfully to her sister.

Khamsing beckoned to Khamhom, who was still hesitating. Indeed, it took her a whole week before she was able to embrace her father, and it took her even longer to accept this strange man who occupied her place in Prawee's bed every night.

Baby Phupian, meanwhile, cried every time Khamsing came near her, although he was to look much more presentable, after a much needed shave and haircut, and change of clothes from the weathered military fatigues that he arrived in.

Khamsing himself was just as bewildered that morning. He had been a stateless fugitive for almost a year. After six months on the run in the malarial jungles of northern Thailand, followed by five months

---

3 Rice with broth, standard Thai breakfast.
4 Mother.
5 Daddy.

as a reluctant guest of the Laotian government, he had just the day before yesterday boarded a Russian plane at Vientiane airport for the long inhospitable flight on Aeroflot to Stockholm via Moscow. He felt like hell, and he had been through hell, only to find himself in a very alien and cold place indeed.

Khamsing Srinawk's world had begun to fall apart on 6 October 1976. That day in Thai history, forever marked in infamy, was when a right-wing anti-Communist backlash climaxed in the death of hundreds.

The build-up was set in motion after 14 October 1973, when student activists joined peasant leaders and labour unions in toppling the old military regime, in order to usher in a new era of democracy based on a revised constitution[6]. Instead, the years that followed featured weak, unstable governments, chaos and confusion.

After three years of political and social strife, an orchestrated media campaign on radio and television depicting the student activists and their allies as "burdens on the land" and "scum of the earth," culminated in the 6 October massacre. On that day, armed right-wing fanatics, hired hooligans and specially trained warfare police fired their guns point blank into the Thammasat university compound and eventually stormed the campus. Hundreds of trapped students were shot, lynched and butchered in unimaginably horrifying ways. Some were burned on the spot. Fear and anarchy gripped the city of Bangkok. It was a shameful moment in modern Thai history.

The students who managed to escape the massacre fled the capital and sought sanctuary in the jungles of the north. Though branded as "leftists", they were really radicals and liberals from middle-class backgrounds. They had no choice but to join the

6 Khamsing was selected to help and advise on the drafting of this new constitution.

Communist Party of Thailand (CPT), a few thousand diehard Maoists, who "owned" the jungle. In the final analysis, the students' only crime had been to protest against nothing more than the return of the old military clique.

How did Khamsing Srinawk, Thailand's best-known short-story writer, a man who was not even at the scene of the massacre, become involved in all this?

After Khamsing accepted the nomination to be the vice-chairman of the Socialist Party of Thailand in 1973, his dairy farm in Pak Chong in the northeast became an open-house venue for social and political debates. "There I would be, peacefully sleeping at my farm, when a group of students and journalists would turn up at 4 a.m., help themselves to coffee, and stay to discuss politics until the late morning. They just had nowhere else to go. This is poor old Khamsing's bad *karma*. No wonder I had to flee the country!" he recalled amusingly.

During this time, Khamsing styled himself a "*social democrat*", but he was never an orthodox "socialist". He did encourage free speech, however, and his short stories often depicted the conditions of poor Isan rice farmers, and the injustices they faced. Khamsing simply believed that by joining the Socialist Party, he could help bring about a more equitable society and a happier Thailand. As a harbinger of peace and social reform, and a spokesman for poor rice farmers in the impoverished northeast, he truly despaired at the government's "callous indifference to the plight of the poor peasant farmers."[7] As a result, even before he escaped to the jungle, Kamsing was already being labelled a "leftist" by the right-wing press.

By November 1976, following the 6 October massacre, his property had become a target for right-wing militants. A few minutes before midday on the eve of Loy Kratong, a traditional Thai festival in November, friendly local police approached the entrance to his farm

7 David K. Wyatt, *Siam in Mind*, Silkworm Books.

with deliberate noise and fanfare, giving Khamsing adequate warning and allowing him and his friends to narrowly make their escape.

Prawee quickly cleared the tables and shelves, making sure all incriminating evidence and Khamsing's "seditious" writings were well hidden. When the armed right-wing hoodlums arrived in the early evening, they entered the bedroom where a pregnant Prawee and her two children were pretending to be fast asleep, petrified, not daring to move. It was the most frightening moment of Prawee's life. The simple farmhouse was completely ransacked but they found nothing. It was already too dark to search the rest of the property. Prawee was sure that they would come back.

Prawee was not to see Khamsing for another twelve months after he fled. Clearly she was no longer safe at Pak Chong, and after that terrifying night, she hastily moved to Bangkok to stay with her relatives and give birth to Phupian. A friend suggested she get in touch with the Swedish ambassador, who had already assisted several Thai journalists who were seeking asylum in Sweden. Together, they came up with a secret plan to help Prawee leave the country.

*The right-wing militants did come back to the farm.* Khamsing was now suspected of harbouring communist insurgents on his property. This time they came looking for arms and ammunition. Such was the intensity of the hate campaign on radio and in newspapers, there were calls for all Thais to "kill the communists". Khamsing's name was included on anti-government wanted lists, and lies upon lies were heaped upon this liberal, intelligent and creative writer who loved his country dearly.

One newspaper even reported that there was a military helipad on his property. The thugs returned in December, and although they found no weapons, this time they completely destroyed his homestead, and the writings that Prawee had carefully hidden were found and trampled underfoot. The manuscript of *Maeow,* a new book that Khamsing had started to work on, was never found again.

Khamsing meanwhile fared badly in the jungle. He was

terrified that he would suffer from the malaria that he had contracted in his youth. The CPT, which he had joined, wanted to train him in guerrilla warfare. He would mockingly ask them how could he, a frail, small man, possibly be expected to carry a big heavy gun?

More importantly, he had serious ideological disagreements with the CPT hierarchy. He would repeatedly describe himself as a peaceful "social democrat", and insist that he was *not* and *never will be* a communist, least of all a militant activist.

The CPT tried to put him to work as their official spokesman, but again the two parties had serious ethical and professional differences of opinion, in matter of both style and content. It was against Khamsing's principles to direct or impose a way of life that was alien to him. He believed that his fellow human beings were intelligent enough to do the proper thing without being forced or told what to do. His short stories had offered no conclusive endings or moral judgments; he implicitly invited his readers to decide for themselves the difference between right and wrong.

When Khamsing learned that the CPT's aim was to take over the country by force within twenty years, he told them that such an objective was excessive and unpatriotic and that he wanted to leave the jungle. Although the CPT were reluctant to let Khamsing go, his sincere powers of persuasion enabled him to depart without rancour. "I am a simple domestic elephant, not a tough elephant of the jungle" were his parting words.

Khamsing was relieved to learn that Prawee was safe and sound in Sweden. He needed to find a suitable route to join his wife. He was missing the comforts of home – he hated roughing it in the jungle – and he longed to be with his family.

He decided to head for Laos where he had become something of a folk hero. There, Khamsing was known by his pen-name *Lao Khamhom* – Lao of the Fragrant Words – and if he could safely make his way into the country, he could call upon some of his old Lao friends to help him get to Sweden.

It is much safer for dissidents on the run to travel under the cover of darkness. Khamsing reached the Thai side of the border near Nong Khai at daybreak and laid low on the banks of the Mekhong until nightfall. He waded across the river in the dark to a little island where he spent a miserable night and proceeded to Vientiane the next morning. He contacted some old friends there and reported his presence to the authorities. When the Lao government discovered what a catch Khamsing was, they appointed a senior Laotian officer, one Salee Vongkamsao, to be his minder.

Alas, Laos turned out to be even more wretched than the Thai jungle. Although he initially basked in his fame there, Khamsing came to realize that the new communist regime was only interested in using him for propaganda purposes.

Khamsing was duped into broadcasting his socialist views that only promoted the Pathet Lao Communist Party, a situation he was to regret bitterly. Indeed, he had been devastated to learn that only the year before, the 68-year-old King of Laos, Sawang Wattana, was forced to abdicate, ending 600 years of royal rule. The king was interned in a re-education camp near the northern border with Vietnam, where he eventually died. Many of his old Lao friends had also disappeared this way. Khamsing wanted to leave Laos as soon as possible. But it wasn't going to be easy.

In Vientiane, Khamsing was shocked to discover that the CPT and the Pathet Lao had joined forces. He also found out that there was a new CPT offshoot, a "Revolutionary Army". It had been formed after the new Thai Prime Minister, Thanin Kraivixian, announced he intended to stay in power for another twelve years and put the country back in time, by closing newspapers, banning certain books and outlawing political meetings. The Revolutionary Army was preparing to fight the reactionary Thanin government with force of arms.

By this time, different Thai student, worker and peasant activists had split up into several factions, from mild social democrats like Khamsing to violent Maoists who believed that power can only be achieved from the "barrel of a gun"[8]. To contain these conflicting groups, the Lao government decided to house all of them together in one location, at a jungle camp in Luang Namtha province. Khamsing was to remain here for several months, a reluctant guest of the Lao government.

Muang Luang Namtha, 700 kilometres northwest of the capital Vientiane, is one of the most beautiful, as well as one of the most remote parts of the country. The low-lying mountains of this province, at the foothills of the Himalayas, are crisscrossed with valleys and hillsides of rice terraces, rubber trees and tea plantations. Once an ethnic Tai principality, it has seen centuries of invasion and domination by the Siamese, the Burmese and the French. On 6 May 1962, it was one of the first provinces to come under the control of the Pathet Lao communist forces.

When political dissidents of varying colours get together to fight a common enemy, conflicting differences in dogma, policy, organisation, leadership and plan of action emerge. The Thai dissidents were unable to agree on a common strategy. Even in communist Laos, there was a schism in the Pathet Lao Party, those who were Maoists under the aegis of China, and those who were Leninists, supported by the Soviet Union and Vietnam.[9]

Khamsing was reluctantly dragged into long didactic discussions with his Lao hosts and the different factions of the CPT. In the end, he declared he wanted no part of any armed conflict in Thailand and requested permission to join his family in Sweden.

His friend and minder Salee, realising that Khamsing was not one to fight on the battlefield, started proceedings to help him leave Laos. His old passport[10] was no longer valid, but it was sufficient

8 Mao Tse-tung.
9 Today, Laos is aligned with China, its biggest benefactor, with investments of more than $4 billion in mining, hydropower, and agriculture.
10 Sent to him by his friends from Bangkok.

proof of his identity as required for stateless individuals seeking political asylum in Sweden. In the beginning, Salee suggested that he cross the border to Kunming, China, and make his onward journey west from there, but Khamsing knew that once he was in the clutches of the Chinese, he would never be allowed to leave.

Salee therefore arranged for him to board a scheduled commercial flight on Aeroflot from Vientiane to Stockholm, via Rangoon, Bombay and Moscow. At Moscow airport, Khamsing wisely braved the freezing cold by deliberately *not* going through Soviet immigration, choosing to remain at the transit gate for six hours before his ongoing flight to Stockholm. When he finally found his seat on the Ilyushin aircraft, he sat back and relaxed for the first time in months. He had just about enough of the Reds in the Thai jungle and the Pathet Lao Communists, and he wanted to get out of Soviet Russia as soon as he could.

Khamsing's flight to freedom had begun.

*I am like a vegetable in the fridge, fresh but not alive.* This is how Khamsing described the way he felt about himself in Sweden on a particularly cold morning in December 1977 just after Christmas. He had barely arrived in Sweden and he was in one of his dark moods.

It had snowed all night. He looked out of the only window of his tiny apartment. All he could see was a vast blanket of fresh snow. The parked cars, the trees, the shopping centre overlooking Vallingby Torg and the railway station on the far side of the square were totally buried in a massive snowdrift, reaching almost halfway up the telegraph pole.

Khamsing was cold and miserable, a virtual stranger to his children, and for the first time in his life, he felt lonely and alienated, more than he had ever been in the jungle or in Laos. He didn't understand the language, he hated the weather and he couldn't stomach the food. He was totally estranged from his new Swedish surroundings and indifferent to its culture. Worst of all, he had no one outside his family to talk to.

Prawee was glad that Khamsing had arrived. "Now *you* can look after the children for a change, while I go out to learn Swedish and look for a job," she told him. Khamsing plunged into an even deeper depression. He didn't come all this way to be a babysitter.

His first month as a Swedish father was not a great success. While Prawee was attending Swedish classes – *free*, as she insisted on pointing out – Khamsing reluctantly assumed the role of homemaker. Shopping for food was not just an annoyance, but an expensive one as well. He kept on bargaining with the grocers and shopkeepers and could not bring himself to pay the fixed prices for food that he didn't even like.

He didn't leave the house if he didn't absolutely need to. Much to the amusement of his children, he often slipped on the icy pavements when he ventured out. They would all laugh together. For the first time, Khamsing felt he was getting closer to his children. At other times during his walks, if he forgot to wear his rubber galoshes, his dry shoes would sink deep into the fresh snow, getting his feet soaking wet. His cold feet started to numb and Prawee would have to rub his feet down.

During the day, he was left alone in the apartment after Tuensiri and Khamhom were at school and Phupian was deposited at the day-care centre. He couldn't read the Swedish newspapers and he desperately wanted to know what was happening in the world.

He was thrilled when he brought home an old Telefunken bakelite shortwave radio set that he found and even bargained for in a second-hand antique shop. Now he could tune-in to his favourite BBC news programs as he once did in the jungle. To get better reception, he climbed out of the window of his apartment and onto the roof to find a suitable spot for the antenna.

The inhabitants of Vallingby are not used to seeing tousled-haired Asians crawling about on their rooftops. As he started to hammer the antenna into place, he heard the piercing sound of a police car siren in the street below. He looked down and saw a crowd gathering on the pavement. Some of them, he noticed, were pointing their fingers at him. He was persuaded to come down by a friendly policeman. After he sheepishly climbed back through the window into his apartment, the crowd dispersed, relieved to see him safe and sound. There had been too many recent reports of suicides by foreign immigrants not able to face another winter.

"Can we feed our friend the *igelkott* please, *poh*?" said Khamhom and Tuensiri when Khamsing came to fetch them from school one afternoon. Instead of going straight home, they took a detour along a narrow path through the park. The *igelkott*, sitting comfortably beneath an oak tree, turned out to be a hedgehog. "It's called a *men* in Thai," said Khamsing, but the children were not convinced. To them it was their friend the *igelkott* and much to Khamsing's frustration they never called it by its Thai name. In time, Khamsing himself was to call all hedgehogs by their Swedish name.

For people from the tropics, the first winter in Sweden is the most difficult. Never to see the sunrise and the sunset for six months makes for a depressing period of darkness. Khamsing was stoic enough to stand up to the cold, but it was the mental anguish that made him suffer the most. He was deprived from doing what he did best, which was writing. Without being able to fulfil his passion, life seemed to have no purpose. In Sweden, he was a *nobody*, an unknown. He was just another unfortunate immigrant. He was not only stuck in the fridge, but his brain was in the deep freeze.

Then there were the cultural shocks, seemingly one after the other. He noticed that Prawee was beginning to behave like a Swedish woman. She was now asserting a new independence, a facet of his wife he never knew. She was learning Swedish very quickly and in six months she had found a job as a social worker, helping out in old people's homes. Within a year her proficiency in Swedish was such that she became an interpreter for newly arrived Thai immigrants. Secretly he was proud of her, but he would never allow himself to admit this. She was even earning good money.

The high price of eating out was another shock. Khamsing's first meal at a restaurant cost more than a month of lunches back home. He never went to a Swedish restaurant again, not unless he was a guest. Throughout his four years in Sweden he only went to a restaurant – as a guest of course – four more times. Each meal was to become an important event.

The defining moment during Khamsing's exile in Sweden arrived when Professor Arne Trankell came into his life. Versatile and intense, Arne was an intellectual all-rounder who first came to prominence in the sixties during the famous Lars trial, a sexual abuse case of a five-year-old boy by an adult window cleaner. Professor Trankell exposed inconsistencies in the little boy's evidence that led to the acquittal of the defendant.

Arne, a Professor of Educational Psychology at Stockholm University, was also a well-known author of a system of airline pilot selection that was adopted by Scandinavian Airlines System, and, in 1965, by Thai Airways. His pilot aptitude tests were designed to detect and examine all serious deviations in candidates' testimony on their qualifications and experience. It became the standard textbook on airline pilot recruitment and is still today the safest pilot selection method.

Through his connection with Thai Airways, he visited Thailand regularly and came to appreciate Thai culture. On one of his trips to Bangkok he picked up a copy of Khamsing's book *Fah Baw Kan*[11], which had been translated into English by Domnern Garden and

11 *The Sky is Not the Limit.*

titled *The Politician and Other Stories*. Arne had read many Thai literary works in the past, which were often written by royal and elite authors for the Thai urban gentry. But *Fah Baw Kan* was different and the most insightful book on Thai country life he had ever read. Khamsing had created anti-heroes and anti-heroines from the earthy Isan peasantry, and Arne was captivated by them.

In January 1978, Arne came to Khamsing's home in Vallingby to introduce himself. He'd read about Khamsing's arrival in Stockholm as a political émigré in *Dagens Nyheter*, Sweden's morning newspaper. He had always wanted to meet the author of *Fah Baw Kan* and he was not disappointed. Arne and Khamsing hit it off immediately.

Arne was appalled by Khamsing's tiny apartment in Vallingby and immediately offered the use of his space at home should Khamsing need a decent place to work. In truth, Arne had already started to translate *Fah Baw Kan* into Swedish from English, and now he realized he could complete the translation directly from Khamsing's own words.

Khamsing happily offered his help and approval. It was a joint venture made in heaven. But it was not an easy start. At first, Khamsing found it difficult to write, and felt like a "mental amputee, cut off from the things that were important to him", recalls Ing-Britt, Arne's wife.

Arne, a professional psychologist, however, was able to get Khamsing back on his feet, helping Khamsing reach deep into his unconscious and restore the feelings that connected him to his past, his home and his culture. They met at Arne's home. He started by encouraging Khamsing to talk about his early years in Siam.

"I was born an Isan farmboy and at heart I am still one. All of us on the farm went to the village school to complete the government's minimum primary education program for four years. After, we all had to return to the farm and continued to work in the fields. Little boys like me looked after the water buffaloes and that is what I did for three years after I left school."

Kamsing gloomily looked out of the window. It had started to snow. He was starting to suffer from pangs of homesickness.

"But unlike the other boys who preferred to sing popular songs and did not really like to learn how to read and write, immediately forgetting what they had learned at school, I continued to practice my reading and writing."

Kamsing's tone was beginning to get emotional. It became clear to Arne that Kamsing was finding it difficult to talk about his childhood.

"On my days off, I walked several kilometres back to the village to read every single book and newspaper I could get hold of. It became an obsession. I used to rip off the newspapers that were used to cover the walls of the public toilets. I would run after the trains hoping that the passengers would throw away rubbish that contained printed matter: newspapers, wrappers, paper packages – *anything* that was printed – I read them all. My other passion was to listen to an old man from Ubol who came to our village and told us old Isan folk tales."

Arne was not only able to bring Khamsing back to his present consciousness and help repair the damage to his morale, but he also learned much more about his emotional and intellectual state of mind when he wrote *Fah Baw Kan.*

"I realized the power of language. I discovered that writing is the only medium that can hold one's attention and change the way people think. When the local abbot saw that I was passionate about reading and writing, he took me on at the temple school and gave me the chance to get a proper secondary education. I was only fourteen when I started to write and it was like being in possession of some kind of magical power. I loved the sound of certain words. I would repeat them over and over in my mind, then roll them over in my lips, and then, most miraculous of all, write them down on paper. Once they were written, they were there for posterity. I would smile smugly to myself."

Professor Trankell could hardly believe what he was hearing. A veteran psychologist, he was moved by Kamsing's words. He encouraged his young Thai friend to go on.

"I then went on to study journalism at university. But I was so poor and underfed that I no longer had the strength or the money to continue my studies. I did what people do when they are poor, I looked for a job – any job – and spent the next three years working in the forests of Chiang Mai as a ranger during the day so that at night I could write."

Arne nodded in sympathy and smiled at him encouragingly. It was a heartening story.

"Then I got lucky. When I returned to Bangkok some short stories that I had written were published in the *Piyamit*[12] newspaper. I was given total intellectual freedom. This was a period in our history when our country enjoyed free press, between 1955 and 1958, the strange years when there was a political power struggle between CIA-backed Police General Phao Sriyanond and Pentagon-backed Army General Sarit Thanarat. Paradoxically, Thai writers like me were free to express our ideas. I now realized the incredible power of the printed word and the short stories in *Fah Bo Kan* was my way of expressing the true feelings I had for the poor people of Isan."[13]

Arne and Khamsing worked together on the translation for two years, word by word, extracting "Khamsing's spoken version of the book", as Ing-Britt puts it, returning to his Isan roots, to the soul of each character and to the plot of each story.

It became a pleascent routine. When Arne was able to get time off from his professional university lecturing and academic studies, they would have lunch or dinner first, clear the dining table, and then Arne would start to ask searching questions. The table was piled up with books and papers. There was no Google to help them so they

---

12 Dear Friend.

13 These recollections were recorded by the writer in an interview with Kamsing at his farm in Pak Chong in March 2012.

would trudge over to the *stadsbiblioteket*, the city library, when they needed to look something up.

In between the work sessions, the Trankells invited Khamsing and his family to their country home on the island of Blido in the archipelago. The peace and quiet was so absolute, that for the first time since he arrived in Sweden, Khamsing slept soundly. He loved the Swedish countryside and he was beginning to feel human again.

When he was first approached by Arne to work on the book, he arranged for Benjaporn, his favourite niece from Thailand, to come over and look after the children. Both Khamsing and Prawee were now a working couple, and for the first time, they both felt good about themselves.

Now that their state allowance was augmented by Prawee's small salary, they could afford to move to a bigger place. Their new address at 15 Stupvagen in the Sollentuna Kommun was a three-bedroomed apartment on the sixth floor in a solid concrete block surrounded by a spectacular pine forest. For the first time, life was starting to improve and the children had never been happier. Even Khamsing had now overcome his dislike of the snow and sensitivity to the biting cold, going for long walks with the children in the forest every day. Khamsing wasn't complaining as much as he used to. They were a happy family.

Prawee had become an expert on the mushrooms that she picked in the nearby forest, able to distinguish the good ones from the poisonous varieties. She read everything there was to know on the subject from public library books. "Not mushroom soup *again*!" was a frequent comment by Khamsing at dinner.

Khamsing's big day in Sweden had finally arrived. *Ett dammkorn under dina fötter* (*Specks of dust under your feet*), the Swedish translation of Khamsing's short stories, was launched by Norstedts, Sweden's leading publishing house, in March 1980.

The book was successfully introduced at the Svensk Pen Club, a prestigious writers' club, and Khamsing was invited to become an honorary member, the only Thai ever to have that courtesy. There was one speech after another to introduce Khamsing. He talked about how his book was originally conceived in Thailand, and the work Arne had undertaken on the translation.

The media had appeared in full force and Khamsing became a celebrity overnight. This was followed a few days later by an official launch hosted by the publishing house and a gala dinner at the Grand Hotel. This historic dinner was Khamsing's *second* meal in a restaurant in Sweden, following that first unpalatable and expensive lunch a week after he arrived two years before.

Khamsing was now a regular guest speaker on radio shows and cultural events. He met Vilgot Sjöman, the working class writer and film maker, famous for directing *I am curious (Yellow)*, a controversial film that examined Swedish society from a critical, leftist viewpoint. The film was censored in the UK and banned in the US for its sexual content. Vilgot Sjöman's books dealt with social class issues, morality and sexual taboos, and the political left. Khamsing was fascinated by this existentialist intellectual. They had a lot to talk about.

He was also invited with his family to the annual Socialist Party conference in 1980, set informally at an open-air summer camp on an island in the archipelago. At the mealtime buffet, queuing for his supper, he noticed a very tall and very old man, with thick horn-rimmed spectacles, accompanied by his equally old but tiny wife, in line behind him. They both smiled at him and his family. They smiled back.

Khamsing could not understand why the locals seemed to be giving this old couple an inordinate amount of space and undue respect, as if they were revered. This kind of deferential behaviour to these two old folk, he felt, was very Thai, and most un-Swedish. When Kamsing asked people around who this old man was, there was a surprised look of disbelief on their faces. *You mean you don't know Tage Erlander, the most famous man in Sweden?*

Tage Erlander was known as the "Big Man", both for his height – 6 foot 4 inches, and for the length of time he was Prime Minister of Sweden – 1945 to 1969. Khamsing immediately went to his table to pay his respects. Tage politely got up on his feet. It was a touching scene, the biggest man in Sweden towering above the small Isan political émigré, squeezing each others hand in amity and friendship. He invited Khamsing to join him at his table[14].

When Tage was told that Khamsing was Thai, he told him that at the turn of the twentieth century, Sweden was one of the poorest and most backward countries in Europe. Swedish farmers were just as poor as Thai farmers, and that many Swedish families now have relatives in Minnesota and Michigan, descendants of poor rural immigrants who left Sweden for America between 1860 and 1910; nearly a fifth of the population escaped starvation. Only free education and social welfare for the masses, he told Khamsing, could lift the Swedish peasant from poverty. "Free education was the first job I did when I became prime minister. I remember the times when we Swedes were so poor that our parents could not afford to pay for our schooling."

Khamsing listened in admiration to this man's simple words. "And finally, at the end of our citizens' lives, we must reward our bus and train drivers, our farmers and factory workers, for all the hard work they had done during their lifetimes, with a good retirement pension. It is our duty to look after our hardworking people. More than any other national resource, it is our people who are the real wealth of our country."

Khamsing was moved almost to tears by the words of this uncomplicated and charismatic man. It was one of the highlights of his stay in Sweden, and he still talks about this meeting with fondness and respect.

---

14 Like all Swedes, Tage spoke excellent English.

On a fleeting visit from one of his diplomatic postings, Ambassador Jean-Christophe invited Khamsing to dinner at the Catelin, a traditional restaurant in Gamla Stan, the historic centre of Stockholm. Arne and Ing-Britt were also invited. It turned out to be a disastrous evening. Famous for its selection of fresh seafood from the Baltic and seasonal game, they arrived too late to order any of the specialities. Jean-Christophe decided on the herring, saying flippantly but without malice, that Thais can "anyway happily survive on fish and rice".

Arne, however, did not take to this comment kindly. What the ambassador said was offensive and insulting, and he should apologise to Khamsing immediately.

Ing-Britt tried to stop her husband from starting an argument with disapproving looks and animated winking. Unfortunately, Arne did not stop there. He proceeded to berate Jean-Christophe for not providing better accommodation for Khamsing and his family.

At this point, Ing-Britt silently kicked her husband under the table. But there was no stopping him. A heated argument ensued between these two well-intentioned men who only had Khamsing's best interest at heart.

Of course, Khamsing didn't understand a word and to this day does not know what the disagreement was all about. The two senior Swedes were simply envious of each other's over-protective concern for Khamsing's well-being, like two competing parents.

Khamsing's *third* meal at a restaurant – one of the most exclusive in Stockholm – was not a great success. He was so upset that he ended up eating nothing. Ing-Britt recalls that the herring dish was unpalatably fried in butter, so nobody ate well that evening.

Despite Khamsing's high regard for the Swedish socialist system, he was not ready to integrate into Swedish society. In his heart of hearts, he was homesick and hoped to one day return to Thailand. He never learned Swedish, claiming (rightly) that he could communicate in English perfectly well with all the Swedes he'd met.

Prawee, on the other hand, came to speak excellent Swedish, as she still does today, and was happy to adopt Swedish customs, making many local friends.

Khamsing found it difficult to let go of his cultural roots and he often overreacted when his children, who were by now totally integrated with their new surroundings, started to behave like Swedish children. On one occasion, just before Christmas 1979, Khamsing decided, on the grounds that they were Buddhists, that there would be *no* Christmas tree in their new Sollentuna home, even though the apartment was big enough to have one. *Every single Swedish home* had a tree at Christmas time and the children decided to earn enough pocket money by doing simple chores, like clearing the snow on the neighbours' front steps, running errands and collecting their rubbish, to buy one of their own. When they brought their tree home and proudly decorated it, Khamsing was livid.

"I told you *not* to do this, and yet you deliberately disobeyed me." The children were surprised that their father was unhappy about this, expecting him to be proud of them for showing their resourcefulness and independence. But it was this very *independence* that caused him concern. He was losing his authority over his family and he didn't like it.

On another occasion, little Phupian, now four, expressed her desire to be an artist. She was gifted with an unusual talent for a child of her age in watercolour painting, but Khamsing would have none of this. There is no future for an artist, he would say.

Khamsing's *last* dinner at a restaurant in Sweden was both memorable and historic. It was with General Kriangsak Chomanand, the Prime Minister of Thailand from 1977 to 1980. After the reactionary Prime Minister Thanin had resigned, Kriangsak had introduced a shrewd liberalization policy to grant amnesty to all the students who had fled into the jungle and joined the CPT.[15]

The general was visiting Stockholm on his way to the States and expressed his desire to meet Khamsing, who replied to the Thai ambassador that while it was a great honour to be invited by Prime Minister Kriangsak, it would be difficult as he was a political refugee and could not in good conscience meet him at the Thai embassy as requested. The Swedish government decided that this was a purely Thai affair and protocol would not allow them to meet at the Foreign Office.

Kriangsak wisely found a solution and invited him to the Grand Hotel, where he was staying. The meeting was easy and relaxed. The following conversation ensued:

KRIANGSAK'S first words were: "There is no point in continuing our quarrel with you. Let us make peace."

KHAMSING: "I just want to know what I did wrong, for me to become such a wanted man."

KRIANGSAK: "We have nothing against you now and we want you to return to Thailand."

KHAMSING: "I have been deprived of my Thai nationality. I want to have back my Thai passport."

KRIANGSAK: "That can easily be arranged," and putting his arm around Khamsing, he said, "If you return to your Pak Chong farm, I will arrange a military guard to protect you."

KHAMSING: "Your excellency, I just want to clear my name and dispel the lies that my farm was a communist base. With respect, I would prefer not to have soldiers guarding me."

At the beginning of 1981, Khamsing returned to his farm after

---

15 "By 1981, the overwhelming majority of those who had fled in 1976 were back where they had come from, sadder, older, and less illusioned." Benedict R.O.G. Anderson, *In the Mirror*, D.K. Editions (1985).

being in the wilderness for four years and where he still happily resides.

His last words to a group of young Thai acolytes that he had gathered in Sweden and had come to see him off at Arlanda airport were those of a true patriot:

"If one wants to work for one's country and for the benefit of the people, it should always be at home, not abroad. I've always maintained with everyone that I want to return home. It is our duty to stay in Thailand if one wants to help the mother country."

In 1992, Khamsing was awarded with the title of "National Artist of Thailand in Literature" by the National Cultural Commission, in a moving ceremony presided over by H.R.H. Princess Sirindhorn. His name is also listed in the *Encyclopedia of World Literature in the 20th Century.*

# ACKNOWLEDGMENTS AND BIBLIOGRAPHIC SOURCES


**CHAPTER 1**

**Interviews and discussions**

Dr. Chaiya Sethaputra, Sor's son, 10 January, 2011, 29 March, 2013

Patcharapim Sethaputra, Sor's daughter, 10 January, 5 February, 10 August, 2011, 29 March, 2013

**Bibliographic sources**

Adirex, Paul, *The Pirates of Tarutao,* Aries Books, 1996

Grey, D., Piprell, C., Graham,M., *National Parks of Thailand,* IFCT, 1991

Landon, K.P., *Siam in Transition,* University of Chicago Press, 1939

So Sethaputra, *Leekit Cheewit (Destiny of Life),* Nanmee Books, 2005

So Sethaputra: Private family papers

Terweil, B.J., *Thailand's Political History,* River Books, 2005

Tongpan, Saran, *The Dictionary of Life (Dictionary haeng chivit),* Sarakadi Press, 2008

**CHAPTER 2**

**Interviews and discussions**

H.E. Nitya Pibulsonggram, Pibul's son, on-going 2010, 2011, 2012

H.E. Pradhab Pibulsonggram, Pibul's grandson, 16-17 January, 2011

Phra Udomyanmolee, Wat Pho Somporn, Udorn, 30 July, 2012

The villagers of Ban Mu Bood and Boong Nam Tao, Phetchabun, 16-17 January, 2011

**Bibliographic Sources**

Chakrabongse, Prince Chula, *Lords of Life,* G.T. Foulis, 1960

Collis, M., *The Last and First in Burma, Faber and Faber,* 1956

Crosby, Sir J., *Siam:The Crossroads,* Hollis and Carter, London, 1945

Haseman, J.B., *The Thai Resistance Movement*, Chalermnit Press, 1999
Jayanama, D., *Thailand and World War II*, Silkworm Books, 2007
Jayanama, D., *Thailand in Zweiten Weltkrieg*, Erdman Verlag, 1970
Jumsai, ML Manich, *History of Anglo-Thai Relations*, Chalermnit, 1970
Jeffrey, K., *MI6: The History of the Secret Intelligence Service 1909-1949*, Bloomsbury, 2010
Kasetsiri, Charnvit, *The First Pibul Government and Its Involvement in World War II*, JSS, July 1974
McNally, J., *Dragon in Paradise*, Doubleday, 1963
Phra Sarasas, *My Country Thailand*, Chatra Press, 1954
Ray, J.K., *Portraits of Thai Politics*, Longman Delhi, 1972
Riggs, F.W., *Thailand, The Modernization of a Bureaucratic Polity*, East-West Center Press, 1966
Roengchantr, Dr Pricha, *The Field Marshal Who Built Phetchabun (Nai phol phu srang nakornbal phetchabun)*, 2006
Sunzi, *The Art of War*, Brian Bruya, Anchor Books, 1994
Suwannathat-Pian, Kobkua., *Thailand's Durable Premier*, Oxford University Press, 1995
Wilson, D.A., *Politics in Thailand*, Cornell University, 1962

**CHAPTER 3**

**Interviews and discussions**

Jueysri, Prof. Sompong, Nai Lert's former employee and protégé, 6 and 10 September, 2011
Sampatisiri, Bilaibhan, Nai Lert's granddaughter, on-going, 2010, 2011

**Bibliographic sources**

Baker, C. and Pasuk Phongpaichit, *A History of Thailand*, Cambridge University Press, 2005
Brown, I., *The Elite and the Economy in Siam 1890-1920*, Oxford University Press, 1988
Nai Lert: Private family papers
Phraya Phakdi Noraseth Centenary, 1972
Warren, W., *Nai Lert Park*, 1993

**CHAPTER 4**

**Bibliographic sources**

Chakrabhand, H.R.H. Karawik, *Tai rom chat* (Under the King's Umbrella) Amarin, 1996
Cruickshank, C., *SOE in the Far East*, Oxford University Press, 1983
Fenby, J., *Generalissimo*, The Free Press, 2003

Gilchrist, Sir A., *Bangkok Top Secret*, Hutchinson, 1970

Haseman, J.B., *The Thai Resistance Movement During World War II*, Chalermnit, 1999

Miles, M.E., *A Different Kind of War*, Doubleday, 1967

Nathsupha, Chatrthip, *For the Country, For Humanity (Phua chat phua humanity)*, 2006

Ngamcachonkulkid, Sorasak, *The New History Of the Seri Thai Movement*, Institute of Asian Studies, Chulalongkorn University, 2010

Reynolds, E.B., *Thailand's Secret War*, Cambridge University Press, 2005

Ride, E., *Baag Hong Kong Resistance 1942-1945*, Oxford University Press, 1981

S.Visooth Busayakul, *Tiang Sirikhan, Veerachon prachatiptai kuhn phol phu phan*, Chonniyum, 2010

Smith, N. and Clark, B., *Into Siam, Underground Kingdom*,Bobbs-Merrill, 1945

Stowe, J.A., *Siam becomes Thailand*, University of Hawaii Press, 1991

*Subhasvasti Century*, Amarin, 2000

Svasti Trachu, *Tiang Sirikhan, Lub sood yod mua khapa chao pen seri tai*, Chonniyom, 2010

Tarling, N., *Britain, Southeast Asia and the Onset of the Cold War*, Cambridge University Press, 1998

Tarling, N., *Atonement before Absolution: British Policy towards Thailand in the Second World War*, a paper presented at the 7th Conference of the International Association of Historians of Asia in Bangkok, 1977

## CHAPTER 5

**Interviews and discussions**

Choomsai, Dr. Sumet, Pravas' cousin, on-going 2011, 2012

Choomsai, Tawanchai, Pravas' nephew, 12 August, 2012

Choomsai, Dr. Vorvat, Pravas' son, 12 August, 2012

Somsri, RTAF Sgt Nathat, Prachuab Airfield, 23 August, 2012

**Bibliographic sources**

Jayanama, Direk, *Thailand and World War II*, Silkworm Books, 2008

Kurlantzick, J., *The Ideal Man*, John Wiley & Sons, 2011

McCoy, A.W., *The Politics of Heroin in Southeast Asia*, Harper & Row, 1972

*Ninety Years of Air Power*, Royal Thai Air Force, 2004

Pravas Choomsai: Private family papers

Pyle, R. and Farst, H., *Lost Over Laos*, Da Capo Press, 2003

Robbins, C., *Air America*, Macmillan, 1979

Robbins, C., *The Ravens, Pilots of the Secret War of Laos*, Bantam Press, 1988

Somsri, Nathat, *History of Squadron 5 (Pravatsat kong bin ha)*

Stieglitz, P., *In a Little Kingdom*, M.E. Sharpe, 1990

Sucharittham, Srisak, *Private Memorial to ML Pravas,* 2011 (unpublished)
Viviano, F., *Dispatches from the Pacific Century,* Addison-Wesley, 1993
Weldon, D., *Tragedy in Paradise,* Asia Books, 1999

**CHAPTER 6**

**Interviews and discussions**

Alice Viratsilp, Doodee Dennis, Radklaow Suebsang: Captain Dennis' daughters at his farm in Sri Racha, 18 March, 2011

**Bibliographic sources**

Ancestry.co.uk, *UK, Naval Medal and Award Rolls,* 1793-1972
Captain Stratford Hercules Dennis, *Memoirs,* 1954
Dear, I.C.B. and Foot, M.R.D., *The Oxford Companion to World War II,* Oxford University Press, 1995
Gorman, Major J.T., *Modern Weapons of War,* Blackie & Son Ltd, 1942
Holmes, R., *The World at War,* Ebury Press, 2007
Kanchanavanich, Rachan, *Pae laow pae ik nai songram lok ti song,* Private memoirs
Kershaw, A., *The Bedford Boys,* Simon & Schuster, 2003
Kruger, R., *The Devil's Discus,* Cassell & Co., 1964
Liddell Hart, B.H., *History of the Second World War,* Cassell & Co., 1970
Stanton, E.F., *Brief Authority,* Robert Hale Ltd., 1957
Stafford, D., *Ten Days to D-Day,* Little, Brown, 2003
Tarling, Prof N., *Rice and Reconciliation; The Anglo-Thai Peace Negotiations of 1945,* History Dept., University of Auckland
Thompson, Sir G., *Front Line Diplomat,* Hutchinson, 1959
Unithistories.com/officers/RN
Wyatt, D.K., *Thailand: A Short History,* Yale University Press, 1984
Ziegler, P., *Mountbatten,* William Collins, 1985

**CHAPTER 7**

**Interviews and discussions**

M.R. Saisvasdi (Noy) Svasti, Tan Chin's daughter, on-going, 2011, 2012
Somboon Palasthira, writer's father, who worked with Tan Chin in England during the war and frequently talked about His Highness

**Bibliographic Sources**

Baker, C., and Pasuk Phongpaichit ed., *Pridi by Pridi: Selected Writings on Life, Politics and Economy,* Pridi Banomyong Foundation, 2000
Elphick, P., *Far Eastern File,* Hodder & Stoughton, 1997

Gilchrist, Sir A., *Bangkok Top Secret,* Hutchinson London, 1970

Jayanama, Direk, *Thailand and World War II,* Silkworm Books, 2008

Jumsai, M.L. Manich, *History of Anglo-Thai Relations,* Chalermnit Press, 2000

Haseman, J.B., *The Thai Resistance Movement,* Chalermnit Press, 1999

Mondey, D., *British Aircraft of World War II,* Hamlyn, 1982

Reynolds, E.B., *Thailand's Secret War,* Cambridge University Press, 2005

Stowe, J., *Siam Becomes Thailand,* University of Hawaii Press, 1991

*Subhasvasti Century*: Official documents, personal papers, letters, memoirs, published by Tan Chin's descendants in 2000

Svasti, P. and Amranand, P., *Siamese Memoirs,* Amulet Production, 2011

Sweet-Escott, B., *Baker Street Irregular,* Methuen & Co, 1965

Wright Jr, J.J., *The Balancing Act,* Pacific Rim Press, 1991

**CHAPTER 8**

**Interviews and discussions**

Dhitavat, Dr Visist; Thai Red Cross, February, 19 July, 2012

Muntarbhorn, Dr Kanit; Dr Smarn's son, 29 February, 2012

**Bibliographic sources**

Gaskin, J., *Blitz,* Faber and Faber, 2005

Lewis, P., *The Peoples War,* Methuen London, 1986

Nhs.history.com, *Emergency Medical Services 1939-1945*

Smarn Muntarbhorn: Private family papers and personal memoirs

Srichandra, Dr Lert, *The Rotarian,* July 1964, pages 53-54

*The Thai Journal of Surgery,* Vol. 31, 2010, page 39

Ziegler, P., *London at War,* Alfred A. Knopf, 1995

**CHAPTER 9**

**Interviews and discussions**

Dhitavat, Major General Vichaporn, Colonel Vicha's son, 16 February, 2012

Dhitavat, Dr Visist, Colonel Vicha's brother, 19 July, 2012

**Bibliographic sources**

Baker, N., *Human Smoke,* Simon & Schuster, 2008

Dhitavat, Colonel Vicha, *A Thai in the Nazi Army (Kon thai nai kong tap nazi),* Sarakadee, 1949

Dhitavat, Colonel Vicha, Private family papers and writings, including *Pajchim Vaja,* his thoughts and comments

Hastings, M., *All Hell Let Loose, The World at War 1939-1945,* Harper Press, 2011
Healey, T., *Life on the Home Front,* Toucan Books, 1993
Kershaw, I., *The End, Germany 1944-45,* Allen Lane, 2011
Lewis, J.E., *World War II, The Autobiography,* Constable & Robinson, 2009
Overy, R., *The Third Reich, A Chronicle,* Quercus, 2010

**CHAPTER 10**

**Interviews and discussions**

Amornsri Subhavat, Boonpong's granddaughter, 26 December, 2012
Lamyai Sirivejjapan, Boonpong's sister, 12 December, 2012
Panee Sirivejjapan, Boonpong's daughter, 26 December, 2012
Rod Beattie,Terry Manttan, Andrew Snow:Thailand-Burma Railway Centre, Kanchanaburi, 12-14 December, 2012

**Bibliographic Sources**

Alexander, S., *Sweet Kwai Run Softly,* Merriots Press, 1995
Beattie, R.,*The Death Railway,* T.B.R.C., 2009
Brooke, M., *Captive of the River Kwai,* Merman Books, 1995
Dunlop, E.E., *The War Diaries of Weary Dunlop,* Viking Books, 1986
Forbes, C., *Hellfire,* Macmillan, 2005
Geddes, M., *Remembering Weary,* Penguin, 1996
Hardie, Dr. R., *The Burma-Siam Railway,* Imperial War Museum, 1983
Kinvig, C., *River Kwai Railway,* Brassey's, 1992
Leemon, J., *War Graves Digger,* 2010
Lomax, E., *The Railway Man,* Jonathan Cape, 1995
Pavillard, S., *Bamboo Doctor,* Macmillan, 1960
McCormack G., Nelson, H., *The Burma-Thailand Railway,* Silkworm, 1993
Peek, I.D., *One Fourteenth of an Elephant,* Pan, 2003
Sparrow, G., *Land of the Moonflower,* Elek Books Ltd, 1955
Summers, J., *The Colonel of Tamarkan,* Simon & Schuster, 2005
Summons, W.I., *Twice Their Prisoner,* Oxford University Press, 1946
Urquhart, A., *The Forgotten Highlander,* Little,Brown, 2010

**CHAPTER 11**

**Interviews and discussions**

M.R. Biranubongse Bhanubandh, Prince Bira's son, 21 March, 2012
Peter Cummins, Royal Varuna Yacht Club, 26 February, 2012

Prasom Yuangtrakul, Prince Bira's secretary, mechanic and companion, 19 September, 2011

Robert Kennett, Royal Varuna Yacht Club, 4 March, 2012

M.L. Poomchai Chumbala, on-going, 2011, 2012

**Bibliographical sources**

B. Bira, *Bits and Pieces, Motor Racing Recollections,* GT Foulis, 1972

B. Bira, *Blue wings to Bangkok,* GT Foulis, 1954

Birabongse, Princess Ceril, *The Prince & I,* Veloce Publishing, 1992

Chakrabongse, H.R.H. Prince Chula, *Lords of Life,* Alvin Redman, 1960

Chakrabongse, H.R.H. Prince Chula, *The Twain Have Met,* GT Foulis, 1956

Cummins, P., *Royal Varuna Yacht Club, A Glorious Half Century,* 2006

Hunter, E. and Narisa Chakrabongse, *Katya and the Prince of Siam,* River Books, 1994

Ying Mud, *Chao Dara Thong (Prince of the Golden Star),* 2003

**CHAPTER 12**

**Interviews and discussions**

Benjaporn Hiltunen, Khamsing's niece, Stockholm, 17 May, 2012

Birgid Oberg, Stockholm, 16 May, 2012

Ing-Britt Trankell, Stockholm, 18 May, 2012

Khamhom Srinawk, Khamsing's daughter, 22-25 March, 2012

Khamsing Srinawk, at his farm in Pak Chong, 22- 25 March, 2012

Prawee Srinawk, Khamsing's wife, 3 April, 2012 (by telephone)

Raruen Garden, 1 April, 2013 (by telephone)

**Bibliographic sources**

Anderson, B., *In the Mirror: Literature and Politics in Siam in the American Era,* DK Editions, 1985

*Art & Culture (Silpa wattantham) magazine,* July 2000, cover story

Lao Khamhom, *Fah Bo Kan,* Kwian Tong, 1958

*Lao Khamhom Seventieth Birthday (Gnan lae kwam kid kong silapin haeng chart pee por sor 2535),* 1992

Peleggi, M., *Thailand, The Worldly Kingdom,* Reaktion Books Ltd, 2007

Platt, M., *Dictionary of Literary Biography,* Vol 348, 2009

Srinawk, Khamsing, *The Politician and Other Stories (translation of Fah Bo Kan 1958),* Oxford University Press, 1973

Srinawk, Khamsing, *Ett dammkorn under dina fötter (translation of Fah Bo Kan into Swedish),* P.A. Norstedt, Stochholm, 1980

Wyatt, D., *Siam in Mind,* Silkworm Books, 2002